LIVING YOUR BEST CAREER

A practical guide for landing jobs and loving your career

Mike Cox
&
Jonathan Phillips

Living Your Best Career Copyright © 2018 by Michael Cox and Jonathan Phillips. All Rights Reserved.

All rights reserved. No part of this book may be reproduced in any form or by any electronic or mechanical means including information storage and retrieval systems, without permission in writing from the author. The only exception is by a reviewer, who may quote short excerpts in a review.

Edited by Joshua Weinstein
Cover designed by Laeeq Hussain

This book includes stories that are works of fiction. Names, characters, places, and incidents either are products of the author's imagination or are used fictitiously. Any resemblance to actual persons, living or dead, events, or locales is coincidental.

Visit the website at livingyourbestcareer.com

Printed in the United States of America

ISBN- 9781790302703

FOREWORD

Congratulations! Merely by picking up this book and reading these words, you have done something important. You have started to take control of your career.

By taking control, you can build the career of your dreams – a career that's long, rich, fulfilling, and satisfying. And you have more control than you may realize *if you utilize the strategies we outline in these pages.*

We developed these strategies over many years of supporting job seekers and employees from our senior positions in human resources and search firms. We have built recruiting programs in large and small corporations, sourced candidates for a variety of industries, and counseled individuals on all aspects of their job searches and career management efforts. We have hired hundreds of people, helped hundreds more get hired, and counseled dozens of companies on the design of their hiring processes.

We have researched not only what gets people jobs, but what makes them successful and fulfilled in those jobs. We identified patterns that breed success and methods that work – and patterns and methods that are *un*successful. We began our careers as engineers, and we understand the value of a practical, data-driven, objective approach. This book empowers you to not only change your mindset, but also take specific, meaningful actions. Our collective experience of more than 40 years of developing, testing, and refining the content of this book gives us confidence that wherever you are in your career, something in this book will help you.

People change over the years. They develop new interests and new needs. Occasionally, they lose interest in topics that once fascinated them. In this book, you will learn how to recognize your changing interests, how to shape your career to fit your needs and passions, and how to take advantage of opportunities that you may otherwise have missed. Our experience taught us that people who do not actively drive their careers often find themselves frustrated – "victims" of their careers rather than masters of them.

You'll learn how to take a new perspective on your career overall, and specific, practical tactics and approaches to the unavoidable, fundamental steps involved in finding and getting a job. We demystify the "black-box" elements of the recruiting process, and we teach you how to create custom resumes that hiring managers, HR departments, *and* Candidate Tracking software will respond to. You'll learn how to interview, how to write cover letters, and how to negotiate when considering a job offer. You'll also learn how to get noticed by headhunters and how to access job opportunities that do not yet exist.

Whether you are just starting out, have a decade or two of experience, or are a long-time professional securing your legacy, this book will empower you to make the most of the opportunities before you – and to *live your best career.*

CONTENTS

Foreword 1
Adopt a new philosophy for your career 4
    1. Changing your mindset from taking jobs to making careers 5
    2. Building a career plan 18
    3. Generating advocates from within your network 27
    4. Engaging outside support 36
    5. Maintaining Career Health 49

Manage your Career 57
    6. Understanding your wants, needs, and ambitions 58
    7. Describing and conveying your personal brand 70
    8. Earning dividends from your relationship capital 87
    9. Interviewing Jobs for Your Career 101
    10. Deciding to go or stay 108

Land your next job 114
    11. Building a job search plan 115
    12. Exploring opportunities through your network 122
    13. Researching Potential Employers 136
    14. Writing a compelling resume 152
    15. Leading with a cover letter 177
    16. Planning for Integration 192
    17. Impressing during your interview 203
    18. Handling your offers 223
    Want more help? 243
    About the Authors 245
    Appendix A - Self-diagnosis and triage (what to read) 248
    Appendix B - 10 interview questions you must be able to answer ... 253
    Appendix C – Sample Interview questions to help you prepare 262

ADOPT A NEW PHILOSOPHY FOR YOUR CAREER

1. CHANGING YOUR MINDSET FROM TAKING JOBS TO MAKING CAREERS

Developing a meaningful, fulfilling career does not happen by accident, even for top performers. Careers require intention, strategy and thoughtful execution. Intention, strategy, and execution start with the realization that you are the only person responsible for your career. Just as important: You have both the responsibility and the power to make the career you want – a career you will love.

Steve logged into the large job board and thought, "Here we go again." It wasn't that long ago since the last time he searched the job market and found his current job. Then, as now, Steve was employed, and his family was comfortable. By many standards, he "should" be happy. Yet while Steve was never in danger of being called lazy, he still woke up each morning dreading going to work.

Steve was an operations manager for a PVC pipe manufacturer. It wasn't his dream job, but Steve didn't really have a dream job, at least not one that he regularly thought about. When he was 10, he had wanted to be a firefighter – which was an improvement over his age five ambition to be an elephant when he grew up. But he scrapped those ambitions many years earlier, and nothing had really replaced them.

In college, Steve studied engineering. Math came easily to him, and engineering jobs were typically more lucrative and readily available than jobs associated with other majors, so it seemed like a good idea. Nearing graduation, he applied to a wide array of companies that were hiring engineers. He was more concerned with getting a job than getting any specific job – much less his dream job. He ended up accepting a position designing fixtures and housings for an appliance manufacturer.

The job wasn't great, but it paid the bills. After a few years, the company moved him out of his original design role into a supply chain position. Steve hadn't requested the move, but he felt good that the company seemed to value his contributions, or why would they move him?

A few years later, Steve's wife received a significant promotion at her company, requiring them to relocate. Worried about going too long with only one income, Steve scrambled to find a job in the new city. He pulled together his resume and surmised that because his most recently job was in a supply chain role, he would have the easiest time landing a similar position. After a few failed attempts, he found himself in a procurement organization for a plastic toy manufacturer. The pay was not as good as in his previous role, but it was a job.

Later, when a neighbor told him that the company he worked for was actively hiring for a potentially lucrative sales role, Steve jumped at the opportunity. He had never worked in sales, but he did not really like his current job, and the money could be much better in the sales position. Largely because of his neighbor's support, Steve landed that job.

Unfortunately, Steve quickly learned that his lack of sales experience was a real impediment to his performance and the money was great only for high performers, which Steve was not. Though the company was patient with him and he eventually did well enough to avoid being let go, he knew that he would never be a top performer in this type of role.

Not wanting to settle for a role where he believed he'd never be more than mediocre, Steve went back to the job market. The combination of design, supply chain, and sales experience gave him a lot of different skills, but no obvious direction like he had when he moved to the toy manufacturer. As he read job description after job description, he felt like he was partially qualified for many roles, but not fully qualified for any of them – at least for anything that paid what he thought he should earn. Still he needed to move, so he applied to a few jobs that seemed like a stretch for his skills, hoping his experience with selling would help him sell himself.

Steve ultimately did just that and got himself a position in operations management for a PVC pipe manufacturer. It wasn't a dream job, but Steve wasn't worried about having a dream job.

* * *

"Choose a job you love, and you will never have to work a day in your life"
-Confucius

Confucius's idea may be one of the best-known and most poorly applied philosophies about careers. The concept is sound. If you assume that jobs are just "work," and not to be enjoyed, then discovering a job that you love means you don't have to "work." The practical application is more complex though, principally because a transition naturally occurs over time as people move from Job considerations to Career considerations:

1. Most people do not understand at a *conscious* level what they "love."
2. Practical constraints imply that being able to "work" at what you "love" often necessitates meeting many requirements – like making enough money.
3. What people "love" looks different at different stages of life, so consistently performing a job you "love" requires a job to evolve over time or to become a sequence of jobs.
4. And finally, the greatest complexity comes from the need for coherence between personal, familial, and professional needs.

Few senior executives wake up in the morning, go into the office and think, "I really love my job. I wonder how I got here. I am sure lucky." Instead, most senior executives, at least the ones who enjoy their careers, could tell you a story of deliberate actions they took with each job they held along their career journey. They would talk not just of the satisfaction that they have now in their "destination," but the satisfaction they enjoyed along the way.

Paradoxically, many people struggle to articulate what they *want* to do. Even those who can describe in detail how they reached their current position may not be there because of a plan meticulously designed early in their career to achieve specific goals. Many are there because they made the best decisions they could as situations arose. These talented people often develop their careers to please their families or make their clients happy without ever truly figuring out what matters to them. Sadly, for some, when they finally ask that question, it is too late to make changes to orient the careers in a direction with better balance.

The most successful careers would make Confucius proud, but they require a minor adjustment to his statement: "Choose a **series** of jobs within professions that you love, and you will never have to work a day in your life." To avoid "working" a day in your life, you need to become conscious, deliberate, and savvy in choosing the series of jobs that, when stitched together over time, constitute a successful and fulfilling career.

It won't make a meme, but it *will* make a worthwhile career.

Let go of misleading analogies

Humans naturally understand stories better than facts, and they relate to imagery better than to numbers or prose. So it is no surprise that from an early age, people are bombarded with visualizations of what to expect from their careers. However, careers are complicated and full of nuance. Metaphors fall short of representing more than one or two dimensions accurately and often send a counterproductive message in totality. Here are some of our least-favorite metaphors, and why you should let go of them.

Careers are ladders – While a career necessarily involves taking many steps to reach a destination, careers have more than one possible path. A career ladder implies only steps forward and backward without the potential for change in lateral direction. One could argue this is the ideal mindset from the perspective of companies who want to see their employees progress within the company, but never leave the company. You have many more options than just up or down within one series of steps.

Careers as a maze – Most careers will inevitably involve numerous turns and changes in direction along the way not unlike a maze which forces changes in direction constantly. Also like a maze, the final destination often is not visible until you are close to the end. However, in a maze you are constantly constrained by barriers. We will show you that while you may perceive barriers to the direction in which you move during your career, most barriers are there only because of actions you have taken or not taken. Unlike a maze, which has only a fixed number of exits, your career can have any destination you chose, and your path is not limited to what the walls allow. You can design your own path.

Careers as a game of chess – Just as in chess, achieving career objectives will not happen without intention and forethought applied to your actions. Many different players will be involved in the efforts of advancing your career, just as a variety of different pieces must contribute to the chess game. However, unlike in chess, achieving victory in your career does not require the defeat of others. And while there are many players involved in your success, the identity of those individuals is constantly changing, and no single mind has control over any of them. Each piece in the chess board of your career has its own agenda which could overlap with or undermine yours. Your responsibility is to create shared opportunities for success – not to dictate their efforts in the service of your objective.

Careers as a road – Roads, like careers, do not always have an obvious start or beginning, but have many opportunities to make turns. There are signs along the way to help you navigate, but none that tell you the "correct" way to go. There will be times when you move fast and times you move slowly. You're allowed to drive indefinitely without reaching a destination if you don't know where you are going or how to get there, but when you have good directions, your path to get somewhere becomes straightforward. However, unlike a road, you have support in your career. Driving on a road is an isolated activity carried out by you and whoever is with you in the car. In your career, you should have many people supporting you along the way. Not only that, roads force you to take paths others have defined for you. You have the power to design your own unique path for your career.

Move from taking jobs to owning your career

Whether you actively manage it or not, if you work long enough, you will end up with a career. Unlike job changes or even shifting professions, maneuvering your career is a long-term proposition. Without planning, you can find yourself in a career you might not like. However, with even a small amount of planning, especially when done early in your career, you can create a lasting legacy that will transcend the jobs you take and the professions you choose.

Jobs, careers, professions, livelihoods, occupations, trades, and vocations are distinct, but related terms that often are used interchangeably. To many people, these different terms are just semantics, but there is some power in recognizing that there are different fundamental concepts in play.

This book focuses on jobs, professions, and careers – and how you can shape yours. The definitions we use are not universal, and are likely to overlap or even patently disagree with definitions or frameworks you might find elsewhere. However, using them in the way we do in this book has proven to be very empowering for many people. By seeing the difference among jobs, professions, and careers, people are enabled to unlock success that had previously eluded them.

Job - A specific set of duties and responsibilities for a specific company for which one is compensated

Profession: An area of expertise defined by a coherent set of skills and/or experiences resulting from the past jobs

Career: The collective body of experience of an individual

It is important to note that jobs are *transient*, professions are *persistent*, and careers are *lasting*.

Jobs are the fundamental building blocks of careers. Sometimes, people hold jobs as part of a larger plan aimed at optimizing long-term careers. Alternatively, jobs can simply be a means of earning money to sustain one's life. Either way, jobs create valuable opportunities to develop and cultivate skills. These skills create options for developing your job or jobs into a profession and ultimately your career. Without careful attention to the selection of jobs in the context of a long-term plan, though, even jobs that could contribute to loftier long-term career goals can remain only a means of sustenance.

A job or series of jobs does not instantly become a profession. Jobs naturally evolve into professions after around 10 years as people start to do their jobs well, train others, develop leadership skills, and gain unique expertise. People may have multiple professions or remain true to a single profession during their careers.

Neither a change of role within a company nor a change in employer automatically means a change in profession. Eventually, your career becomes the sum of all jobs and professions (past, present, and future) *and* should reflect elements of your personal and family priorities.

Only when you start to think about jobs in the context of leading to professions and contributing to your career do you begin the process of controlling and managing your career.

Planning for the later stages of your career does not require you to clearly define and map out the specific jobs that will take you there. Instead of focusing now on what moves to make later in your career, think about the goals you expect to have and the criteria you will need to apply to identify the best moves. Job moves always will be emotional, but the best decisions are made based on objective criteria which can be understood and anticipated, even if they may change over time. Making decisions now which set you up for better options in the future should be your focus.

Recognize that where you are in life affects your immediate goals

There is a natural cadence that most people follow during their careers:

Years 0 – 10	Years 11 – 20	Years 21 – 30	Years 31+
• Build skills • Test out industries • Find yourself • Take risks	• Convert skills to profession • Define long term goals • Begin to manage to work-life balance	• Prioritize family needs • Set end state goals • Maximize wealth creation potential	• Define legacy • Focus on what you love • Plan to stay engaged

No two people will manage their careers the same way, and people should not have the ambition to do so. However, the following is true of most people who manage their careers effectively:

- (Years 0 – 10) Early in the career, they focus on developing skills and experiences that will be valuable later. This is akin to retirement planning. Most financial advisors stress the importance of saving early because of the compounding effect of savings over time. This is similarly true of skills within your career. During the first decade of your career, your occupational story can afford to take some unexpected turns as you are investing in interesting skills and experiences. It is rare for somebody to make decisions in this time period that severely constrain career options in the long term.
- (Years 10 – 20) Careers begin to take a clear shape after about 10 years. By this time, people often identify with a profession. They have enough skills and experience to be valuable to employers for what they can do and have done, not just based on potential. Learning to work productively with others also takes shape during this period.
- (Years 20 – 30) By the third decade of their careers, individuals should have a strong identity and high market value. During this period, they should be able to harvest wealth and push/define the limits for their careers.
- (Years 30 – 40) As they wind down a successful, well-planned career, people should be able to shift their focus to their passions and begin working out of desire rather than necessity, with the option to fully retire if that is a goal.

Unfortunately, many people move from job to job without conscious consideration of the implications of any move on their larger career. Consequently, they never achieve a career they find meaningful. While individual jobs may be fulfilling and attractive, until those jobs combine to become a profession, their value is distinct, rather than cumulative. Without the compounding effect of a naturally cohesive set of skills and experiences, an unplanned series of jobs may prevent someone from achieving maximum potential in the second half of their career.

Equally disappointed are people who wait too long to identify their passion and ultimately fail to build the skills they need to make meaningful transitions late in their careers.

Think like a marketer and brand yourself as a valuable product

Think about the last time you bought something of substance – maybe a television, or a new set of golf clubs. Why did you pick that particular TV or those specific clubs? Was that the absolute cheapest option available to you? Or was there something about that product that made you willing to spend more to get the *right* level and selection of performance?

Assuming your purchase was motivated at least marginally by something other than the price, how did you know the product had the attributes you were looking for? Generally, somebody or something – possibly packaging or advertising – told you.

Too many job seekers fail to present themselves in a way that sufficiently excites their potential employer to "buy" them – even when they are a great fit. Essentially, the employer doesn't fully understand what's in the box, and passes.

The job seeker is frustrated that the employer didn't recognize what they already knew: that they are a great candidate. But the real failure is with the candidate for not effectively conveying their qualifications. Would you have bought a television that had smart capabilities (assuming that was important to you) if the box only told you it was a 60-inch television and nothing more?

Often, job candidates fail to stand out because they rely too much on their qualifications to sell themselves. They bury their qualifications in a resume or unintentionally hide them as implied aspects of experience instead of pointing them out. Until you are presented with an offer for the job you seek, it is your job to promote yourself to the company you seek to have hire you.

Unless you have successfully practiced it, talking or writing about yourself can be challenging: How do you avoid sounding arrogant without sounding boring? How do you convey authenticity while still sounding impressive? How do you explain purpose and objective without seeming demanding or entitled? How do you describe yourself comprehensively without a making your resume painfully long or dense?

When you stop thinking about the recruiting process being an opaque enterprise over which you have little control and start thinking about it as an exercise in you selling yourself as a unique product to interested buyers, what you want to say becomes much clearer.

Furthermore, when you start to think about yourself as a valuable product rather than a take-it-or-leave-it commodity defined by your experience and skills, you empower yourself to stand out in a crowd. Like a savvy marketer, you will understand what your customer (in this case, your potential employer) is seeking, and you will emphasize your abilities to not only deliver on those basic needs, but to over-deliver and provide a uniquely comprehensive package of services that sets you apart from other candidates.

Savvy candidates research the company, seeking out people who not only were hired in similar positions, but have been successful there. They search for patterns that make people successful there and opportunities where they could add distinct, needed value.

Marketing changes the hiring process. When you shift your thinking and properly market yourself, you no longer feel like the employer has done you a favor by offering you a job. Instead, you understand that *you are doing the employer a service* by accepting their offer. Effective marketing allows both sides to feel like they are winning in the transaction. Because they are.

Think about interviewing as a two-way activity

Although we just used the example of purchasing a television to justify the importance of thinking of recruiting as an exercise in marketing yourself, it's important to remember that interviewing is not one-sided, like the purchase of a television or set of golf clubs.

When someone buys a TV, the television has neither say nor interest in who purchases it. The same is not true in a hiring decision. Both candidate and employer have much to gain or lose based on which employers hire which candidates.

It obviously is crucial for candidates to tell their potential employer a story about why the company should hire them. But it *is just as crucial* for candidates to demand that an equally compelling story exists for why their career should involve the company. Before ever interviewing with a company, a person should be able to answer the following two questions:

- Why should this company hire me?
- Why should I work for this company?

That second question is as important as it is often overlooked.

Many candidates understand that it's their responsibility to demonstrate how they fit the needs of a potential employer. Unfortunately, many fail to recognize that they should demand that the employer also demonstrate its ability to meet the needs of the candidate. While it may be fine for the customer to never give a second thought to any needs the television might have, you have a responsibility to yourself to ensure that your needs are addressed. Since the employer has no way to know what those needs are, you must take responsibility for handling that aspect of the process.

A successful hire is, by definition, a "win-win." The employer wins by filling a position and getting access to the efforts and capabilities associated with the new employee and the candidate-turned-employee wins by receiving the remuneration and career growth involved in the job.

Still, the process is very self-focused. At a certain level, most companies do not lose sleep over the idea that an employee they hired, despite performing well, might be in a suboptimal job for his or her career. Similarly, most employees will not lose sleep over the idea that there might have been a better candidate to fill the role that he or she just accepted. Employers and candidates pursue win-wins not out of an altruistic desire to help the other party, but because they want to win personally.

Yet truly winning or losing in this situation goes far beyond the initial hire. A perceived win-win due to a successful hire can quickly become a win-loss for the company if the employee fails to perform well or leaves quickly. Similarly, a win-win deteriorates into a win-loss for employees who find themselves unfulfilled or unhappy in the position they accepted.

To avoid perceived win-win situations that become win-lose or lose-lose situations, employers invest heavily in designing recruiting programs to test candidates for fit and potential with the company. Surprisingly few candidates construct equally functional approaches for vetting employers. Shouldn't candidates be equally diligent in testing employers for fit with their needs? The answer is they absolutely should.

The people who are happiest in their jobs tend to be the ones who knew what they wanted out of a job when they sought the position and were diligent about vetting the company's ability to deliver on those needs before accepting an offer. We will cover this in more detail in the next chapter.

Harness the power of being human

Once you recognize that in the recruiting process you are as much as buyer as a seller of an opportunity, it should become obvious that listening is a crucial element of any interview. For many people, however, that is an unexpected nuance of the process. How will you determine if an employer is able to meet your needs if you do not listen to what they have to offer (and ask meaningful and directed questions)?

Since the industrial revolution (and some could argue before then), businesses have sought to create efficiency through the selective use of machines to improve or augment productivity, often at the expense of the human element. Automation and Artificial Intelligence continue that pursuit and have created significant business benefits and consequent disruption to the people in the business. Still, the business world still relies on humans – and likely will for quite some time.

The discipline of human resources is a laggard in terms of leveraging machine technologies to augment the human element, especially compared to manufacturing, supply chain, and trading, where technology has dramatically changed the landscape. This shouldn't be surprising. After all, how logical would it be to have human resources without humans?

We humans are an interesting but often predictable species. Our egos love to be massaged, but we also love to hear a good story. Humans focus on helping themselves, but are happy to help others when convenient, especially if that help is mutually beneficial. We are more likely to relate to the familiar than to put forth the effort to unpack and understand the unfamiliar. We prefer others to relate to us than the other way around, even though we seek mutual understanding. Humans can connect on a logical level or an emotional level, but prefer to connect on both or neither.

All these statements, though made completely independent of a career or recruiting context, have value when you start to apply them to that context. The following principles are simple but often powerful when pursuing job opportunities:

- Understand your audience – You get to choose what you say and how you say it, but the things that interest you most may not excite your audience the same way. Whether composing a resume or engaging in an interview, you want to cater to your audience's agenda and interests to maximize your impact.

- Be positive – Regardless of where negativity is directed or how it is manifested during the recruiting process, being negative subconsciously associates you with negative emotions. Be positive, even as you describe unpleasant situations. For example, avoid talking about problems and instead talk about opportunities to innovate and persevere. Let yourself be associated with successes not challenges.
- Be relatable – Short of being "folksy," avoid overly complex speech and do not be afraid to use analogies to help make yourself and your background relatable to those who were not there to experience it with you.
- Humanize the situation – Do not be afraid to speak about the emotional side of situations. While one should not dwell too much on emotions, introducing some emotion not only makes you more relatable, it can help to bond you with an interviewer.
- Speak in stories – Humans love stories. We react to them and we understand them. Data is much harder. Accomplishments without context and data on their own are difficult to process and find exciting. But when delivered in the context of a story, both can become inspiring. Avoid being unnecessarily long-winded, but as much as possible, speak in compelling, objectively interesting stories, both in documents such as resumes and cover letters and during interviews and conversations.
- Be engaging – Whether using interesting, action-oriented language on your resume or showing excitement and upbeat emotion in an interview, bring a positive energy to the recruiting process. This invites people to want to spend time with you and empowers them to envision working together as a fun and rewarding scenario.

* * *

Steve's latest job search was going poorly. He was fortunate to be employed during his search because he could not find traction anywhere. Not only was he not being called for many interviews following his resume submissions, the few interviews he had did not amount to progress toward an offer.

Three months into his search, he finally seemed to be gaining traction with one company. While he was not thrilled with the idea of working for a construction company, the company seemed interested in him, and that interest is what he really needed. He felt like he had built a good relationship with the recruiter and had made it to the final interview stage with the hiring manager. Feeling good about how that interview had gone, Steve was very disappointed when the recruiter informed him that the company would not be making an offer.

Steve asked the recruiter if she would tell him what happened. Instead of answering directly, the recruiter asked him, "Why do you want to work here?" Steve was surprised by the question but was happy to answer because he had spent a lot of time crafting the story of how his skills and experiences would help the company be successful and why he was qualified for the job. He delivered his answer so fluidly he might as well have been reading from a teleprompter, so he was shocked when she wasn't impressed.

"That's great that you are so confident that you can do the job, but why do you want to work here?" An awkward pause ensued as Steve both understood the nuance of the question and realized he did not have an answer. The recruiter explained that the company was small and could not afford to have regular turnover of people. The hiring manager had liked Steve but hadn't been able to convince herself that Steve would be happy in the company. That's why she had passed.

Reflecting on the conversation with the recruiter, Steve realized that he had never looked at his career as something he needed to (or even could) design or manage. He had always reacted to a need, never created a purpose. Whether it was his manager, his wife, or his neighbor, somebody else had always driven his career in some direction. His job changes had been pragmatic solutions to a need at a singular time, rather than part of a bigger plan. Steve realized that he had been going about job searches the wrong way all along.

* * *

Opportunities to Apply Chapter Concepts
- Describe why you selected your current/last job. What was your primary motivation for selecting that opportunity over others? Were there strong outside influences that pushed you in a certain direction or were you fully in control?
- Describe your current profession (if you feel like you have one). Did you develop this profession through intention or by chance?

2. BUILDING A CAREER PLAN

Building a compelling plan for your career is exciting and empowering, but the impact of that plan is only as significant as your ability to deliver. A written – not just imagined – plan helps you recognize progress, helps you assess when you need to change directions, and helps keep you accountable to yourself.

Ahmed had spent years building a successful professional reputation in digital technology. He had recognized the growing importance of issues related to automation and digitization dominating CEO agendas across the resources sector, and had focused his professional identity in that space.

Though Ahmed was happy where he was, his ambitions drove him to ensure he maintained a positive direction in his career, so he developed the excellent habit of thinking about his long-term career plans at least once a year.

Money was nice, but it was not the principle motivator that Ahmed thought it was for other people. He was living comfortably and had no ambitions for significant change in lifestyle. However, he did have a burning desire to elevate his level of responsibility. Ahmed assessed his career success based on how much impact he felt he had on the business – not on how much money he made. He really wanted a seat at the C-suite table.

Ahmed further recognized that to really belong at the C-suite table, he needed to engage often with people who were regulars at that table. Every time he revisited his career plan, he made sure to identify three interesting people he would like to know. Usually these were CIOs or CEOs he believed he could learn from. He would plan to study them and try to develop business relationships with them.

* * *

The idea of planning out a career manages to be obvious, novel, and impractical all at the same time. It is wholly unrealistic to imagine accurately scripting the future job moves and professional advances that in retrospect will define your career. It is equally unrealistic to expect that without taking actions that are part of a larger plan, the pieces will serendipitously fall into place to build a career that is satisfying and fulfilling.

You are unlikely to build a career that achieves your potential without planning.

Whether by intention or chance, all people end up with a career. A career is simply an individual's collective body of work experience. You get to decide whether this body of work is something you develop as part of a plan or is merely to a reaction to the environment. It's a decision everyone must make.

Very few people graduate from their studies with a clear vision of what they want to achieve over the next 40 years. Even fewer spend those 40 years following the expected path and retire having done the exact things they expected to. Not only is this infeasible for most people, it is generally unattractive and limiting.

Over time, people should expect their interests and priorities to evolve in ways they could not anticipate earlier in life. Furthermore, changes in technology, government, business, and society are likely to create new markets and evolve existing ones in ways that were not possible to anticipate in the months and years leading up to changes.

Consequently, effective career planning is not an exercise in scripting the decisions you will make during your career. Instead it is an exercise in building a compass that will guide you at intersections in your career, when you must choose to move in one direction or another. It orients you in a positive general direction without requiring specific action.

Successfully developing a career plan involves capturing the ideas that you have for your career and creating guardrails for key decisions – not specific expectations or timelines. The format you employ for capturing your career plan is immaterial, provided you address the following topics thoroughly and keep the plan evergreen over time.

Career plans commonly address a few key topics

While the format of your career plan has limited bearing on the impact that plan can have, most effective career plans will include sections addressing the following topics:

- Motivation – What are you seeking from your job(s) now and in the future?
- Aspirations – What goals and objectives do you have?
- Network – Whom do you know or want to get to know?
- Relationship Capital – What can you offer employers in terms of intellectual, social, and political capital? How do you plan to grow your relationship capital?
- Opportunities – What opportunities do you think would be interesting to pursue, and on what timeline do you estimate pursuing them?
- Action Plan – What are you going to do in the short term to advance your career?

Beyond simply addressing these topics, there is value in documenting your thoughts. Not only does this force additional rigor in thought, it enables you to compare changes in your priorities and career direction over time and hold yourself accountable for taking important actions.

Understand your motivations so you can find a job to motivate you

People tend to be most satisfied and fulfilled in their job when they have a balance among their personal needs, family constraints, and professional ambitions. While the specific elements within each category are likely to change over time, the need for balance remains consistent.

Personal needs often include recognition, positive social impact, intellectual challenge, and curiosity. Personal needs are things that excite you and give you energy irrespective of how they impact anybody else. These are the things that you *want* to have in your in life for your individual enjoyment and fulfillment.

By contrast, *family needs* reflect those things which affect you because of how they affect others. Elements including level of compensation, standard of living, geographic location, amount of travel, and indicators of social status affect you and those close to you. These reflect the things you *need* in your life.

The third component to be balanced is your *professional ambitions*. This aspect of your job reflects what you can do, both in terms of skills you are expected to utilize and the opportunities you have the potential to pursue. Specific industry expertise, functional expertise, soft skills, and opportunities for advancement all can be hallmarks of what you *can do* in a position.

Jobs that are healthy for you and your career should be fulfilling and enjoyable, and should contribute to future opportunities. Healthy jobs almost always will balance your wants, needs, and ambitions, making it important for you to easily recognize balance or lack of balance.

It is common for emotionally appealing jobs to have a spike in one dimension, but not ultimately provide balance. For example, a job with high compensation but no potential for advancement offers a spike in needs, but at the cost of ambitions. This renders the job out of balance and makes it a questionable fit for your career. In another example, a job that intellectually appeals to you, but would force your family to move to a location where they would be unhappy may satisfy your wants, but at the cost of your family's needs, putting it, too, out of balance.

This topic is discussed in significant detail in chapter six.

You can only achieve your aspirations if you know what they are

From an early age, people begin to envision their future career. While few people at the age of 40 are in the profession they imagined they would be as 8-year-olds, enabling yourself to be in a fulfilling and improved position 10 years from today requires imagining what that position might be well in advance of getting there.

For some people, career aspirations are clearer than others. Taking control of your career does not require that you have a perfectly clear vision for your entire career. Instead, owning your career involves being able to consistently remain in balance even as your wants, needs, and abilities evolve over time.

In considering your career aspirations, it is generally best to begin by capturing your aspirations furthest into the future. Envision aspects of your desired legacy.

Think about what you want to be remembered for and where you want to be at the end of your career. Think not only about professional attributes like being CEO or a business owner, but also about family and personal attributes such as owning a vacation home or publishing a book.

Next, think about the changes you would like to see in your situation 10 years from now (assuming you are not within 10 years of retirement). Again, think not just about career aspirations such as reaching vice president level, but also personal and family aspirations. For example, do you no longer want to work on weekends? Then do the same for five years from now.

Part of the value in capturing these three snapshots is to confirm that there is some coherence in your ambitions. If your 5-year ambitions are not leading toward your 10-year ambitions, or if those ambitions are not moving you closer to your desired legacy, this becomes a signal that you should revisit your career aspirations.

Significant pivots do happen during many careers, but they should be triggered by unforeseen changes in priorities. At any point in time, you should aim to have your career moving in a direction that has the potential for long-term sustained balance and fulfillment. Aiming for a long-term goal that will require a significant pivot from your short-term direction creates inefficiency and adds difficulty to the execution of your career plan. Most likely, either your vision for your legacy is clouded by outside or subconscious influences or there is a more appropriate way to get to that goal.

Whom you know should be an active ongoing process

Whom you know is a contributor to your long-term success as will be explored in detail in the following chapter. Because relationships take time to develop and require regular maintenance, it is important to plan the necessary efforts to sustain and develop them.

Not every relationship you have needs to be treated as a strategic part of your career plan, but a few groups of relationships are important to think about:

1. Personal board of directors – Who are the people you can reach out to for guidance to help you test and confirm the decisions you ultimately make for your career?
2. Key advocates - Who would support you in a meaningful way in securing future jobs and integrating successfully into them?

3. New relationships – Whom do you want to forge a relationship with (specific person or just a role or type of person) to grow your network in a useful way?

At key decision points in your career, a much more detailed look at your network will be necessary. Chapter 12 speaks to how best to engage your network to support job searches. However, even between job searches it is beneficial to remind yourself of the people who constitute your personal board of directors and to have a plan for remaining engaged with them. These are your most important advocates, and along with your key advocates are people you want to stay regularly engaged with to at least maintain (and ideally grow) the quality of your relationships.

While it is not always feasible to anticipate the new relationships you will want to have years down the road, by the time you figure out which relationships would be most helpful to have, it may be too late to start cultivating the relationship to receive the support you would like. Therefore, it is best to continuously be developing new relationships and enhancing existing ones.

Recognize the value of your relationships and invest in them

Developing relationship capital is a form of investing in yourself and your career. Chapter 8 delves into the topic in greater detail, but as part of the planning process, it is important to consciously create situations through which you can generate additional intellectual as well as social and political capital.

Whether you commit to reading books, taking classes, writing white papers or simply paying attention to articles on interesting topics, you should have a strategy for increasing your knowledge on topics that can develop and advance your career. Growth in intellectual capital is key to accessing many different types of future opportunities.

Similarly, you should plan to grow your influence and standing within your organization to better access opportunities. Whether strategically supporting key individuals in the organization, mentoring colleagues, or offering to take a manager from another division out to lunch next time she is in town, you are building your political capital. It takes time but can deliver significant impact in certain situations.

Growing your social capital with activities outside of the office is an easily overlooked, but no less important element of building relationship capital. Participating in charity events, golf tournaments, children's activities, school events and other seemingly non-business-related activities exposes you to many people, creating the opportunity to build relationships. Often, relationships founded on a social premise provide unexpected business value at some point.

While it may not be feasible to plan activities specifically to develop relationship capital, planning to be in situations conducive to building relationship capital increases the likelihood of realizing that potential. Relationship capital often is best developed opportunistically, but doing so requires being in situations that can produce such opportunities – and then recognizing and acting on those opportunities.

Imagining the future doesn't constrain you, it gives you direction

Many people find it useful to include in their career plans a snapshot view of interesting next positions. While objectively less important for career ownership than the other four topics, many people find it helpful (and motivating) to envision and capture three interesting potential next positions within their current company and three positions outside of the company that appeal to them.

Having a list of future opportunities lets you test your career plan for coherence. If the future opportunities you identified do not align with the motivations and career aspirations expressed in the plan, then some aspect of the plan requires revision. If the networking and relationship efforts do not support increased likelihood of successful pursuit of one of the future opportunities, then there is an inconsistency in the plan which ought to be addressed.

Even if you are not actively pursuing an exit from your current role and/or company, identifying a few target opportunities prepares you to act on unexpected prospects that may serendipitously show up. It further empowers you to engage your network (especially your board of directors) to watch for such opportunities.

Build an action plan so you can hold yourself accountable

As useful as the introspection encouraged by the career plan is, the most valuable aspect is the action plan that results. Every time you refresh this document, you should include specific actions with measurable target results and an associated timeline.

While the action plan can be high-level or very detailed (as suits your preference and the current needs of your career), the most important aspect is that it inspires you to take specific actions that propel your career forward.

Capture value – not dust - from your career plan

The initial capture and creation of your career plan is most likely a significant effort and should require a meaningful amount of time. However, refreshing the plan is much less time-consuming. You should expect elements of the plan to evolve over time, but drastic changes in the plan should be rare.

It is useful to revisit and refresh the plan at least every two years or anytime you experience a significant change in priorities. Such changes come from a variety of situations, including marriage, divorce, birth, graduation, significant expense, and/or significant windfall.

Finally, the career plan becomes an effective starting point for justifying the initiation of a job search. Whether you find yourself in the job market unexpectedly or as the result of reaching a planned milestone, this plan can help justify your decision to act.

* * *

When Ahmed's company decided to go in another direction, Ahmed quickly agreed to a severance package and decided to find a company that would allow him to continue pursuing his chosen career path.

He called professional contacts from the network he had spent years building and quickly set up interviews for opportunities designed around developing new digital strategies. After three months, Ahmed had six job offers. He was initially delighted, but he needed to confirm that offers involved a clear path to C-suite access because this was a non-negotiable requirement for him. He knew that he only wanted a job that brought him closer to that goal. Unfortunately, as he talked through the career paths offered, it became clear that while the subject matter and compensation were good fits for his needs, the path to the C-suite was not clear, and none of the six moves would enable the career opportunities he sought.

Despite feeling discomfort from remaining unemployed longer, Ahmed spent another six months maneuvering toward the C-suite level. He eventually joined a company that offered him the opportunity that his career needed. As counterintuitive as it felt at the time to turn down six offers without accepting one, Ahmed was confident that the gamble had been worth it as his career not only remained intact, but resumed well ahead of where it had paused.

* * *

Opportunities to Apply Chapter Concepts
- Create a career plan document.
- Set your calendar to remind you to review and refresh your career plan document in two years.

3. GENERATING ADVOCATES FROM WITHIN YOUR NETWORK

Especially in the latter half of your career, who you know can be more important than what you know. Active management of your relationships throughout your career, not just when you need support, is critical to maximizing the support when you need it.

Gail was 12 years deep into an exciting career in data science, which at the time was still a young and somewhat poorly understand discipline. Although she was neither classically trained as a business person nor as a data scientist, she had developed the ability to directly link data science and the business agendas for transformational impact. While much of her experience was at a small scale, Gail knew her work was powerful and would scale easily, allowing her to achieve success at much larger scope. Yet after four disappointing interviews with companies that she was confident would understand her vision and benefit from her skills, she wondered whether she was up against a glass ceiling or was mistaken in her assessment of the function she had chosen to pursue.

Adding to her frustration, she was receiving conflicting feedback. An energy company told her that her experience in management and financial services did not apply to the energy industry, so while her data science skills were attractive, she didn't have enough of the full package to be hired. At the same time, a financial services firm told her that while her management experience fit their profile, her data science experience lacked the fundamental credentials for them to trust her in the type of role she sought.

Gail seemed left with only two choices: earn the managerial credibility in the energy industry or earn the data science credentials in the financial services sector. To Gail, both seemed like a step backward. Her experience told her that these steps were unnecessary and that the companies were just missing the opportunity.

Gail decided to pursue a third option. She reached out to her network for guidance and support. She began by listing the people she had worked with or kept in regular contact with, organizing them by industry, function, and level. She also listed the issues she thought would be facing the individuals on her list and the companies they worked for.

Gail began working her way through her list of contacts, connecting with each person to talk not about specific jobs, but about the issues her contacts were facing, and to seek their guidance on what she might do with her career. She knew that some of the people she was contacting could not directly help her in her job search, but she was pleasantly surprised that many of them were able to connect her with people who were in positions to help her.

While this process took longer, the career conversations that resulted ultimately were more productive. In some cases, the conversations were more about the issues Gail's contacts were facing than her own, but even in these conversations, she gained useful insights. Other conversations helped her to crystalize her story for the data science integrator role she wanted, so that instead of having to move backward, she was able to articulate the right story to the right company that brought her on in a role that advanced her career in the right direction.

* * *

"Networking" can bring to mind awkward "networking events" or boring conventions. But proper networking is extremely helpful. Remember this: You do *not* have to manage your career in isolation. Other people – mentors, friends, current and former co-workers – can and will support you. When you properly engage your network, you have control over how you utilize that outside support. And when you engage, you create brand visibility that advances your career as opposed to being desperate and needy.

Most people are naturally connected to a significant number of others, yet too often, people artificially classify some friends and acquaintances as "personal" and others as "professional." While "personal" relationships often are not thought of as relevant to one's career, a surprising number of them could be. Most people underutilize their network either out of fear of burdening others or because they simply fail to challenge the paradigm through which they have organized their relationships. By shifting the network paradigm from calling for favors to sharing issues and insights, "networking" becomes a mutually beneficial activity.

In most cases, people are happy to help others in their social circles regardless of whether the relationship has personal or professional origins. Most, however, will not identify an opportunity to help unless they are asked.

Anyone within your network can become an advocate for you and your career. By growing your understanding of people's issues and situations within your network, you may find ways to evolve your natural social relationship into a mutually beneficial professional relationship. This evolution is unlikely to happen unintentionally; however, with intention, the change should benefit both parties.

As you work on the development of your career, you should become aware of the ways you can help others and how others may factor into your career. These sorts of mutually beneficial network interactions should be done throughout your career – not just when you would like to benefit from them. Waiting to enhance your relationship until you need help typically leads to an inauthentic and/or unnatural outreach.

Build your network now so it can support you in the future

The best way to position yourself to have support when you need it is to help others along the way as a matter of course. There are numerous ways you can support others, many of which not only help them, but position you in a way that makes it easier for them to return the favor. It also is important to know that senior management often notices and remembers which of their colleagues help other professionals in their organizations.

From a professional standpoint, creating professional connections between contacts (sales leads, suppliers, job candidates, referrals, testimonials), collaborating on business-related projects, providing expert guidance (on topics where you are an expert), helping to promote others' public exposure (attending speaking events, sharing articles on social media), volunteering for special projects, and mentoring are all ways you can help make others successful.

Enhancing and strengthening your relationships for eventual professional benefit does not always require a significant investment of time and effort. Even simple things such as celebrating milestones (birthdays, anniversaries, new jobs) and discussing major career or personal decisions with people in your network can have a profound strengthening effect on the relationship.

People who do this naturally without specific expectation of the favor ever being returned are those who typically find themselves best-supported at the times when the benefit will help them most. If you are not already engaging regularly in these activities, now is a good time to start.

Start by inventorying your existing network of connections

When you decide to enter the job market, it is obvious to review your network and think about whom you can engage as an advocate to improve your decision-making and/or help you gain access to additional job options. However, it is even better to make such a review a regular component of your career management.

The following list of actions enables you to describe your network but is not an exhaustive approach. Be sure to include both people you think of as professional and personal contacts:

1. Start with the people who have helped you in the past
2. Add people you regularly consult for advice (mentors)
3. Scroll through your phone and note people obviously relevant to your specific objectives, as well as people who are generally influential (even if on topics unrelated to your profession or job search)

4. Then add acquaintances who may not know you that well but are people you would like to know better
5. Review your LinkedIn connections:
    i. Note relevant 1st degree connections
    ii. Search for companies you are interested in to see if you have 2nd or 3rd degree connections who are close enough for you to reach out to
    iii. From that list of 2nd and 3rd degree connections, see if any are in sufficiently impactful positions to request an introduction from your mutual connection (ideally someone who will advocate for you)
6. Think about people (specific people or just roles and companies) you would like to have in your network. Even if you do not know them yet, you can develop a plan for building a relationship, making it relevant to include them as aspirational members of your network.
7. Ask trusted supporters if they can think of people who would be useful to you in the process. Sometimes your friends know your network better than you do. Other times they are open to creating access for you to their networks.

This list should constantly evolve. It may not be necessary to go through all seven steps in the same level of detail when updating the list, but over time, you should expect to add and remove names from the list. One other criterion is to consider noting in your advocacy network those people who you know will call you back fairly quickly. This is helpful when opportunities arise that you need advice on quickly.

Understand the value of advocates

In much the same way that track sports and swimming are individual competitions where individuals must rely on others to help them achieve a goal seemingly entirely on their own merits, making career decisions and job moves are individual pursuits which should never be pursued in isolation.

As you go through career decisions and/or work to make job moves, a network of advocates can add clarity to decisions, constructively challenge your thinking, and encourage you. They also can support you with connections, guidance and intelligence during the actual recruiting process.

Advocates are people who take a personal stake in your success and are willing to contribute their time and/or relationship capital to help you succeed. They have the highest engagement level with you and are people with whom you have a mutually beneficial relationship. While the best advocates are those with whom you have had longstanding relationships, newly developed advocates can be equally impactful.

Supporting others to make positive career decisions is often rewarding for advocates. The sense of community that is built in this endeavor is generally enriching, and many advocates recognize that by supporting someone in complex career decisions, they are more likely to be supported when they inevitably make their own career decisions. In most situations, you will only engage with people in group A (see below) for this sort of support.

Turn your contacts into advocates

Not everyone on your list of contacts will readily advocate for you, but most people on your list of potential advocates will if you invest the time and energy to elevate your relationship to that level.

Whether exploring this concept for the first time or refreshing your understanding of your network, it is beneficial to start by grouping your contacts based on level of current closeness:

- A. Potential advocates – people you expect to answer a phone call or return it within a day or two.
- B. Probable supporters – people who will likely respond to a phone call, but may not quickly address your issues.
- C. Potential resources – people with whom you would need to cultivate the relationship before being able to seek support.

Some of the contacts in group A will likely readily advocate for you because you have unintentionally (naturally) put in the work to develop the relationship to a level of advocacy. This is quite common with family members and current or formerly close colleagues and mentors. However, being in group A does not necessarily make a contact an advocate. Still, people in group A are the natural initial targets for advocate conversion.

Advocate relationships are generally mutually beneficial. This implies that the best way to convert someone from contact to advocate is to find ways to advocate for that individual. Supporting potential advocates in their careers increases the likelihood that those people will support you in yours.

It should not surprise you if these potential advocates do not come to you to seek your support, but that does not absolve you from needing to find ways to support them. Once you elevate your relationship to an advocate relationship, it is likely that they will start to seek you out, but you must take the lead in getting there first. Do not try to force yourself into awkward situations. Instead, look for natural opportunities to help, such as:

- Staying connected on their current challenges and successes – Regularly asking about what is going on in their personal and professional lives so you can identify opportunities to celebrate their successes with them or offer your help when your expertise could be valuable.
- Follow the activities of their employers – Pay attention for their employers to show up in the news, and reach out to discuss interesting events, especially if those events could create issues for your contact or opportunities for you to be relevant.
- Share passions and interests – Support charities or social organizations that advocates are involved in. Try to create opportunities to engage in sports or social activities of mutual interest.
- Use your relationship capital to help them be successful – If you work together, find ways to use your knowledge, connections, and/or influence to support them. Even if you do not work together, you can often find ways to positively impact their efforts both in and outside of the workplace. This topic is explored in greater detail in Chapter 8.

Advocate relationships require time and cultivation making it valuable to build a strategy for developing advocates well in advance of needing their support and revisiting your advocate landscape on a regular basis. Regular contact and genuine interest are more important than making a material or noticeable impact at any one point in time.

Create a personal board of directors

Sometimes, understanding yourself is more difficult than understanding others. Being objective when making inherently emotional decisions is difficult. Finding others who can challenge your objectivity makes these complex, emotional decisions easier. Whether empowering you with additional data or simply validating what you already know, they can expose overlooked or undervalued information and offer meaningful perspective.

One approach for accessing this type of support is to build a personal board of directors. This group is an informal collection of advocates who hold you accountable to your best personal, professional, and family interests, and should include at least three people.

Most people include their spouse, mentors, respected family members, and successful friends with relevant professional experience in their personal board of directors. It is possible, but not expected, that advocates supporting you with respect to specific opportunities also be a part of this important group of advisers. However, it can be valuable to exclude people who have multiple interests in the decisions (such as a person you are close to but also is an executive in a company you are considering joining). Avoiding these possibly conflicted opinions helps to keep the board purely focused on your best interests.

Unlike a traditional board, it is uncommon for this group to ever meet. However, like a board of directors, it is common for you to seek guidance on the following topics:

- Confirmation of priorities and criteria for your career's success
- Confirmation of priorities and criteria for resultant job selection
- General strategy and approach for your job search
- Testing the impact of your personal brand and your effectiveness in communicating that brand
- Validation of trade-offs when comparing options
- Stress testing of final decisions
- Appropriate level of network sharing for mutual benefit

As you engage with your board members, it is important to be clear with each member about the role you would like them to play. Encourage them to be direct and honest with you when expressing their ideas. You do not benefit from a board full of "yes" men and women. It is furthermore important to be appreciative and considerate of the input provided, even if you ultimately move forward in a conflicting direction.

People who employ a board of directors approach will engage members of this group on an ongoing basis. Board members can only be helpful if they remain current in their understanding of your ambitions and activities. In addition to keeping them updated on your career, regular contact enables you to continuously support them, strengthening the relationship.

* * *

Opportunities to Apply Chapter Concepts
- Create list of connections within your network and identify level of closeness (A, B, or C level contacts).
- Identify your personal board of directors.
- Create list of additional connections you would like to make and describe a plan for engaging them.
- Avail yourself of any opportunity to become a personal board member for someone in your network.

4. ENGAGING OUTSIDE SUPPORT

You don't need to do this alone. Identify and use the resources that are out there.

Min was a natural leader and a very successful businessman, but he never considered himself the smartest man in the room. He knew he had a knack for simplifying complex situations into simple concepts, but he did not think of himself as exceptionally intelligent. However, this unnecessarily humble perspective became a source of empowerment because it led Min to regularly seek out the support of others as he progressed through his career.

Min was on the verge of a C-suite promotion, but when he was passed over for the position, he realized he would either need to delay that elevation indefinitely or move to another company. But because Min's employer was one of the largest players in his industry, Min needed to move not only to a new company, but to an entirely new industry if he was to keep his career progression on track.

Min spent time reflecting on his situation and querying people who had been involved in the decision not to elevate him. He concluded that his deficiencies were not in traditional skills, but in the soft skills that a C-suite executive at a major company needed. Looking at the people who would be his peers in the next role, he realized that many of them had coaches. He realized he could probably benefit from similar expertise. He hired a stylist who helped him with personal grooming and appearance and he enlisted a media coach who helped him with posturing and presentation skills. He also engaged a career coach to assist him with identifying, understanding, and responding to the political aspects of the complex situations he was and would be facing. Min built an external team to physically and mentally empower him to look and act the part of the senior leader he was aiming to become.

Min then set out to make a transition from his current industry to the energy industry – an industry he knew little about. While Min was confident that his functional skills were more important for the role he sought than specific industry knowledge, he knew he needed some industry context to be credible. Min tapped his network for ideas and was able to schedule meetings with two different consultants who were experts in serving the energy industry.

During these meetings Min grew to appreciate just how much he did not know, and he realized that getting up to speed on the industry would takes months or years rather than days or weeks.

Still, at this point he knew enough to leverage his strength, which was to distill complex situations into more simple concepts, and he put together a pitch for his target company. Min interviewed with the board of this target company, benefitting from the instruction and expertise of the broad team of outsiders he had assembled to support him. He delivered his pitch with poise, professionalism, and authority. While it was obvious that he was not an expert in energy, it was clear that he understood enough of the industry to produce a compelling agenda and vision for implementing it if hired. The board perceived Min as bringing the full package necessary to be successful, and made Min an offer.

* * *

As important as it is to become proactive in your management of your career, doing so does not require doing it alone. Treating yourself as the CEO of your career instead behaving as a sole-proprietor will increase the likelihood of achieving your goals and reduce the stress involved in getting there. The final decisions must come from you and those who support you in your career will only support you under your direction, but with a team helping you along the way, you are in a far better position to succeed.

Your support team, like a healthy company, should involve people with different skills and different levels and forms of interest in your success. Often family members will play a part. With a naturally vested interest in your success, they can offer experience and guidance (if appropriate to their skills and background) or simply emotional support and a sympathetic ear. Your broader network of contacts is very likely to include people with an array of useful skills who also are inherently interested in your success and others who can be drawn to help you in the spirit of achieving mutual success. We will explore these relationships in much greater detail in Chapters 8 and 12.

Finally, there are individuals and businesses outside your immediate circle who can provide deep expertise, generally for a fee, but sometimes at little or no cost to you. These resources are the focus of this chapter. Recognize that utilizing these services is not an admission of failure along certain skill dimensions, but instead a strategic decision to maximize potential.

While spending money on such services, especially if facing a break in employment, may seem counter-intuitive, this should be viewed as an investment in yourself and your future. Good services can easily generate a significant return on investment in a very short period of time if they give you enough of an edge to secure a job that increases your compensation and/or or satisfaction that you might otherwise not have gotten or help you to accelerate your job search process and/or reduce the effort required to successfully complete the process. While many free resources do exist, you often get much better results from services that can cater to your specific, individual needs and situation.

Consider working with the right coaches

Career coaches are skilled individuals practiced in the art of helping others find success in their careers. Commonly employed by senior executives in large corporations, often with the expenses borne by the corporation, career coaches provide both broad guidance in directing your career and recommend specific actions to make transitions happen fluidly. However, most coaches support people in being successful within their roles, not just in making transitions between roles.

Traditional career coaching is a costly, time-intensive, and very powerful tool. It requires developing a relationship with a coach over many months or even years so that the coach thoroughly understands your priorities, motivations, capabilities, and career aspirations. Obviously, the impact depends on the quality of the coach and the commitment of the person being coached, but it is a proven, albeit expensive model. Though a powerful tool, career coaching is rarely effective at rendering rapid change.

In some cases, when a coach empowers you to perform better in your ongoing role, a company will be willing to pay for that service. If you are interested in retaining the services of a coach, build a compelling business case for why it would be in the best interest of the company to pay for that service and see if they are willing to do so.

Many modern coaches offer similar but discrete services, allowing people access to similar support at a fraction of the total cost and time. Typically, the impact is less significant than with an ongoing relationship, but often can be enough to make the difference in achieving a specific objective. Such services typically focus on immediate impact rather than maximum impact which is frequently a good tradeoff when constrained by budget or time.

These service providers focus on specific topics within the scope of career management. Among the services these consultants and coaches (not all will call themselves coaches) offer are:

- Resume and cover letter writing services – provide support in composing, editing, customizing or even creating your resume from scratch
- Personal branding services – act like marketing firms for a business but for you as an individual

- Digital presence services – build or curate a digital presence on social media sites such as LinkedIn, on personal websites, etc.
- Interview preparation services – work with you to improve your personal skills, specifically as they relate to the act of interviewing, often involving mock interviews and/or video reviews
- Job search workshops – provide intense guidance on a variety of activities related to job searches

It is entirely possible (and common) to successfully own your career and secure jobs without using any of these services. However, because you are reading this book, you already are clearly open to the idea that learning from experts can be valuable to more quickly and confidently achieve your goals.

The principle benefit for most people who work with coaches is that they receive guidance tailored to their own specific and unique goals and context. Not only that, buyers of these services receive feedback on how effectively they apply the guidance from others (like this book or the coach) in a way that is not possible from a static resource.

It is important that if you engage one or more of these services, you do the following to improve the likelihood of a good return on your investment:

1. Be clear on what success looks like for you. Be able to articulate what you want out of the transaction, rather than simply consuming whatever is offered.
2. Ask about the individual's qualifications and make sure he or she has a background that makes their advice valuable and credible.
3. Inquire about common profiles of candidates they work with. Especially in certain specialized fields, a coach's familiarity with your specific industry or functional role can make a substantial difference.
4. Understand their philosophical approach. This book describes a proven philosophical approach and a proven set of tactics, but these are not the only approaches in existence. Make sure that you and your coach align in approach.

Locating companies that provide these services is much easier than qualifying the services. Internet searches should easily lead you to many options, but you will need to qualify and select services to use in a way that makes sense for you. People in your network may also be able to refer you to services they trust. Those who would appreciate support in applying specific concepts from this book can seek coaching support at livingyourbestcareer.com/support.

Search Firms can be a powerful, but complex tool

Search firms, often known as "headhunters," are a common and attractive option for candidates, particularly executive-level candidates, to be matched with opportunities. Search firms identify and engage candidates on behalf of a client company. They are paid by their client companies – not the candidates they place. This makes getting placed by a search firm a very attractive proposition for candidates. When successful, they receive an influential advocate and job opportunities they did not work to find – all for free.

For most candidates, this sounds like an excellent arrangement. However, it is important to remember that as a candidate dealing with search firms, you are not the client. Rather, you are a valuable commodity. While it is in the best interest of the search firm to get you placed, their priority is filling *their* searches – *not* finding *you* a job.

Many candidates become frustrated in their interactions with search firms because they do not fully understand the business model of these firms leading to behaviors on the part of the search firms that do not make sense to the candidate and/or do not support the objectives of the candidate. We want to pull the curtain back to help you understand the way the search industry typically operates to limit or prevent frustration if you decide to work with a search firm.

Search firms generally operate within two basic models. *Retained searches* involve some fee being paid to the firm regardless of success. With retained searches, companies usually pay firms an additional fee with successful hires. *Contingent searches* involve fees being paid to the firm only for successful placement (offer issued and accepted).

There is no requirement for a search firm to work only under one type of contract, and most will engage in both retained and contingent searches. Search firms working under a retained search contract typically have a stronger connection to the employer and often have greater influence in the selection process. Firms working under retained contract also typically have stricter boundaries on candidate profiles they can put forward, limiting the number of candidates they can support. Contingent searches often are more flexible. As a candidate, you need not be concerned with how the firm gets paid, however you can better set your own expectations by understanding the differences.

Retained Search	Contingent Search
• Usually creates exclusivity for one search firm to fill the position(s) and the firm is paid for both their efforts and successes • Companies typically create a very narrow solution space, limiting the ability of firms to submit candidates • Supported candidates can expect active support from the search firm and rapid movement of process • In the absence of an active retained search for which you fit the narrow profile, it is unlikely that the firm will provide much help to you until they are hired for a search that fits your profile	• Contingent searches are popular with companies that use a number of 'agencies' for searches • The search firms are only paid upon successful placement of candidates • The candidate criteria for submission tends to be flexible to encourage high numbers of candidate submissions • Firms typically have less influence or voice in the hiring decision process and are less likely to be consulted on compensation packages • Firms focused on contingent searches may expose candidates to multiple companies • Companies use contingent search mostly for lower level positions

You should not expect to produce results through a search firm on your timetable. The timing and/or success at all will depend more on their searches than your qualifications and efforts.

Every candidate wants to find a search firm that is qualified, responsive, and able to align on a vision with them, but because search firms are paid by their clients, rather than the candidates they place, candidates cannot always select which search firm they work with. You always can opt out of working with a search firm that you do not feel is trustworthy or a good fit, but that typically implies walking away from whatever opportunity the firm was promoting. Companies that retain a search firm to find candidates rarely also entertain applicants from other channels.

While you cannot engage a search firm to operate on your behalf because their ability to place you is fully tied to the collection of clients they are working for at any point in time, having preexisting relationships with search firms can help your long-term career. Firms that already know you and are familiar with your profile are more likely to put you forward for appropriate opportunities than firms which must also find you to consider you for a role.

There are a few other rules of thumb which can help to increase the likelihood of successful placement via search firms:

- Discuss the management of confidentiality up front. Ensure that the firm will not send your resume anywhere without your explicit emailed permission.
- Identify relevant firms for your professional space and develop relationships with those that seem best able to help you.
    - Being known by firms empowers them to reach out to you when a search that fits your profile comes up. The chances of success are much better in this scenario than trying to force a match on your timeline.
    - Maintain relationships over time. It easier for placement firms to sell the idea of hiring somebody when they have a longstanding relationship with that candidate.
- If you happen to be approached by multiple firms at the same time, work with each, but be transparent about what you are doing and do not actively market yourself to other firms during that time
    - Control which search firm sends your resume to which employers.
    - Ask if the search is a retained or contingent search. Try to understand how well the firm knows the client and/or marketplace before allowing them to represent you (if you have multiple options). If presented with a choice, going with a firm that is working under a retained search contract is usually preferable.
- Be as clear, specific, and honest as possible about your objectives and constraints.
- Do not try to subvert a search firm process and become a direct hire. While it may seem logical to help a company avoid paying a fee to the search firm, this is rarely how things work out. Companies hire search firms because they want to use that channel and you may burn multiple bridges even if you have understandable intentions.
- Polished, high-quality collateral such as resumes, LinkedIn profiles, personal websites, cover letters, etc. make it easier for placement firms to work with you. Most search firms use referrals and LinkedIn as their primary sources for finding new potential candidates.
- Be responsive without being burdensome.
- If you do not fit the profiles a firm is seeking to fill at that time or if you are not interested in the positions they can discuss, offer referrals.

Helping a search firm builds relationship capital that you may want to access in the future.

Search firms typically try to complete projects in 120 days or less, so depending on when you come into the process, remember that the placement firm is focused on placing a candidate within that timeframe.

Search firms will want to "check off" quantitative criteria from their position. If you do not have a key criterion, it will be very hard to complete the process with them. Therefore, be realistic when self-evaluating your candidacy for any role discussed. Retained firms also will have detailed qualitative criteria they will seek in each prospective candidate. Expect that if you are not a clear fit, it is unlikely there will be much you can do to alter the outcome.

Search firms place a high value on you responding quickly. The process often begins with a researcher call (especially with retained firms). This can often be a bit frustrating as the researchers frequently have only limited understanding of the reality of the role they are working on. Still, it is crucial that you respond quickly and completely to the researcher for that person to set the stage for a productive call with the "principal" who is handling the search (assuming there is enough potential fit to warrant a call). This person should be much more knowledgeable about the role.

Developing relationships with search firms should not be left to chance

For most job-seekers, search firms are a "nice-to-have," but because you are a passive party in the transaction, relying heavily on search firms is not advisable for people who are truly owning their careers or need to make a change quickly.

There are a variety of ways to become involved with search firms:

- Network through peers – Search firms often have an industry or functional bias, so asking people within your network who have a similar profile to introduce you to search firms they know and/or work with can connect you to the right people.
- LinkedIn (proactive) – Headhunters regularly connect on LinkedIn both with the candidates they place and their clients. Perusing the connections of people who work in target companies for people with titles that

indicate being involved in search firms can help you find the right firms and connect with people in the most relevant search industries. We discuss this in more detail later in this chapter.
- LinkedIn (passive) – Having a current, thoroughly populated, and interesting LinkedIn profile allows search firms to find you. It is helpful to indicate on the LinkedIn platform (in the settings not your profile) that you are open to opportunities to increase the likelihood of contact.
- Search Engines – Simple internet searches should be able to identify relevant search firms allowing you to engage with them through their websites.

Trying to proactively build your search firm network through LinkedIn is more trial and error than proven methodology. Job titles for search professionals often include "Recruiter", "Recruitment Consultant", "Placement Specialist", "Talent Acquisition Advisor", "Resourcing Consultant" and a wide variety of similar combinations. Often titles may be more ambiguous such as "Manager" or "Managing Director," making it even more difficult to identify people by their title alone. You'll also need to look at the employer's website to confirm the nature of that business.

It is also feasible to start from the other direction by searching for placement firms and then seeing who within your extended network works for those firms. Internet searches for "search firm" and the industry you are interested in are likely to return multiple options which you can then carry into a LinkedIn search. Search firms vary in size and scope. Some very large firms service many disconnected industries. These often are attractive because their high volume of clients creates access to many more jobs; however, small, highly specialized firms frequently have stronger relationships or greater influence because of that specialization. Until you become familiar with the landscape of your industry, we would not recommend discounting any seemingly credible firm.

When proactively contacting a search firm, it is helpful to be clear about why you are getting in touch. Be clear about what you hope to achieve by contacting them. It is perfectly acceptable to connect without the intention of making a near-term move, but that will most likely be the default expectation.

It also is helpful to be able to describe what would make an opportunity seem compelling to you and to describe how you think the search firm could best "sell" you to one of their clients. Finally, if you are willing and able to refer other interesting potential candidates from your network to the search firm, you are more likely to earn the time and attention of the search firm.

Ultimately, the level of support and attention you receive from a search firm is tied to the potential you have for earning them fees. Anything you can do to increase your potential to earn them money can elevate the level of attention you receive. If you are not getting the attention you would like from a search firm, you are likely either 1) not presenting yourself in a sufficiently compelling way, in which case Chapters 7 and 14 will be very helpful to you or 2) engaging with the wrong firms, meaning that either the firms you are trying to work with are not well specialized in your area of interest or the timing is simply poor and they lack relevant clients at the time.

Placement firms can be costly, but give you greater control

In contrast to search firms, which work for potential employers, placement firms work for *you*, the candidate. Their priority is to get you placed. Success is no more guaranteed than with a search firm, but you have more influence on the level of activity on your behalf.

With placement firms, you pay a fee. Some firms charge is a fixed fee (typically without guarantee of results). More often, however, the fee is a percentage of your earnings from the job that you ultimately accept (two months of salary, for example).

Sometimes these firms also (or principally) provide services to design or refine your personal brand and collateral (resume writing, online digital presence, interview coaching, etc.). It is important that you understand the costs, potential and guaranteed benefits, timing of payments, responsibilities, and objectives well before entering into an agreement with a placement firm. Each agreement may be different and should fit your individual needs and situation.

There are a few other rules of thumb which can help to increase the likelihood of successful placement via placement firms:

- Discuss the management of confidentiality up front. Ensure that the firm will not send your resume anywhere without your explicit emailed permission.
- Clearly understand the commercial side of the engagement. Commercial arrangements vary, and it is important to understand what costs are contingent and which are obligatory. It also is important to understand when payments will be expected and what criteria trigger contingent payments. Additionally, it should be clear what support services (such resume support, mock interviews), if any, are included in the service and what additional costs could be triggered.
- Be careful to select a relevant placement firm. Ask about the past successes of the firm and understand their specializations in terms of

industry and function. A firm that does not specialize in an area relevant to you is less likely to have useful employer relationships or be able to quickly build relationships in the industry.
- Be able to clearly and thoroughly articulate what you need and want out of future jobs. Be realistic in both your non-negotiable requirements for a job (including compensation) and in what your wish list includes.
- Provide polished, high-quality collateral such as resumes, LinkedIn profile, personal websites, cover letters, etc. to help the placement firm understand the scope of your background and market you (unless the engagement involves creating these).
- Identify a few jobs and employers that would be very attractive to as reference examples.
- Be responsive. Even though you are the placement firm's client, your responsiveness impacts their ability to serve you. If you want them to be responsive, you should likewise be responsive.

Because of the personal costs associated with placement firms, many people wait to engage them until they have made some attempts on their own to place themselves into jobs. However, if you want to target specific companies or roles that do not appear to be hiring, placement firms can be very useful in helping to find or open opportunities that do not yet exist.

Do not lose control of the process

No outside support is a panacea that can magically generate the job opportunities you seek. Not only is it important to avoid delegating too much control to any party, you must recognize that in a job search, very little can truly be delegated. Most collaborations are better thought of as partnerships than delegations.

For example, engaging a resume-writing service (or even utilizing an advocate within your network for that type of support) may accelerate the creation of a polished resume, but you still need to take the responsibility to thoroughly review and own the content of the resume. Employers will attribute all content to you, so any errors, typos, omissions, or gross embellishments become issues that you – not your writing service – must explain.

Even though you are hiring experts, you have a responsibility to yourself to only do things that feel right to you. If you are not comfortable with how a resume or cover letter is written, you have no obligation to accept that expert's advice.

If you are uncomfortable with an expert's advice, explain your reservations and ask the expert to explain his or her rationale for the content that does not sit well with you. Most likely, there has been a misunderstanding or incomplete communication that once resolved will enable the expert to provide guidance that you then feel comfortable using. If this does not happen, you should seek a different source of help.

Be cognizant of your network as you expand it to involve third party resources

Working with either search or placement firms will impact your network. When you are presented with an opportunity at a company where you already have close existing contacts, you should talk to those contacts before beginning any process with a search firm. In addition to wanting to feel personally involved in the process, they may want the opportunity to hire you without paying a fee to a search firm.

If you elect to move forward with a search firm-led process with one such company, you might also consider advising firms not to call your closest contacts, or at least not contact them without first seeking your permission. You should not allow unintentionally reckless communications from somebody who does not know your history thoroughly to potentially sour existing, valuable relationships.

Finally, as these firms act on your behalf, they are facing your potential employers. Consequently, you need to know how they talk to them and what they intend to say. You are trusting these firms to build your brand. Not only do they have the potential to create new and interesting connections and opportunities, they also have the potential to negatively impact your positioning in the market. While accepting an unsolicited phone call and having an initial conversation need not be avoided, flippantly entrusting a firm with your reputation without vetting their process and intentions first is a dangerous decision.

* * *

Opportunities to Apply Chapter Concepts
- Apply the approach described in this chapter to identify search firm contacts who are within your untapped network and/or contacts you might want to cultivate.
- Search for third-party coaching or search services to improve your awareness of what is available even if you do not have an immediate need for services.

5. MAINTAINING CAREER HEALTH

No matter how great a fit for your career any job is on Day One, it can change over time – and so can your goals. To keep your career moving in the direction of your ultimate (and evolving) objectives, you must regularly reassess, and intervene when necessary.

Katrina landed her dream job after 20 years at her previous job. The decision to leave felt risky, and Katrina agonized over planning her integration into the new company to reduce that risk. She was moving out of a regional firm to a fully integrated global company, but in many ways, she was remaining in the same familiar role – one she knew well and in which she had a strong, proven record. On top of that, Katrina was being positioned to lead the industry vertical once she was fully acclimated and proven.

Katrina built her business case and 100-day plan with her new boss's direct input. It included lining up accounts Katrina could work with without violating her previous employer's non-compete clause. Everything was set for a perfect start as Katrina was slated to engage with a neutral client to while waiting for the 12-month non-compete to expire.

At her new company, Katrina jumped right in. She led a project, met all the senior leaders at a global meeting, and prepared a paper on a huge issue facing her clients' industry. Katrina performed admirably and exceeded her first-year targets while setting the stage for reengaging with her previous clients. Then her new company went through a promotion cycle and the leadership all around Katrina unexpectedly changed. Further complicating the situation, the organization chart evolved, and Katrina's industry was folded into another group.

Katrina was confident that her performance and her paper would see her through the changes, but the plans that had carried her well thus far suddenly seemed obsolete. Katrina knew she needed to be on top of the changes taking place, and engaged her new boss three months into her tenure in that new role. Though she received positive feedback, Katrina got the distinct impression she was being held in place until her new boss could figure out what to do with the industry vertical. The promotion that seemed almost a formality earlier now seemed in jeopardy as her new boss was neither familiar with Katrina nor the industry. Katrina sensed she could be in trouble.

At this point, Katrina reached out to her advisor network to talk through how to maintain her career trajectory toward leading the industry vertical she was brought in to take over. Katrina's career health was good, but it wasn't as good as it had been a few months earlier. Katrina had some advocacy, and her new boss liked her, but the reorganization had increased uncertainty. Katrina became concerned her new boss might bypass her in favor of someone he knew to take the lead role.

To head this off, Katrina increased her level of engagement within the new company's network. She already was leading a large charity in her hometown, where her new employer had a big office, and Katrina quickly asked some of the local partners to join her in sponsoring a charity event. Katrina hoped that increasing her social capital would build additional advocacy and access to the political capital necessary to get to the leadership role she wanted. She worked diligently to connect herself with the people in her vertical, and with people outside of her vertical but who also were connected to her boss. Ultimately, Katrina was offered the position she had aimed for, but without the proactive planning she did, it is unlikely her job performance alone would have secured that outcome.

* * *

Whether you joined a company two years ago or 20 years ago, your continuing success depends upon regularly assessing whether the company and the role can continue to carry your career forward toward your long-term objectives.

Companies are constantly evolving. Markets change frequently and sometimes drastically. Disruptions can happen in any industry, and leaders of disruption and reactors to disruption experience those changes in different ways. Innovators can become stagnant and veteran dinosaurs can reinvent themselves.

Katrina experienced some significant changes soon after joining the company. Though she was able to adjust her approach within the company, the health of her career was challenged much earlier in her tenure at that company than she expected. For other people in similar situations, such a significant shift might have forced them to look outside the company to return their career to healthy status.

Still others manage to avoid experiencing such significant shake-ups at their employers, but that does not mean that they can avoid actively monitoring the health of their career and expect everything to work out. Even these people need to stay on top of their careers to get the most out of them.

Recognize that your needs and opportunities are constantly evolving

People naturally evolve over time. We have a natural cadence to the progression of our lives that commonly manifests in 5-year increments. Marriages, divorces, the birth of children or grandchildren, children meeting various age milestones (they too move in roughly 5-year increments), completing education programs, paying off debt, reaching wealth milestones, and many other events happen naturally, and they rightfully lead to changes in priorities.

This does not mean significant changes will occur on regular 5-year intervals, but most people find that their priorities and behaviors are noticeably different at the beginning and end of any 5-year period.

With companies and people both evolving, it makes sense to expect that sometimes they will evolve together (remaining in alignment), and at other times they will evolve apart (reducing the fit of company and personal objectives). This in mind, it is prudent for people to regularly test the continued fit for their current job to their career objectives.

Establish a process and cadence for giving your career a health check

For most people, an annual analysis of whether their current job still fits their career aspirations would be overkill, and waiting five years would risk letting things get much worse than they need to before taking action to move in a good direction. Of course, when significant events occur in your personal or professional life (as happened for Katrina), you will naturally think to reassess the health of your career. However, changes aren't always drastic, and it is possible for a good fit to become a bad fit slowly and quietly. Therefore, it's a good idea to give yourself a career a health check every two-to-three years, even if there has not been an event triggering concern.

Testing the health of your career does not necessarily involve putting yourself into the job market. In fact, understanding your options and value in the market is often counterproductive to maintaining career health, as the "grass-is-always-greener" effect often skews people toward pursuing new, inherently riskier options.

Instead, maintaining your career health begins with revisiting your personal wants, family needs and professional ambitions. Chapter 6 will introduce the North Star concept, which is very powerful for determining which situations are best suited to creating happiness and fulfillment. Your need to maintain balance among your personal wants, family needs, and professional ambitions persists even as your targets for each change. Revisiting the North Star exercise and adjusting for the changes in your life and skill set begins the maintenance process.

You can always "re-interview" your current job for your career. Chapter 10 offers a quick test to assist you in gauging how well your current job is meeting the needs of your career.

If you find that your current situation no longer meets your non-negotiable needs, then you need to consider acting. Likewise, if many of the high-priority attributes that brought you to your job in the first place are no longer satisfied, actions could be warranted. However, if your non-negotiables and most of your high-priority attributes remain satisfied, you may still be in a good situation.

For most people, getting some outside support to confirm or challenge their conclusions about career health helps them see things they otherwise might miss by being inside their own careers. The personal board of directors discussed in Chapter 3 are generally the best people to involve in this process.

While testing for the continued fit of the job to your career ambitions is important, being in a role where you are successful and can grow is not enough for claiming sound career health if your personal or family needs are no longer being adequately addressed.

Don't assume that an unhealthy situation requires changing companies

When your health check suggests that your current job is no longer well-suited to your career, the approach to improving your situation should happen in two distinct steps.

First, it is important to disconnect the job from the company and understand if a change in job without a change in employer is a potential solution. Is the job, the employer, or both causing the lack of fit between job and career? Especially for strong performers who develop well and have been in their job for an extended time, it is possible to switch jobs within a company and address career needs.

Many employers are happy to work with employees who bring reasonable concerns and requests to them in a timely and constructive manner. Whether your issue is of personal, family, or professional origin, companies realize that if it does not get addressed, you are likely to leave, and they want to avoid that. However, even when a company wants to work with you to address your issues or needs, improvements are rarely immediate. While you have some bargaining power, nobody is completely irreplaceable. When you bring a concern to your employer, you also should bring a solution –ideally multiple solutions in case the first is not feasible for the company.

While it is always an option to enter the broader job market – even when an internal move could address the gaps in job to career fit – there is a practical limit to the frequency with which a person can effectively enter the job market. Finding a job at a new company also is far more personally burdensome than making an internal move. Thus, if you believe you can effectively address the gaps and remain with your current employer, that is generally your best option.

If, however, the employer is the root cause for the disconnect between job and career, then it becomes sensible to move on to the second step and launch a full job search. In that case, the third section of this book, *Secure Your Next Job* will help you through that process.

Assess your relationship capital and network as part of your health check

Even when your health check shows that your current job remains a good fit, avoidable challenges which warrant intervention before becoming difficult to manage can be brewing. Throughout your career, you should continuously establish, develop, curate, and utilize *relationship capital*, a concept explored thoroughly in Chapter 8. However, it is easy to lose sight of these efforts when focused on delivering the core aspects of your job responsibilities.

If you cannot describe growth in the number and/or quality of your relationships, then you should see that as a risk to your career's health, and plan to address it. Your intervention does not necessarily require a job change (though it could). Most frequently, simply acknowledging that you have not invested enough time and effort in relationship development and creating an explicit action plan to reinvigorate your efforts is sufficient.

It is natural to have some ebb and flow of activities that build your relationship capital, but a lengthy absence of such activities can constrain job progress and/or performance, even within a role that should fit your career well. You want to correct these situations before they're obvious – and while they're still relatively easy to fix. Waiting until challenges turn into problems always is a mistake.

Depending on your job and your career aspirations, having *many* people in your network may not be as important as having the *right* people in your network. Don't assume that if your network doesn't have more people in it than the last time you took inventory that you are in trouble. Some people naturally fall out of your network, only to be replaced by contacts who are more relevant to your current aspirations. This is a form of network growth and is healthy.

Avoid the trap of looking externally for justification of career health

Though formalizing a process for checking the health of your career is a new concept for many people, most people are already naturally, but inconsistently checking the health of their career in different ways. Unfortunately, many of these well-intentioned checks do more harm than good.

People often look outwardly to assess the health of their career. This commonly takes the form of comparing one's compensation either to colleagues or to reported earnings of peers at competitor firms. Driven by ego, this is a self-destructive approach to assessing career health because there is no way to win in such a comparison.

In one scenario, you are paid less than others in a similar role to yours, which is likely to frustrate you. In another scenario, you are the highest-paid individual, which should indicate limited room for growth in your compensation – which also is likely to frustrate you. In a final scenario, everyone is paid the same, but you're still frustrated because most people believe they perform better than their peers. Ultimately, this sort of comparison test offers no scenario in which the current situation is positive.

Instead, your career health check should focus on your wants, needs, and ambitions. Determining that your compensation is unacceptably low should be a function of personal and family objectives, not a comparison to others. This may lead to you to accept less money than others in a similar role, or to you insisting on a higher wage. Either way, your decision is based on what matters to you and your family.

This is important for two reasons. First, there is no way for you to accurately and comprehensively understand the context surrounding the compensation of other people. The backgrounds, capabilities, and contributions of two people are never the same. Differences in pay are often objectively defendable, and companies have every right to compensate employees differently, if they follow the law and do not discriminate based on legally protected categories such as gender, race, age, etc. Secondly, your happiness and job satisfaction are tied to *your individual needs, wants, and ambitions*. Whether the free market would objectively define you as underpaid, fairly paid, or overpaid does not influence your happiness and satisfaction as much as having balance across those three dimensions.

Furthermore, the fit of your job to your career involves managing the impact of your total rewards on yourself, family and career. Comparing only discrete components like salary can lead you to undervalue other aspects of your job. Factors including vacation time, flexible working arrangements, autonomy, amount of bureaucracy, and intellectual freedom, among others, contribute substantially to your satisfaction in the job and in your career. Comparing the impact of these attributes on other people is nearly impossible and is irrelevant in terms of anticipating your future happiness and satisfaction within your career.

Get started in assessing career health with this quick test

For those who do not want to take the time to test career health thoroughly using a refresh of their North Star and an assessment of their relationship capital and network, the following quick test provides a good first indication of your current job career health. If you strongly agree with most of the following statements, your career is likely on a positive track. If you disagree strongly with many of the statements, a more thorough health check is probably warranted, and you may need to intervene in your career:

- I find fulfillment in the work that I do today
- I enjoy and respect the people I work with
- I enjoy the work that I do
- I find purpose in the work that I do
- I am proud to tell others what I do
- I live a comfortable lifestyle
- If I had more income, I would not significantly alter my lifestyle

- My family speaks favorably of the work I do
- My skillset is thoroughly utilized
- I regularly utilize the skills I most enjoy using
- I easily imagine myself doing what I am doing now for many more years
- I am on a path to accomplish the goals that I have for myself
- I have good balance in my life
- I am not jealous of the success of my friends and/or family
- Others would describe me as successful
- I am developing current skills and/or growing new skills in the workplace
- I am developing current skills and/or growing new skills outside of the workplace
- Most days, I wake up excited about the day
- I feel well-connected to my family and the people I care about
- What I am doing today prepares me for interesting opportunities in the future

Maintaining career health is a never-ending part-time job. People need to constantly think about how they can build advocacy for their career. Stay in touch socially with influential people. Create intellectual property that benefits you, your company, co-workers, and others. Be sure to get to know your co-workers within and outside of work. Much of this can be done in minutes a day, but by being "health-wise" about your career, you can often stay in the loop within your company socially, intellectually, and politically – heading off issues and making your career more enjoyable.

* * *

Opportunities to Apply Chapter Concepts
- Take the quick test and see how healthy it indicates your career is.

MANAGE YOUR CAREER

6. UNDERSTANDING YOUR WANTS, NEEDS, AND AMBITIONS

Unless you know what you want from your next job, you'll never find it. However, knowing what you want is not always as easy as it seems. Satisfaction and happiness come from creating sustainable balance across all important facets of your life - not from merely maximizing one aspect.

Shareen sat across the table from the interviewer at a mid-sized logistics company interviewing for what would be her fifth job in 12 years if she were given and accepted an offer. Now a seasoned interviewee, Shareen was ready for the inevitable questions about why she left each of her previous jobs, including why she was interested in moving again.

Receiving those questions as expected, she delivered well-rehearsed, thoughtful, genuine answers with ease, but was caught off-guard when the interviewer asked her, "What will be different here? Why will you stay here longer than you've stayed at any of your previous jobs?"

Shareen was working on her fifth position in 12 years not because she was a poor performer and couldn't keep a job. It was quite the opposite. She was an excellent performer and the jobs couldn't keep her. Unfortunately for Shareen, the frequent changes were starting to wear her down, and employers were starting to be more skeptical of their ability to get a return on their investment in hiring her.

As Shareen tried to conjure up a brilliant answer to the unexpected question, she couldn't help but agree with the interviewer. "Why would she stay longer" was an excellent question, and unfortunately for Shareen, it was one for which she did not have a compelling answer.

Shareen fumbled through an answer before breezing through the rest of the interview with the polish and poise that had landed her each of her previous positions. However, this interview process did not end with an offer.

* * *

Many people should be able to relate to Shareen. Her mentality and actions are common among even the most successful people and are almost guaranteed to result in some level of frustration and unhappiness. Shareen searched for a job based on what she expected her abilities would lead her to secure, excluding all other factors. Unfortunately, she excluded the factors which are most important in landing a job that will cultivate and sustain happiness and satisfaction.

Many people pursue jobs based on at they expect is their ability to interview well and secure an offer. From one perspective that is perfectly logical. If you want a job, shouldn't you pursue the jobs you are most likely to actually land?

While this is important, it should not be the only criterion used when selecting jobs to pursue. Consider this question: Why would you ask to do something that you do not want to do – even if you can do it? If being capable of doing the job was the only consideration, why are there both unemployed people and unfilled janitorial roles?

A job is a relationship, and like any relationship, it is two-sided. A healthy job, like a healthy relationship, benefits both parties. People who consider only the needs of the company and their own ability to meet those needs are addressing only half of the equation.

Shareen, like many talented, successful people, was addressing only half of the equation. She moved frequently because *her* needs were not being met in the job-relationships. Consequently, she moved job to job, inevitably finding herself quickly bored, frustrated and/or unfulfilled, leading her to restart the process, but really doing nothing differently. Fortunately for her, she was talented enough to keep finding positions, but at a significant transaction cost to herself, her family, and those employers.

In many situations where people leave a company, it is easy to place blame on the employer and say the employer should have done more to retain the employee. However, in this case it is difficult to fault the employer for not providing the right environment and experience to an employee who doesn't understand what she wants.

Finding fulfillment in any job requires achieving balance across three dimensions:

- Personal Fulfillment and Enjoyment – What do you want?
- Family Priorities and Practical Constraints – What do you need?
- Professional Skills and Ability to Deliver – What are you able to do?

The answers to each of these questions are inherently personal, but only questions about what job candidates can do are intrinsically relevant to most employers. Thus, job-seekers expect to face questions about job skills – and they prepare answers to answer those questions (and only those questions).

There is a natural dynamic tension among personal, professional, and family needs and aspirations. All people experience motivation, but many do so without consciously examining the origins of their motivation. Consequently, they focus only on their level, rather than their source, of motivation.

This frequently leads to problems.

Successful careers balance the pursuits of personal, professional, and family needs and long-term aspirations. People who place excessive importance on any one dimension – personal, for instance, over professional and familial – almost always do so to their detriment because doing so throws their total motivation out of balance.

You may believe that it is a potential employer's responsibility to pay attention to broader questions of "fit," but employers cannot read candidates' minds. So, while they can ask candidates for this sort of information, their ability to make good decisions is limited by the quality of the candidate's understanding of himself or herself. The candidate is always the limiting factor in his or her half of the job-relationship.

Increasingly, savvy employers are asking about wants and needs to assess the retention risk associated with candidates, but it is still common for employers to unknowingly allow candidates to receive and accept offers that fail to meet their needs and wants from day one. And while a savvy employer might pass on a candidate due to a recognition that the job is a poor fit for the person's career, no employer is going to offer a job to an unqualified candidate simply because the job would fit well with the candidate's career balance.

First, determine what motivates and fulfills you before any other considerations

When asked during an interview why they want a job, many people will answer in one of two ways:

- The assumed correct (but inherently useless) answer: I want to make a positive impact on the company and utilize my amazing skills for good
- The honest (but short-sighted) truth: I need money and you will pay me to do work that I'm able to do

While no candidate should articulate those sentiments so bluntly, the spirit of the answer given is commonly one or the other. However, the fundamental wants of a candidate are generally much more intricate (and interesting). Sadly, many candidates fail to take the time to do the necessary introspection to understand their own wants.

Sources of personal fulfillment and enjoyment often include some of the following:

- Status
- Power
- Wealth
- Recognition
- Respect
- Camaraderie
- Positive social impact
- Autonomy/clear direction
- Cultural specifics
- Individual development
- Making a difference
- Purpose

Anything that leads you to get excited about waking up and going to work is a personal want. Likewise, anything that when absent the workplace makes you upset, disappointed, or frustrated is likely also a personal want.

The list of wants is unique to each individual. You and only you can determine it. This is not to say that the wants of others are irrelevant. They are very relevant, and we address them in the next section. But there is great value in thoroughly understanding what naturally motivates you, irrespective of the impact on anybody else.

Many cultural influences lead people to fear expressing certain wants. Some people, for example, think it is uncouth to be motivated by money. Understanding and acknowledging your wants does not mean that you must pursue them, but there is power in understanding what motivates you – even if you choose not to actively pursue certain motivations.

As you seek to understand your sources of personal fulfillment and enjoyment, the following questions may be useful to ask yourself:

- What gives you energy and/or excites you?
    - Trying new things, being under pressure, competing with others, exercising, high energy in a room
- What motivates you?
    - Potential to earn a bonus, recognition in front of peers, praise from others, reaching a goal you set for yourself
- When are you happiest?
    - Watching a football game, accepting an award, cashing your bonus check, reading a book to your child
- When are you most frustrated?

- When you feel like people do not listen to you, dealing with internal office politics
- How can/does your environment affect your energy level?
  - Late nights drain you, Natural light energizes you, Offices bore you
- What helps you engage effectively with other people?
  - Clear roles help to know protocol, Blunt communication avoids confusion, feeling like a family increases commitment

Having thought through these questions and reflected on when you have felt fulfilled and unfulfilled in the past should enable you to compile a list of your wants.

Second, determine what your family needs

Everyone who has scanned a job board at least once in their life has likely dismissed a potential opportunity because the salary was insufficient to meet their expectations. For some reason, it is natural for people to have firm minimum expectations for quantifiable things like salary, total earning potential, and number of vacation days. However, work/life balance, amount of travel, and specific cultural elements often have a greater impact on fulfillment and happiness. Yet because those factors cannot as easily be quantified, job-seekers often forget them or do not include them among their minimum expectations.

Your personal needs differ from your family needs in two ways: 1) they typically relate to others 2) they establish minimum boundaries outside of which you should not be in the job. There can be some overlaps between personal and family needs. You may want wealth *and* your family may need a minimum salary to support the desired minimum lifestyle for your family. Alternatively, you may want recognition, but not have a minimum level of recognition.

Family needs are principally defined by your family situation, but even single adults still have a list of family needs. People with smaller families tend to have smaller lists of needs, but this is not always the case. Common needs include specific:

- Geographic location
- Benefits
- Line of sight to career growth
- Work/Life balance (maximum hours working per period of time)
- Cultural fit
- Education needs
- Flexible working arrangements
- Travel
- Compensation
- Minimum level of one or more of your wants
- Significance of work
- Access to childcare

It is important to note that all people have family needs. Not everybody will have a partner and children to consider, but parents, extended family, and especially you contribute to family needs. It is both possible and relevant to be a family of one, and the approach you should take to pursuing balance need not be different from somebody who has an immediate family that includes a spouse and children.

Many find answering the following questions to be helpful:

- How much time are you willing spend away from home?
    - 2-3 nights per week/month, want to be home for dinner more than 90% of nights, prefer long days in town to travel with short days when not travelling
- What level of income do you need to sustain your lifestyle? What level do you need for your ideal lifestyle?
    - $100k gross income to sustain, $150k to meet savings and lifestyle goals
- What long-term objectives do you need this job to prepare you for?
    - Eventually want to own my own business, want to have Profit & Loss responsibility, want to gain international experience
- Do you have specific timelines for milestones that you are seeking to achieve?
    - Purchase vacation home by next summer, publish a book in next five years, complete degree program in two years
- What do your social circles value in forming opinions about jobs?
    - Number of direct reports, cache associated with client base, earning level, amount/location of travel
- How do you personally measure your success in a job?
    - Number of direct reports, cache associated with client base, earning level, levels removed from CEO

- What fears/concerns are most likely to keep you up at night?
    - Loss of job, embarrassment during meeting, missing milestones in child's life
- If you are geographically mobile, what do you look for when considering a city in which to live?
    - Cost of living, public transportation, diversity issues, quality of schools

Not all needs will have specific quantifications, but wherever reasonable, it is helpful to describe minimums and targets. This exercise of understanding your needs will help prevent you from wasting time pursuing jobs that you ought to eliminate from consideration from the start.

Third, identify your professional ambitions

The final balancing factor in your effort to set a direction for your career (and your next job search) is understanding your skills and what you can deliver. For most people, this is the most familiar aspect of motivation and fulfillment because people are taught to write this stuff down on their resumes.

Your professional ambitions become a reflection of the skills, knowledge, and capabilities that you seek to apply now and in the future. Hopefully, many of the skills you have are skills you want to continue to utilize going forward, but it is very common for people to possess skills they have no interest in applying in or out of the work place in the future.

Setting a direction for your career should demand that you think more broadly than you do when populating your resume. You have more skills than you have included in past resumes or are likely to include on future resumes. These skills have value to you and add to your happiness – even if they are not relevant to employers.

Skills and areas of knowledge can shape your career, not just by your ability to apply them for the professional benefit of your employer, but by their influence on decisions that you might make in the future. Most skills can be traced back to origins including:

- Technical skills and experience
- Education
- Professional accreditations
- Languages and competency
- Hobbies
- Personality attributes
- Management skills and experience
- Awards and honors
- Publications
- Interests

In addition to thinking about what knowledge and capabilities you possess today, think about what you have the ambition of doing in the future. If you are learning to speak Spanish, but aren't yet fluent, that may have relevance to your career in the future. If you have the ambition to speak regularly in public but have never had the opportunity to do so, capture that too. It's also important to take what could be mistaken for superficial into account. If, for instance, you are an avid tennis player but have no ambition turn pro, that can still be influential to your career.

As you think through your skills and capabilities, it may be useful to collect them in a list such as the following template:

Skill / Area of Knowledge	Proficiency (High/Med/Low)	Strength / Development Area	Priority? (yes or no)
e.g. Project planning	Med	Dev Area	No
e.g. Snowboarding	Medium	Dev Area	Yes
e.g. Financial analysis	High	Strength	Yes
e.g. Coaching soccer team of 10-year-olds	Low	Dev Area	No
e.g. Oil and gas market dynamics	High	Strength	Yes
e.g. Conflict management (mostly with 3-year-olds)	High	Strength	Yes

Knowing whether skills are strengths or areas you want to develop, as well as whether they are a priority (professionally or otherwise) can help to inform the importance of those skills in shaping future career decisions.

Many people might not think to include snowboarding or coaching their daughter's soccer team on a list such as this, but there can be immense value in doing so. Having a strong desire to improve your snowboarding skills may suggest pursuing a job that geographically lands you closer to snow (or at least provides flexibility to travel to snow during the winter). Coaching a youth soccer team may expose innate leadership skills that you haven't flexed in past jobs but could be utilized professionally given the opportunity.

Recognize that your professional ambitions should constrain you in two ways. First, understanding where you want to go in the future should constrain you to move only in a direction that progresses you toward your goals. Secondly, your abilities constrain you to the jobs that you can execute. You may have the ambition to be a CEO, but until you have the skills and qualifications to be successful as a CEO, your abilities will constrain you to the jobs in which you can currently be successful *and* build the skills to eventually end up qualified for your longer-term ambitions.

Describing your North Star

You now have three lists (personal, family, professional) that you can use to compile a collection of attributes that you would like your job to have. That's good data to have, but you can refine it even more. Next, assign a general level of importance – low, medium, high, or non-negotiable – to each attribute on the list. Refine them even more by ranking the attributes that are negotiable. The grid you have just developed provides you with an objective and straightforward way to test possible jobs for their fit with you and a way to compare jobs against one another.

Most people find that choosing among job options involves evaluating options across attributes that can be grouped into the following six dimensions:

- Location
- Industry
- Function
- Level
- Compensation
- Culture

As you compile the attributes that you expect to influence your future job decisions, you should ensure that you have at least one attribute from each of those six categories.

Attribute	Importance (high/med/low/non-neg.)	Rank
e.g. Based in Northeast US	Non-Neg	
e.g. Involves international travel	Low	2
e.g. Pays greater than 125k	High	1

As you build this list, pay close attention to your non-negotiables. These attributes are your most important considerations because they will eliminate some jobs from consideration. A greater number of non-negotiables reduces the number of job prospects you pursue, which can be a positive if you have a wide array of potential jobs or problematic if the set of potential jobs already was small.

Most people find it valuable to test this list with family members. Things that may be less important to you might be non-negotiables to your spouse – which may transform them to non-negotiables for you. Figuring this out early helps you avoid pursuing jobs which you ultimately would turn down even if offered a position.

This list becomes your *North Star*. You will use this to orient yourself in the pursuit of future jobs. You should also use it as a reference against which you test and compare opportunities. It becomes the mechanism through which you objectify decision-making and avoid blind, overly emotional or gut decisions.

Orient your future job searches using your North Star

While understanding your North Star has obvious benefits in deciding when to make moves in your career and enabling those moves, it also has an opportunistic value in several common situations.

It is common for recruiters to reach out to people, especially those with strong digital presences, to introduce potential opportunities. People who have a clear understanding of their North Star can quickly and credibly assess which opportunities merit consideration and which do not.

In such a situation, by utilizing your North Star, you can assess – based on data – whether the opportunity meets your criteria to fit your desired career progression. By confirming that an opportunity has a high likelihood of fitting into your career plan before addressing your fit for the job, you save time and you maintain focus on what will fulfill you – not just what is new and different.

∗ ∗ ∗

Miguel was the CIO of a major auto company. Reaching the CIO position took longer than anticipated and ultimately did not bring the fulfillment and excitement that he had hoped it would. Rather than accept it for what it was, a disappointment, Miguel chose to step back from the problem and find a better solution.

He started by looking at what his family needed. At this stage, the family was mobile and very supportive of his career, so while many things were important, the only critical component from the family perspective was the compensation.

Miguel then thought about what was getting him up in the morning. He realized that while he liked the automotive industry, he did not find it fascinating. Rather, it was his function. Looking internally, he understood that anything he did next needed to keep him within that CIO domain and add fuel to his internal fire for technology. He also realized that level and impact are very important to him. He needed to believe that he was moving up and could continue to move up in standing and impact with his future roles, even if his title did not change.

As he thought about his professional capabilities and what he could do within the space he was defining for his career, he concluded that two things really separated him from other CIOs he knew. First, he had been exposed to – and in fact created – technology innovations. He had more than merely applied the great ideas of others, he had personally been involved in creating those ideas. Secondly, and perhaps more importantly, he excelled as a manager in a function that historically has received no accolades for its collective emotional intelligence.

Equipped now with his version of a North Star, Miguel launched into the process of identifying and crafting a path forward for his career. While the obvious next step was to continue in the auto industry as CIO of a larger company, the options that would address his need to grow his impact were limited, and his recent insights had shown him that staying in the industry had no intrinsic value to him. So Miguel expanded his scope and began considering industries with touchpoints to auto that might offer more attractive options.

The energy sector emerged as a frontrunner for offering opportunities that could fit. While lack of experience could obviously be a barrier, Miguel was confident that he could sell himself through the value he would create as a manager and the insights he gained as a senior IT executive in the automotive and manufacturing industries. He began preparing for this career move, and when a great opportunity in an energy company opened, Miguel was able to land that job and move his career in a direction that he really excited him.

* * *

Opportunities to Apply Chapter Concepts
- Compile your list of personal wants.
- Compile your list of family needs.
- Compile your list of professional ambitions.
- Generate and prioritize your list of North Star attributes.
- Set your calendar to remind you to pick up this book again two years hence and update your North Star.

7. DESCRIBING AND CONVEYING YOUR PERSONAL BRAND

Having a compelling brand is essential to standing out in the recruiting process and is key to earning opportunities. Being impressive but not memorable, or being capable but not obvious, are barriers that regularly prevent talented people from moving forward.

Oscar regarded himself as a humble guy, but he also thought that he had an objectively impressive resume. After all, he had earned an engineering degree from a prestigious university, and after a couple of years working in a premier engineering, procurement, and construction company, he went to a top MBA school for his master's. From there, he decided to try his hand at management consulting.

Oscar neither struggled nor excelled at the consulting company he joined. After two years, he determined that consulting simply was not right for him in the long term, and he decided to enter the job market. He found it easier than expected to get interviews, and he was very excited about the prospects for moving his career forward.

However, despite believing that he objectively was a good fit for the businesses he interviewed with and having a genuine interest in those organizations, company after company passed on Oscar. Six months after deciding to leave consulting and after in-person interviews with seven different companies, Oscar still did not have a single job offer.

In one case, Oscar could tell that the fit was poor during the interview, but in the other six cases, he was unclear about what had happened. The interviews were pleasant and seemed to Oscar to have gone well. The companies that offered feedback had only positive comments about his qualifications and even his interviewing. Yet none had extended him an offer.

Frustrated, Oscar reached out to career coach for advice and analysis of the situation. Skeptical that the interviews were going as well as Oscar thought they were, the coach suggested they do a mock interview. At the end of the mock interview, the coach agreed with Oscar that he was a good interviewer. However, he explained that Oscar lacked a personal brand. The coach speculated that Oscar wasn't doing anything wrong. The problem was that he wasn't doing enough right. ==He simply wasn't memorable or exciting.==

* * *

Would you ever buy a product before knowing what it does? Most people would not.

Have you ever been in the aisle of a store needing detergent and having a selection of a half-dozen different options all purporting to accomplish the same purpose? Which one did you choose? Most people go with the cheapest option or the brand with which they have the strongest affinity.

All, Cheer, Gain, Persil, and Tide (listed here in alphabetical order) are all widely available laundry detergents which claim to clean your clothing. It would be possible for you to construct an objective test for performance, compare the performance of each, and base all future purchase decisions on the outcomes of your test (or purchase a report from a company that did this exercise on their behalf), but have you done that? And if you have done that for detergents, are you doing it for all your purchases? Most frequently, consumers do not buy projects based solely on objective scientific data. Instead they buy based on a combination of objective price and subjective affinity for the brand.

A brand can be defined as a person's perception of a product, service, experience, or organization. For products and services, that perception usually involves an expectation of both what it will do and how well it will do it. For experiences and organizations, perception typically involves an expectation for what it will be and how effective or enjoyable it will be.

Because brands are perceptions, they need not reflect objective reality. If a person perceives one detergent to be better at removing stains than the others, that person is more likely to purchase that brand. Whether they can objectively prove that the detergent is more effective or not and whether a second person would agree with the perception of the first are immaterial to the purchasing decision for the first person. This makes brands incredibly powerful when it comes to humans making decisions.

When you enter the job market, you and your abilities become a product to be purchased. Like any product, potential buyers develop perceptions of you and what to expect from you based on what they read about you and how they interact with you. Those perceptions become your *personal* brand.

People can manage their brand by pointing out specific skills, strengths, and experiences and emphasizing those skills, strengths, and experiences on resumes, cover letters, social media, etc. However, like the lineup of detergents, it is rarely possible to cultivate a brand that objectively and consistently appeals to all buyers in the same way and at the same intensity because interaction with brands is inherently subjective and emotional.

Having a personal brand is inevitable. Even if you never pay attention to or actively promote your personal brand, it exists. While you cannot prevent a brand from existing, you *can* and *should* influence and shape the impressions, expectations, and limitations that constitute your brand.

Your personal brand should be a message that inspires people to want to know more about you and expect the best from you. With deliberate planning and action, you can greatly increase the likelihood that you establish the brand you want and use it to secure the jobs and ultimately career you desire.

It is time to start thinking about yourself as a product to be marketed

If you have not thought much about brands and their impact on people, consider the case of the athletic apparel company Lululemon. Most people familiar with the brand when asked about it would tell you the clothes are comfortable and high-quality. Even people who have never worn a single article of Lululemon are likely to tell you that. How can they pass such an assessment if they have never tried on any of the clothes? Branding.

Strong brands compel people to expect certain things. Without reading any reviews or tests of a new model, a car buyer is likely to assume that a Volvo is safe. Without even seeing the article of clothing, people assume that Gucci products are stylish. A steak from Ruth's Chris is expected to be good. Do you need to drive a Volvo to Ruth's Chris, where you'll be complimented on your Gucci dress to share these expectations? No. But you do need to be exposed to and understand those brands.

The same is true when getting hired. Does a company need you to work for them for six months to develop an expectation for how well or poorly you will perform? No. Just like most consumers won't try five different detergents to objectively measure performance and then stick with one, companies rarely hire five people to try them all out before sticking with the best one. However, they do need to be exposed to and understand the brands of each of the five people to build expectations of who will perform best in the role before hiring anyone.

Be careful to build your brand with your customer – not yourself – in mind

Brands are important to employers for the same reason they appeal to consumers: they reduce a huge volume of information down to important, bite-size servings. Carrying on the detergent example, there are many performance elements that can be assessed for detergents including: cost, stain-removal ability, preservation of original colors, abrasiveness, smell, environmental friendliness, and toxicity to animals or people. Different customers will value these dimensions in different proportionality, and no product will top all categories at once.

For a consumer to understand the performance of every detergent on every dimension is as unrealistic as it would be for every detergent to advertise their performance on every possible performance dimension. Humans simply do not enjoy processing that much data and are not effective in doing so. However, when a brand focuses only on the most interesting and compelling information, it empowers a product to stand out to the customers most likely to buy it for those reasons thus avoiding the need for all the noise of the less relevant data.

Especially as you think about your personal brand, you need to be careful to think about your customer. If you were a detergent that was unique because of your environmental friendliness but otherwise average, it would be obvious to design your brand in a way that appeals to consumers who appreciate and care strongly about environmental friendliness. If you have spikes in both environmental friendliness and color-protection, you must choose one or the other or attempt to do both even though branding yourself as a leader on both dimensions could dilute the impact of your message to audiences who care only about one performance measure or the other.

You need to speak to your customer (in this case, your customers are potential employers) in a way that will attract and capture their attention. Don't be concerned about alienating people who are outside your target market with industry jargon if that jargon helps to establish your credibility and convey your brand in a compelling way to your target audience.

Similarly, don't be afraid to focus narrowly on what makes you most unique and interesting. As with the environmentally sensitive detergent, focusing your message on that key attribute or few attributes will not force people to assume you are terrible on other dimensions. You run more risk of losing a customer's interest by seeming to be acceptable at everything than by being great at the most important thing and mediocre on a few unimportant things.

Enhance your brand mentality using individual brand statements

For people who are new to the idea of marketing themselves as a product, creating a clear and focused message and making that message consistent from cover letter to resume, to social media to interview is one of the biggest challenges of a job search. Individual brand statements are a tool for both organizing your thoughts around branding and assuring alignment to the brand throughout your job search.

Strong brands can be articulated verbally or in writing, but ultimately the subconscious expectations that brands inspire have more substantial impact than the way they are expressed. Brand statements are not slogans such as "Finger Lickin' Good" or "Just do it." Slogans are meant to be memorized verbatim, and though slogans likewise must align with a company's brand statement, your individual brand statement should be more complex and meaningful.

An individual brand statement is a one or two sentence description of what you would want someone to say to describe you if they were explaining to their boss why you would be great to hire. There is no specific formula for individual brand statements, but a brand statement should exhibit the following attributes:

- Be concise enough to be memorable (at least in concept)
- Provide an authentic depiction that your actions will back up
- Inspire interest and excitement
- Reflect something of interest to your intended audience
- Be compelling but not comprehensive
- Be relatable to somebody in your target industry

The following are examples of brand statements:

- Exceptional management consultant with proven client-centric mindset and extensive network able to open new markets and clients, principally through knowledge of operational excellence topics
- Board-level leader in chemicals industry with more than 30 years of experience addressing strategic issues across the entire value chain
- Innovative marketing executive with proven success harnessing creative thinking from elite teams to package into compelling launch campaigns
- Tenacious sales manager known by her clients for overdelivering on promises through her fastidious attention to detail and exceptional work ethic

- Strategic, global human resources leader with a history of transforming average organizations into top performers through optimization of human capital

Some people will include their individual brand statement on their resume and/or social media sites like LinkedIn. Others may even share it during an interview. Some people may never share it with an employer. However, in all cases, having it as a reference proves valuable to your candidacy as will be explored in detail as the chapter progresses.

Understand your innate native brand

As noted earlier, everybody conveys some brand. Even if you do nothing to intentionally manage how you present yourself, you will still have a brand which we call your *native brand*. That native brand is likely to be plain, simple, and ultimately uninteresting to prospective employers.

Think about the generic products you might find at a grocery store. They make no effort to market themselves, yet you still have expectations about them. You expect generic paper towels to be cheap, flimsy, and not especially absorbent. In the absence of alternatives, you probably choose them to serve your purpose because you prefer substandard paper towels to a dirty kitchen. Alternatively, you may choose them if your only criterion is minimizing cost. However, you are more likely to purchase a different brand if you care about performance.

The same is true of employees. Establishing that you are a paper towel – not a napkin or a paper bag – qualifies you to be a paper towel but leads you to appeal only to the fully cost-driven buyer (assuming you are also inexpensive). Most people don't want to be the lowest-paid person in their profession, so while you may be attractive to that one buyer, that buyer is probably not the one you want to have hire you.

Instead of letting this native brand define you to employers, you should define and then promote an *intended brand* which reflects how you *want* to be perceived by others.

However, before developing the brand you want, you should understand your native brand in specific detail. Elements of your native brand that overlap with your intended brand are generally the easiest and most natural to convey. Thus, it is generally most effective to build your intended brand by enhancing your native brand, not starting from scratch.

To capture your native brand, start by imagining the impression you would leave if you were meeting yourself for the first time. What do you expect you would remember about yourself? The following questions may help you determine your answer:

- What topics do you enjoy talking about?
- About what topics are you most knowledgeable?
- What are you most proud of?
- How are you unique?
- In what differences do you take pride?
- What influences your choice in fashion?
- What/who do you look to for understanding new trends?
- Who do you hold in high regard?
- Who would you be proud to be compared with?
- Who do you try to emulate in certain capacities?
- What is your personality style?
- For what professions is your personality style common?

As you think about the answers to these questions, you might want to consider asking friends and trusted colleagues about their first impressions of you. If you were actively managing your brand at the time, their answers should reflect your intended brand. If the concept of personal brand is new to you, then asking them the following questions may help you articulate your native brand:

- What stood out to them when they met you?
- How do they think of you differently now that they know you well?
- How would/do they describe you to other people?

After compiling answers to these questions, construct a personal brand statement to reflect your native brand. Look for themes across the answers you collected. What words or ideas came up repeatedly? What ideas sound most interesting to you?

Do not be surprised if, at first, you create a brand statement that is a paragraph long. Though that fails to meet the recommended attributes of a personal brand statement, it is a natural starting point. Remember that your brand is not meant to describe you in your entirety. It should be a quick highlight of your most exciting attributes.

Develop your intended brand to reflect how you want to be perceived

Describing your intended brand is almost always an iterative process, so do not expect this to happen quickly. Remember that it is intended to inspire people to want to know more about you and expect the best from you. But know the effort is a challenge because you need it to:

- Be supported by your past, but not be defined by it. Having done something in the past (even if successfully) does not ensure that attribute will be accepted as part of your brand. However, it is very difficult to generate a brand around a concept with which you have limited or no experience.
- Incorporate elements of your personality as well as your professional capabilities.
- Be coherent with your personal, professional, and family motivations to enable you to pursue and secure jobs that align with those motivations.
- Be interesting, compelling, and memorable to your intended audience.

Because your intended brand incorporates so many elements that may or may not be naturally coherent, distilling it to a single brand statement can be a challenge. However, developing a brand statement helps you control how people perceive you.

The following tips should help you articulate your intended brand:

- Involve the feedback and thoughts of others who know you well and understand your ambitions, background, and capabilities.
- If there is someone you admire or would like to emulate, start your brand by trying to describe them and then capture elements of their brand which you think belong as part of your brand.
- Fight the urge to simply allow your past to define your brand. Instead, focus on looking forward toward what you *want* to be known for in the future. Your brand needs to be *supported* by your past and consistent with your career ambitions (For more on this, please see Chapter 6).
- Also fight the urge to make your brand complicated and multifaceted. Everybody has many capabilities. Your brand should be compelling, but

not comprehensive. If you feel your brand constrains you, bring it up a level instead of adding detail. For example:
    - Change from a "compensation specialist" to "human capital specialist" rather than "compensation, recruiting, and employee relations specialist" or "procurement, logistics, and inventory management expert" to "supply chain expert" assuming titles that imply aggregated responsibility exist within your industry.
- Once you have a draft, ask yourself who would come to mind (besides yourself) based on the brand description, and ensure that person is somebody with whom you would want to be associated.
- Compare your brand articulation with your career and/or job search objectives. Do the two correspond in a coherent, sensible way?
    - If the answer is "no," it does not necessarily mean that your brand is poorly articulated. It could mean that you should revisit your objectives. If your brand is well-articulated and still is inconsistent with your objectives, you may have suboptimal objectives.
- Be realistic in your brand. Your brand should cast you in a positive light, but you still need to be able to deliver what your brand suggests you can deliver.

Once you have constructed your intended personal brand statement, compare it with your native brand statement. The two almost always will be different, but they should have some things in common. If you find nothing in common, you might struggle to make your intended brand statement appear authentic to employers.

It is always good to test your brand statement with others. Utilize friends, family, co-workers, and others to get feedback on how well your brand suits you and how compelling and memorable it is. If you are comfortable doing so, share your career objectives with them and ask if your brand aligns with those objectives. This feedback can be immensely helpful in avoiding coherence issues.

Understand and avoid coherence issues with your brand

It is difficult to claim that there are inherently right or wrong, good or bad brands for people with one exception: A brand that is incoherent with your story, background, and/or behavior is likely to cause harm. Incoherence typically leads to your audience understanding your intended brand but viewing it (and you) as inauthentic or not believable because something in your stated background or something in your current behaviors undermines it.

Imagine your career as a vehicle. A sedan with low clearance, rear-wheel drive and small tires that conveys itself as an off-road vehicle would obviously be incoherent. The first encounter with even modest terrain would prove that description wrong. If you cannot live up to the brand you convey, employers will not be interested in you despite how well your intended brand may fit their needs.

Sometimes the boundaries for coherence are less obvious. Continuing with the vehicle metaphor, the term "luxury vehicle" is subjective and is heavily influenced by the expectations of the evaluator. A vehicle with attractive styling, leather interior, and a smooth ride may be enough to earn the "luxury" moniker from somebody accustomed to base model used vehicles. However, a person accustomed to riding in new vehicles with 6-figure price tags might argue with that assessment, especially if the "luxury vehicle" costs half the price of their familiar rides. In this scenario, the individual can live up to the brand with some audiences but not others. Even if you can live up to your brand in some situations, make sure that you convey your brand in a way your specific audience will believe you can live up to.

For this reason, you should always give some thought to your audience. When you shift professions, you likely need a simpler brand and may need to avoid conveying it with unique jargon. The way you establish your brand with a CEO may also be different from how you establish it with somebody four levels below the CEO. This doesn't mean you need to change your intended brand statement (which is a tool for you alone unless you decide to capture on a resume, cover letter or online profile), but should inform the language you with the company during the recruiting process.

Convey your brand regularly and consistently

You convey your brand in many ways. What you write on a resume, cover letter, social media sites, and personal websites sets an expectation for you and begins to establish your brand. What you say in an interview can either reinforce or contradict that brand. How you look and carry yourself in that interview also speaks to your brand.

It is critical that your behavior is coherent with your articulated brand and personal story. Recognize that your brand is conveyed less by what you put on paper and more by how you interact with people, including how you dress, how you carry yourself, how you engage with and treat other people, how you speak, and what you choose to talk about.

Your social and professional circles can also influence your brand. If you want to be perceived as a senior executive but cannot describe having relationships with other senior executives, your brand will lose credibility quickly.

Recognize that others use many inputs to interpret your brand, some of which may be the same ones you use, others which may be different. This is one reason it is especially helpful to solicit feedback from people who know you well. For example, you may not care about fashion, but if you want to be perceived by others as a senior-level banking executive, wearing poorly fitting, wrinkled, or unfashionable clothing will undermine your desired senior executive brand.

Managing your behavior is another key to staying true to your brand. If your brand involves being a likeable people person or a caring manager and you are rude or dismissive to people you meet during the recruiting process (including receptionists or people you meet in passing), you can quickly undermine your own brand. If you speak about yourself as family-oriented, but then talk about your willingness to travel 100 percent of the time and work long-hours consistently, then your brand could be called into question.

Your intended brand needs to be authentic and something you can live up to. It is better to have an accurate brand which is less than ideal for the position than to present an ideal brand which you cannot live up to.

Recognize possible gaps in coherence and address them proactively

Anytime you "reinvent" yourself or make a significant change from one job to the next, coherence becomes less obvious. Coherence is rarely lacking in your mind, but you should be prepared to explain how switching professions is logical and aligned with both your objectives and your capabilities.

In these situations, your established brand works against you because you are aiming to change roles and "rebrand" yourself in the process. For many people this seems complicated, risky, or confusing, but it happens with products all the time.

Mobile phones are a great example. Introduced to the market as a communication device enabling voice communication from everywhere, they rebranded to offering both voice and written (SMS and email) communications. Soon they evolved to be multipurpose devices offering communication, camera, and music capabilities. They then grew to involve the use of apps, and soon the devices became marketed more by their ability to stream and interact with online content than based on the communications that were the original purpose. These instead remained a feature, albeit one which was no longer differentiating.

The first phone to likewise function as a camera struggled with the market because it was new, different, and non-obvious. The story for its value was compelling and though it required more effort to tell its story coherently, doing so was possible. Ultimately, that unique, differentiated combination was valuable to the right audience when the brand and value proposition were well articulated. In fact, it was so compelling that it grew to be the norm rather than the exception.

The same can be true of people in jobs. Most businesses see value in cross-functionally trained individuals. Diverse sets of skills are moving from being outliers to being requirements. The responsibility to sell the value of unique backgrounds remains with the candidates, but employers are generally open to seeing coherence where it might not be immediately obvious.

Sometimes lack of coherence can be addressed with additional information or a resetting of context. For example, people with all social styles and all Myers-Briggs personality types can succeed in all roles, but some social styles are more common and relatable in certain roles. For example, introverts who want to be in high-profile leadership roles will have to provide more explanation than extroverts for others to perceive their brand as coherent with that role. Coherence can, however, be achieved.

In cases like this, introversion and leadership are not incoherent, but the coherence may be less obvious to some people. If you believe you may be in such a situation, do not feel pressure to change your brand. Doing so would risk losing authenticity. Instead emphasize the aspects of your brand which most obviously convey the coherence of the brand with your goals and be ready to explain the less obvious components if asked.

Take the case of a highly analytical introvert applying for a VP of Sales role. Her personality was not what most would think of as natural for a successful VP of Sales. However, her command of the underlying data allowed her to design powerful negotiation strategies, margin-rising customer segmentation approaches, and clear sales initiatives. Her customer-facing team executed those initiatives in a way that was effective and coherent in her brand as a sales executive and her delivery in that role. She had to work harder than some other candidate to paint that picture and get hired, but she certainly had a coherent and qualified brand.

Demonstrate coherence to avoid hiring barriers

Many coherence challenges originate with or at least relate to the level of position sought by the job-seeker. In rare cases, an individual may interview with a company without the specific role or level being clear already, but in most cases, this is known. It is critical that your resume and brand reflect a natural and obvious fit with the role you are seeking.

Brands can help or hurt in aligning on level, however it goes beyond the obvious disconnect of a former CEO seeking a mid-level job or a person with two years of experience seeking to be the lead of a large department. How you behave plays as much of a role in your brand as what you write on your resume. A timid, tentative senior executive or an entitled, aggressive junior hire both would raise eyebrows for behavior inconsistent with their purposed level.

From the perspective of level, there are three scenarios. All make sense in certain scenarios, but depending on which scenario applies, you may choose to adjust your brand or how you convey it:

1. Lateral Move - You have held a very similar position or positions and been successful, thus making this a change in employer, but not a change in seniority and/or basic capability expectations.
    - This is the simplest story for an employer to identify with and relate to.
2. Promotion Move - The move recognizes the growth in skills and capabilities that prepare you for added responsibility, making this effectively a promotion, but one you fully deserve.
    - Though often very attractive for candidates, this kind of move requires the individual to provide more justification that he or she is qualified for the role in the absence of proven experience.
3. Repositioning Move - The move returns you to a lower level of responsibility which you are clearly capable of successfully executing, but which makes sense for reasons outside of pure capability set.
    - Companies can be excited to hire "overqualified" people but will generally look for a "catch." Therefore, you want to show there is no catch by explaining why, despite your apparent overqualifications, the move makes sense. This often can be accomplished in a cover letter and interview.

- Also, in some cases you may choose a repositioning move to shift your profession and achieve a different career objective.

While companies regularly hire people in all three of these situations, it is important that you and the company align your understandings of the situation because misaligned expectations can lead to the perception of a poor match.

Candidates need to be honest and objective in assessing their qualifications. Even if you believe a move is lateral, the potential employer may see the move as a promotion. In some cases, it is to your advantage to approach the position as if it was a promotion. For example, if you were recently promoted to a similar position in your current company, approaching the change to a similar role at a new company as a promotion would carry similar expectations for performance over to the new company. If you instead viewed it as a lateral move, the expectations at the new company would likely be set higher as if you were a veteran of your current (but still new) role. As a lateral move, you would be expected to perform at a level you had not yet performed at while concurrently acclimating to a new organization. In other words, you would be making the integration much more difficult than if your expectations were organized around the move being a (deserved) promotion.

In a promotion or repositioning situations, you want to be upfront in identifying the situation as such and justifying the move:

- Promotion situations – Need to understand the principal qualifications of the role being sought and clearly establish that you have the skills and qualifications even without the experience
- Repositioning situations – Need to establish that though overqualified for the role by traditional standards, the position offers something specifically valuable to you, making it more suitable and more attractive than a lateral role and better than no move at all

Revisiting the example above, another option besides the lateral move (viewed either as a lateral or promotion) would be to accept a junior position equivalent to the one you held before your recent promotion at your current employer. While this approach can be difficult on the ego, it does have the advantage for you that if you over-assessed yourself (or underestimated the role), you are less likely to find yourself unable to perform at expectations. Similarly, if the company underestimated you, when you perform as well as you expect, you will be identified as a high performer (rather than as someone who merely meets expectations). Either way, it should reduce the burden of you during the integration period into the new company.

Your digital footprint should enhance – not conflict – with your brand

There are many ways to establish a digital footprint to convey your brand online. Your digital footprint can be thought of as anything which could be discovered by searching for you on the internet or a social media platform. LinkedIn, Twitter, Facebook, and Instagram pages are the most common across industries, but it is also common for people to have blogs and for people, especially those in creative industries, to have websites showcasing their portfolios of work. It is still possible to have no digital presence, but this is increasingly rare. Most employers now expect candidates to at least have a LinkedIn profile.

Because the norms, expectations, risks, and opportunities for digital footprint vary extensively by industry, job level, and job responsibility, we will not go beyond a few surface pieces of guidance on this topic.

When building or reviewing your digital footprint, it is useful to regularly revisit your intended personal brand statement. Some people even publish that brand statement as part of their digital footprint (such as in the summary section of their LinkedIn bio). This is not a requirement, but either way, you should be reviewing your content to make sure it does not contradict or undermine that intended brand.

While it is smart to customize your resume for each company and potential opportunity, you have only one LinkedIn profile. It is expected that one or the other will have more information, but it is important that the information in your resumes and cover letters does not conflict with the information in your LinkedIn profile.

Although companies most commonly use LinkedIn for recruiting purposes, many look at other platforms too. Consequently, it is important to manage the content, especially if your profile is public. Companies recognize that what you post to Facebook, Instagram, and Twitter is not professionally motivated, but your character is consistent across professional and social situations. Character therefore is relevant to recruiting. Social media posts that frame your character – and your brand – can have a materially positive or negative impact on your recruiting process if your potential employer sees them.

It can be revealing to have someone search the internet and develop a profile of how you appear on line.

Watch out for common pitfalls and avoid them

- Having an unclear brand – This happens most often when people rely on their native brand rather than managing their brand. Like in the example with Oscar, employers struggle to get excited about candidates with unclear brands even when those candidates have objectively interesting qualifications.
- Demonstrating an incoherent or inconsistent brand – If the resume, cover letter, LinkedIn page and interviews seem to describe different people, the employer will wonder which source truly reflects the person they would be hiring. This typically causes the candidate to be viewed as a risky hire.
- Assuming all people will receive your brand the way you do – Because much of your brand is a function of subtle behaviors, people often think they are conveying one brand when most others perceive something different. It is always helpful to test your brand with a "friendly" audience who will give you candid and thorough feedback. This helps ensure that your audience will interpret your brand the way you would like them to.
- Failing to create coherence between brand and objectives – Being an excellent ice skater is a great skill, and you could have a brand that clearly conveys that. But it is useless if you are pursuing a career in baseball. For you to extract value from your brand, that brand must clearly relate to your objectives. If your objectives and brand do not relate, that should be a signal that you need to rethink your objectives.
- Failing to understand thoroughly what the employer is seeking – By having a strong and accurate sense of exactly what your potential employer is looking for, you can communicate your brand so it resonates. For example, your brand may involve being an excellent chef, but if you emphasize the quality of your appetizers when the employer really needs a pastry chef, you will look less appealing – despite being qualified to make both appetizers and pastries – than if you drew attention to your pastry skills.

* * *

After receiving the feedback from his career coach, Oscar realized that he was presenting himself as a "jack of all trades." He was inundating potential employers with a wide array of only loosely related skills that were individually impressive but were irrelevant to the position. Furthermore, the skills did not collectively add up to describe a role that was relatable. Oscar hypothesized that he was leaving employers thinking, "This is a good guy. I like him, but I don't know how to use him. And he does not really fit the position I was looking to fill."

Oscar took a step back from his situation, revisited his personal objectives and thought hard about what really made him different from other candidates. While his breadth and range of skills was unique, it was not his objective to use all his skills – and prospective employers were not asking him to.

After some thought and some conversations with his family and friends, Oscar realized that what really made him unique was his ability to be both technical and business-minded. He had the ability to credibly interface with engineers on complex, deeply technical topics, as well as the business and interpersonal skills to work with senior-level executives on very high-level strategic topics. This ability to be the connector between two worlds within an organization WAS something employers were interested in.

Importantly, it also aligned with Oscar's desire to have greater ownership of something in his future role. Oscar decided to work on writing a new intended brand statement, and decided he wanted to present himself as "a determined, personable problem-solver equally conversant at the board level and the line level on topics ranging from complex technical issues to broad strategic imperatives."

Oscar set about recrafting his resume, LinkedIn profile, and overall approach to his job search to reflect this reconstruction of his brand. After a little testing and fine-tuning with some trusted advisors, he resumed his job search, but with greater focus and more compelling alignment to the needs of employers. He ultimately secured a position with an electronics manufacturer as a product line manager – a move he saw as a great step forward in his career.

* * *

Opportunities to Apply Chapter Concepts
- Compose a personal brand statement for your native brand.
- Compose a personal brand statement for your intended brand.
- Review your digital footprint to see if it is coherent with your intended brand (and update it if necessary).

8. EARNING DIVIDENDS FROM YOUR RELATIONSHIP CAPITAL

Careers are shaped as much by who you know as by *what* you know. Invest in your long-term success by taking intentional measures to curate and cultivate your relationships.

Sam was a strong performer in his role in the corporate office of a large retail company. He started with the company 15 years into his career after stints at two other companies. His first role at the company was an internal consulting position not related to the core business, which played to his strengths as a problem-solver and benefited from his deeply analytical background.

Leadership noticed Sam's abilities, and moved him rather quickly into a recently vacated global role in the core business. There, Sam interacted with the highest-level executives in the company and ran his own small team. He continued to contribute well, and despite the broader challenges facing the industry, Sam never questioned the safety of his job or the direction of his career.

At this point, he operated very autonomously. The team reporting to him had a clear idea what his stakeholders needed. Since he reported directly to the CFO, he had little interference from others in his day-to-day activities. Most importantly, he received positive feedback and was confident that he was delivering what the company needed.

When the company entered into a new product space, a new organization was created to manage the new product line. Sam was tasked to be the strategy lead – effectively the second-in-command – of that new organization. In the year following the launch of the product, it grew 50 percent faster than the market, and seemed to most to be a wild success.

However, not everything in the company was as positive Sam's product line. Other areas of the company underperformed, market challenges proved difficult, and overall company performance failed to meet investor expectations. The company initiated a wave of layoffs to reduce costs, and Sam found himself with an exit package instead of the big bonus he expected based on his product's stellar performance.

While such an outcome could often be blamed on sinister motives, this was not the case for Sam. Sam had missed many opportunities to prevent this outcome. It was not that he failed to deliver results, nor that he lacked the skills for the job. Instead, Sam, like far too many people, failed to consider and manage his relationships. Consequently, he lacked the right support when he needed it most.

* * *

You've landed yourself in a job for which you have all the necessary skills and abilities. You like the job and the people you work with. You're totally set up for success, right? Not necessarily. There's a lot more involved in being successful than just having the right skills. You also need the right relationships.

It is impossible to not have your job performance influenced in some way by your interactions with other people. While this impact is typically less for people early in their careers, the most powerful impact comes from people who actively manage their relationships to generate positive influence on their careers. We call the ability of relationships to influence job performance and careers *relationship capital*.

Begin recognizing and creating relationship capital

Business transactions happen all the time. The most transparent ones involve the exchange of money for goods or services. However, the ones with the most impact are often never captured on a ledger and involve no movement of money. These transactions involve the use of relationship capital. These off-the-books transactions frequently influence their more transparent counterparts, usually working in unseen ways to ensure all involved parties feel satisfied by the outcome.

Relationship capital is a familiar but rarely discussed concept borne in childhood, which continues into the workplace. When you do something beneficial for somebody, they become more likely to do something beneficial for you in the future. However, if you seek too many beneficial things, others become less inclined to help you.

Relationship capital must be earned and is specific to the two involved people. Because relationship capital is an unwritten, unmeasured currency between two people, it is straightforward to earn, simple to spend, but easy to overspend.

Relationship capital comes in three basic forms:

- Intellectual capital – What you know
- Social capital – Whom you know
- Political capital – Whom you can influence

Even if you are not thinking in these terms today, you are either benefitting from or being inhibited by your relationship capital. Companies hire people not just because of their skills and knowledge (part of their intellectual capital), but also because of who they know and how they influence others. Likewise, people are successful in their jobs not just because of what they know and can do, but also because of who they know and how they persuade others to act. Some people are even successful despite their gaps in skill or knowledge because of their ability to make up for those gaps using other forms of relationship capital.

The dynamics of building capital change over time. You begin building capital in school and you keep building through retirement. You can imagine relationship capital like poker chips being added to your stack: depending on your actions, they can be taken away as well as added. Sometimes you play chips and get more back than you put in. Other times you put in chips and get nothing back, hoping to gain that amount and more later. Each person effectively has three stacks of chips: intellectual chips affected by what you know, social chips affected by who you know, and political chips affected by how you influence.

Throughout your early education, you used knowledge as the currency to create opportunities. Knowing more, having more skills, and building the capacity to meet given objectives paved the way to success. Knowledge and raw skill often sufficed for getting your first job, but as your career progresses, you need more in order to unlock future opportunities.

As you move from holding a job to having a profession, employers begin to ask:

- What do you know?
- Whom do you know?
- How do you get things done?

While the first question is one people are conditioned to answer from their first job interviews, many people fail to think about the relevance of the latter two questions to their employer or career. Yet, from the midpoint to the end of your career, "Whom do you know?" and "How do you get things done?" often are the most important questions. Your answers to those questions can be the difference between taking a job you need and owning the career you want.

Go beyond knowledge and develop intellectual capital

Intellectual capital is tied to the collection of things you know and can do. Most people are familiar with their own intellectual capital because they have practiced describing it when writing resumes. However, possessing skills and knowledge is not sufficient for claiming intellectual capital. Intellectual capital requires that others recognize and believe in those skills. Your knowledge remains just knowledge (adding only limited value to your career) until you convert it to intellectual capital by making others aware of your skills and convincing them to believe in your capability to utilize them for positive impact.

As you start to take inventory of your intellectual capital, ask the following questions:

- What skills and knowledge do you have that make you rare or unique?
- On what topics do people come to you for advice or support?
- What special trainings have you attended, or certifications have you earned?
- What are you "known for knowing?"

What you know and can do has intrinsic value, but that value is not fixed. Much like a jeweler increases the value of a rare stone by cutting and polishing it, and further increases it by placing it in a setting, your intellectual capital increases in value when you find ways to convert it into material impact on a business. It increases even more when you market that capability.

As you seek to grow your intellectual capital, remember that there are two ways to make that happen: (1) developing new skills and capabilities and (2) making more people aware of your skills and convincing them to trust in your ability to deliver on tasks that require those skills.

* * *

Kendra developed a new process for manufacturing a widget at a much lower cost. She captured this intellectual capital by writing an article[1] about her approach and publishing it.

---

[1] Before publishing anything related to your employer's practices, you should secure the support and approval of your employer. Inappropriately disclosing company trade secrets could eliminate any value created for yourself through the publishing and could lead to significant, negative legal repercussions.

In doing so, she created value for the company by saving it money. She also created value for herself because her knowledge and the proof of her ability to innovate made her attractive and known to other potential employers.

Kendra could have simply developed and deployed the process, effectively "doing her job well," without fully benefitting from the intellectual capital she created. Instead she chose to polish and market that capital by publishing a paper. This brought attention to her accomplishment and capabilities both inside and outside her company. It also brought positive attention to her employer, which could benefit from Kendra's innovation when marketing to customers.

In the future, when Kendra seeks a new job (in or out of the company), she will have a nice piece of intellectual capital to incorporate into her brand and resume, which should help her stand out from other candidates or help justify her requests when moving internally.

* * *

Stop thinking of relationships as only personal or professional and view all as social capital

Your social capital is the collection of people you know and your ability to get to know more people. Basic social capital involves access to people – nothing more. But it is often enabled by *intellectual capital* and can lead to *political capital*. People in sales roles will immediately recognize social capital as a valuable asset that employers ask about and are willing to pay for, but it is valuable for everyone – not only people in sales or business development roles.

You can take inventory of your social capital with the following questions:

- What people do you know whom you could you could contact and expect a response?
- What contact information do you have for each person (email, phone, etc.)?
- On what topics would that person expect to and/or be willing to engage in conversation?
- Who else might they be connected to?

You might also challenge yourself with asking:

- Whose spouses/families do you know?
- What activities do you engage in regularly that lead you to interact with other people?
- How do other people meet you?

Many people have an urge to separate personal and professional relationships. For people who carry a very different persona in a professional setting versus a purely social setting, this might be understandable, but doing so necessarily shrinks the amount of social capital you can access. Few people met in a social setting would be offended to also be engaged professionally (if done appropriately), so there is little downside to being comprehensive in considering the set of relationships that could contribute to your professional success.

Similarly, many professional relationships could also have a social component if you permit them to. One of the simplest ways to invite professional relationships to have a social component is to decorate your office with personal affects. Photos, memorabilia from recent trips, hobby activities displayed on walls, choice of art, and books displayed in a bookcase can invite conversations that build a social relationship on top of a professional foundation.

For most people, social relationships never result in business or career impact, not because those people draw strict boundaries between their work and social lives, but because they do not take deliberate action to enable the benefits.

Adding numbers to your contact list has little value if you do not also capture some ideas for how you might engage that person in a meaningful way in the future. Aligned with the issues-based thinking introduced in Chapter 3, it is a good practice to try and learn as much as situationally appropriate about new people when you meet them. Understand the companies people work for, what roles they are in and what's on their minds to convert just knowing somebody into a potential source of social capital.

Even as more business procedures become automated and computers take on an increasingly substantial role, business remains fundamentally rooted in human interaction. Cold-calling and door-to-door sales have become obsolete in many industries, replaced by social media for engaging passive potential customers, but *access* remains the key to creating business opportunities.

* * *

Mark was an operations manager at a construction equipment manufacturer. He is a social person, active in his community and active with his two high school age boys. He is outgoing and personable, but more importantly for his career, Mark makes it a point to establish contact with the people he meets, and he keeps engaged with them beyond what naturally happens.

For example, at his younger son's baseball team practices, Mark makes sure that any time he meets another parent, he asks for a business card and follows up with a cordial email. Then, when other players have significant events or milestones such as winning a game, making a first homerun, or suffering an injury, Mark reaches out to those parents to express support and interest.

A couple months after the baseball season ended, Mark's company was launching a new product, but was getting delayed by poor delivery performance from one of its key (and previously reliable) suppliers. Upon learning from his procurement department which company was meant to supply the part, Mark realized that one of the other parents on his son's team was an executive with the company.

Having cultivated a relationship with that executive through youth baseball, Mark was able to call the executive and have a strong enough relationship to ask him to help him with the issue. The executive quickly figured out that Mark's account had accidentally not gotten assigned to a new sales rep during a recent internal reorganization. The executive ensured that this issue was resolved, and Mark's organization started getting its parts on time again.

Without Mark's access to the executive through his social capital, the issue may not have been resolved until it had caused substantial problems. Mark's involvement helped his company and increased his social capital with the executive of the supply company, because it preserved Mark's company as a customer.

* * *

Recognize your opportunities to gain influence and build political capital

Political capital is about how you influence others. It is simultaneously the most powerful and ethereal of the forms of relationship capital. Having political capital enables you to influence decision-making to align with your desired outcomes.

The simplest form of political capital is the ability to make the decisions yourself. This form has two components: First, you can get your desired outcome because you control that outcome. Second, your power to control the outcome directly invites others to collaborate with you for "win-wins" so that the decisions you control help them. This should result in you being empowered to drive similar "win-wins" related to decisions under *their* control or significant influence.

Another form of political capital is more elusive but equally powerful – sometimes, in fact, *more* powerful. It involves influencing someone to make decisions that benefit you when you lack personal control over the decision. Sometimes this is the result of an informal quid-pro-quo "you help me, I'll help you" type of arrangement, but often is much more complex.

Eventually, you may be in a position of power, and call most of your shots. But even business owners and CEOs don't have complete autonomy, so all people must find ways to influence outcomes not fully under their control. Since many situations lack a singular, objectively ideal decision or outcome, political capital regularly becomes the mechanism by which a final decision or outcome emerges.

Political capital is more difficult to recognize or describe than social or intellectual capital, but think of it as a recognition that another person believes it is in his or her best interest to act in alignment with your interests.

Another way to characterize political capital is that it is manifested through the perception of shared success. When somebody consciously or subconsciously believes that working in your best interests is the same as working in their own best interests, then you need only establish what is in your best interest for it to become a common best interest.

Achieving that state can happen in many ways. Here are a few examples:

- Trading favors – a strict quid pro quo can lead to moral, ethical or even legal challenges, but a history of helping another on a regular or at least repeated basis does incline that person to help you out in the future (when ethically and practically appropriate).
- Mentor relationship – whether you are mentoring somebody or being mentored, your two successes become linked because the success of the mentee becomes at least partially attributable to the guidance of the mentor. Therefore, when you have mentors or mentees in positions to support you, you have political capital because they share in your success or failure.
- Trading guidance – Similar to a mentor relationship but on a less sustained basis, giving or receiving advice also creates shared success. You thus get some degree of political capital with people you advise or accept advice from.
- Recognizing others – Creating visibility to or helping to advertise and/or celebrate the successes of others attaches a positive association with you and creates a sense of operating on the same team.

- Making others successful – In contrast to the trading favors tactic, simply helping people be (or at least look) successful is a simple and natural way to build political capital. People like to support people who they believe have and will support them when opportunities arise.
- Benefiting the company – Doing things which support the company at a broad level can also build political capital. It is not necessary to always attach your contributions to a specific agenda. For example, participating in recruiting or corporate social responsibility programs may not inherently support any personal agendas, but does help the company overall and can grow your political capital.
- Using your influence to benefit others – At times, you may have political capital that could be used to further somebody's agenda which is either in conflict with your agenda or irrelevant to your agenda. Like the trading favors approach, deploying your political capital to benefit another creates new political capital even as it spends existing political capital. While counterintuitive to do something in conflict with your agenda or not relevant to it, you can think of this as an example of picking your battles. It can be a good strategy to lose some battles that do not matter much to you in order to position yourself to win the battles that are important to you.

Do not be surprised if activities you undertake in one situation with one individual to build political capital do not generate the same benefits in a different situation or in a similar situation with a different individual. Political capital transactions are inherently very personal.

* * *

Jennifer was working in a marketing firm and had steadily been climbing the corporate ladder. As she did this, she paid careful attention to how she managed her relationships. For example, soon after joining, she took a big risk and reached out to Sebastian, who was the most senior partner in her office, and asked him to help her orient her career. She cultivated this initial meeting into a mentorship relationship that persists today with the two of them meeting several times a year to talk about her career.

Six months ago, Juanita, a partner in the office, was championing a charity event sponsored by the company. Steve, one Jennifer's colleagues, had offered to organize the event, but unexpectedly fell ill near the time of the event. Jennifer recognized the opportunity to help, and approached Juanita, offering to take over for Steve. Jennifer worked long hours over consecutive weekends and made the event a huge success despite the last-minute scrambling brought on by Steve's unforeseen illness.

Three months later, the account lead for one of the firm's most interesting clients announced his decision to the leave, creating an opening that Jennifer really wanted to fill. It was a coveted role and would represent a promotion for her, but she was confident she was ready. She knew there would be substantial internal competition for the role, and she knew skills alone would not be enough to land the job.

In addition to going through the normal HR channels to formally apply for that role, she reached out to Sebastian, Juanita, and a few other people in her network who she thought might have influence in the final decision. She sought their guidance in the process while making sure they understood her story and the merits of her candidacy. She did not ask for their support in the decision, however, she did make her agenda clear and equipped them with enough information to advocate on her behalf if they chose to.

Jennifer ultimately got the promotion. Though she had no way of knowing if her use of her political capital was necessary – or even helped – she suspected that Sebastian and Juanita may have been instrumental in her being selected for the role.

* * *

Utilize your relationship capital regularly but with care

Many people struggle with the concept of relationship capital because it has no physical form. There are no bills or receipts to keep in your wallet that signify possession of relationship capital. Neither is there a website where you can log in to confirm you have enough capital to cover the expenditure you hope to make.

Furthermore, like many frequent flier programs, your relationship capital expires if you don't use it soon enough. Only unlike frequent flier program, you cannot predict the date of expiration. Just as you never know how much capital you truly have, you also never know when the capital you do develop will or has expired.

With that in mind, you should aim to continuously add, use, and replenish your relationship capital. Don't save relationship capital for a rainy day because it might not rain before the capital expires, but do save it until you can use it on something meaningful. Spending relationship capital on trivial wins makes it more difficult to replenish that capital because the shared successes you create are not especially meaningful. However, when you create significant mutual wins, as Jennifer did, replenishing your capital can become easier than building it in the first place.

Even though you can think about relationship capital as if it was a currency to be traded and exchanged, you lose capital by discussing it that way with others. Jennifer's approach to using her capital is a model example. She did the right things to establish a bank of capital, but never explicitly confirmed the existence of that capital. Even as she sought to benefit from that capital, she was subtle. She reached out to others so they could recognize her agenda and come to their own conclusion that what she wanted was in line with their own agendas.

Always remember that relationship capital is not a tool for changing decisions that have an objectively clear answer. If Jennifer were not a qualified candidate for the role, no amount of relationship capital would change that, and the business should not have selected her. However, in Jennifer's case, she was one of many qualified candidates. Selecting any of those candidates would have been objectively good for the business. Jennifer's political capital helped her to emerge as the best out of a group of good business decisions.

Many people have squandered political capital and even soured relationships by being too aggressive in their use of political capital. Because there is no explicit contract when it comes to relationship capital, you should never assume that you will get a specific (or even any) return on whatever investment generated that capital. There are countless stories of people who have tried to hold others accountable to unwritten, unshared and unagreed-upon expectations they created in their own minds. When they asked others to meet those terms, the others felt cornered, attacked, or blindsided by expectations they hadn't agreed to. When poorly used, political capital can build resentments rather than positive outcomes.

For example, Jennifer could have opened her conversation with Sebastian with a reminder of the long mentoring relationship by thanking him for all the help over the prior seven years before seeking guidance on her process. Or she could have reminisced a bit with Juanita about the charity event before entering the conversation about the position. In either scenario, Jennifer would have gently introduced the source of her political capital into the other's mind without overtly tying it to the intended use of that capital.

However, if you people feel like you only ever do things to help them because you will expect something in return later, they will probably find you manipulative or self-serving rather than helpful or even savvy. If you are not writing off at least some of your investments in creating relationship capital as altruism in retrospect, then you are probably putting some of your relationships at risk.

Overcome gaps in one form of capital with another

It is natural and common to wish you had more power. Everyone has been in a situation where they wished they were the boss and able to just make the decision rather than being at the mercy of another who clearly sees things differently. When this happens, you have insufficient political capital. In situations like this, while you may not have enough political capital, you might still have enough relationship capital if you invoke some of your intellectual and/or social capital along with the political capital you do have.

For example, in a new product design meeting, an engineer who is relatively new to the company may find her ideas being pushed aside in favor of an alternative. New to the company, this engineer lacks the political capital to push through her design; however, her many years of experience and unique training may give her enough intellectual capital to sway the minds of key decision-makers to her agenda using data, studies, experience and/or knowledge the group did not always have. This could allow her to overcome the gap in political capital with intellectual capital.

In another example, during a debate over level of inventory to maintain for a component key to the manufacturing of a new product, an analyst felt the others in the debate were overestimating the reliability of the supplier to respond to unexpected needs quickly, yet his arguments seemed to be getting overruled. However, the analyst remembered that a colleague from a completely different department had experience working with that same supplier but for different component to a different product. The analyst only knew this person because they happened to both play on the company's softball team. The analyst convinced the group to call the softball player in the other department, and based on his firsthand experience with the supplier decided to increase inventory to the level suggested by the analyst. In this situation, the analyst used his social capital to make up for lack of political capital by both knowing somebody who could help and having a strong enough relationship with that person that they were willing to help.

When it comes to job moves, many people unnecessarily limit themselves to promoting their agendas using only intellectual capital (principally in the form of their experience, capabilities, and accolades). In most cases, intellectual capital is a crucial component for demonstrating your merits and fit for a position, but in a competitive job market, it is rarely enough to secure sought-after positions. Candidates who maximize their use of all forms of relationship capital are better positioned to rise to the top.

Depending on the nature of the job, this can mean different things ranging from having members of your network advocate on your behalf, a concept explored more deeply in Chapter 12, or demonstrating that you know a large group of people who could be relevant to your new position as clients, suppliers, consultants or experts.

Furthermore, your sources of relationship capital can be sources of job opportunities. When your social contacts become aware that you are seeking opportunities, they can share job opportunities that you might not otherwise discover. Your intellectual capital, if marketed well, can make you "findable" by employers seeking candidates like yourself. In a third example, your political capital can encourage leaders within your current company to create new opportunities for you to optimize your contributions and advance your career within the company.

* * *

Returning to the case of Sam, when he reflected on his time at the company, he recognized a few things that he wished he had done differently. While he initially reveled in the freedom afforded to him by having a "hands-off" boss, this ultimately hurt him because when it came time to discuss his contributions to the company, his boss had few specifics around which to build the case for keeping Sam.

Sam excelled as he rose through the company, but he had not often helped those around him excel. Sam pushed the team that reported to him hard, and though they delivered, few on the team felt a personal connection to him. He lacked a group of more junior people who would support him and help him deliver. During the layoff process, concerns were raised that Sam's style and lack of supporters made him less "portable" in the company. This created concerns that putting high performers on his future teams risked limiting the potential of those individuals – or even driving them away.

Furthermore, Sam had focused so narrowly on the joint venture that he had not established much political capital with any senior leaders in his organization. Though he made leadership in the joint venture happy, none of them were able to advocate for keeping Sam during the round of layoffs. Sam lacked any powerful advocates in his company who would accept risk to their careers to support Sam.

Ultimately, Sam's exit from the company was not related to a lack of results, but to a lack of relationship capital. While it is never possible to know with certainty what could have been for Sam, had he taken more interest in the development of the success and growth of his subordinates, he might have gotten more of their support and could have been more portable in the eyes of those making the decisions on exits.

Had Sam paid more attention to the needs of his boss (beyond just the specific tasks his boss assigned him), perhaps he could have found opportunities to make his boss shine, leading his boss to find him more valuable and creating a case for his boss to fight for keeping Sam.

Finally, if he had taken the time to develop relationships with influential people who didn't relate to his day-to-day work, he might have unknowingly developed relationship capital with people who would later decide if he kept his job – and who might have then had more reason to keep him than was the case in reality.

* * *

Opportunities to Apply Chapter Concepts
- Create a list of activities you can start or continue to do to grow your relationship capital in each of intellectual capital, political capital, and social capital.
- Identify the last time you employed relationship capital and identify an opportunity to use relationship capital soon.

9. INTERVIEWING JOBS FOR YOUR CAREER

During the recruiting process, you may think employers are in control because they get to decide if you are qualified for their job. But remember that you have immense power in this process through your ability to say "no" to a job. Before inviting a company to assess you, make sure that *you* would want to say "yes" to *them*.

Mark was an engineer who had been working for a defense contractor for the past 12 years. After his wife received an opportunity in a different state, the two decided she should accept the job and that Mark should resign from his. After the move, Mark entered the job market in a new location far removed from the concentration of government-related jobs he was accustomed to in the Washington, DC area.

Eager to get started with the next chapter in his career, Mark got online and began reviewing job boards searching for open positions in his new city. He almost immediately felt overwhelmed by the high number of open jobs in the area and the absence of jobs that resembled his current job. After having the same experience on four different websites, Mark decided he might need some help.

He reached out to a placement firm in that city and scheduled a time to connect with a headhunter. After a bit of small talk, the headhunter asked Mark, "So what are you looking for in your next job?" Without hesitation, Mark started to recount his work. The headhunter politely listened and when Mark had finished describing most of his resume, the headhunter said, "It's great that you have those done all of those things and have all those qualifications, but what do YOU want from YOUR next job?"

Mark realized that he had never thought about that question. For Mark, like many reading this book, the next step in his career was always a function of the previous step. He worked hard to get promoted, and with each promotion there was a new one to pursue. However, in this moment, Mark realized that there was no rule that said he had to follow a singular, linear path beholden to decisions made many years prior.

In the moment that followed, Mark realized that this was at the same time both liberating and terrifying. The idea that he could pivot his career and pursue new things was exciting. The terrifying part was, he had no idea what that would mean for himself and he didn't know how to choose a job that would both be unfamiliar and an improvement.

* * *

A common irony in many careers is that people often are careful to select jobs that suit their personal agendas only at the beginning and late stages of their careers. At the beginning, people have no work history to "force" them in a particular direction. At the tail end of a career, people realize their value and often feel a greater financial freedom. This creates an increased willingness to exchange financial gain for other drivers of happiness and satisfaction. In between, many people simply follow the path that evolves naturally through serendipity and inertia constrained largely by risk. In most cases, the path evolves without a clear understanding of what truly matters to them.

This still can lead to fulfilling and rich careers, particularly for those who select a well-fitting starting point for their career. However, this leaves your career choices to chance, which is a risky way to manage your career.

There are likewise many cases of people feeling unfulfilled and unhappy in jobs that they are reluctant to leave because they feel trapped by their current role, unwittingly assuming their career is limited to the boundaries of the obviously familiar next steps.

When you are unsatisfied with a job, it is easy to seek a position with a different company but that requires the same skills to execute very similar tasks. It is more difficult to recognize that those same skills could add value in a different industry executing different tasks. It is even more difficult to foresee which of those options will bring you the most fulfillment. However, the payoff in overcoming that difficulty can be immense, and the process to make such a determination is far from rocket science.

Understand what you want BEFORE searching

Before a company ever interviews a candidate, that company builds a vision for the person they would like to hire. This vision naturally results in the company composing a job description including the skills and qualifications they are seeking in candidates.

As a candidate, you should be doing a similar exercise. You should build a vision for the job you would like to accept before initiating your job search. The outcome of this imaginative process likely will not be as specific as a company's job description, but you should be able to describe some key attributes that are important to you.

"Shopping" for your next job is not unlike shopping for other things in your life. If you were looking for a new vehicle, for instance, would you (A) determine things like how many seats you need, what your budget is, what features and performance levels are important to you, and what features and performance levels are important to your spouse? Or would you (B) simply start visiting dealerships and hoping that in a conversation with one salesperson, a car will emerge as the right one for you? And if you adopted approach B, how would you know if a car that sounds right for you is the best fit or just a good fit?

Whether you prefer approach A or approach B, if you want to get an optimal outcome, rather than a merely acceptable one, you must do some deliberate research and introspection that will enable you to objectively and consistently evaluate and compare your options.

Objectively and consistently evaluating options requires that fundamental understanding of what you are looking for. Chapter 6 provided a detailed approach for understanding your sources of motivation. The North Star developed in that chapter should form the basis for developing your list of qualifications for a job to meet your needs.

Qualify jobs for your career, do not just take jobs because you can

It is easy to get excited about an interesting opportunity, but interesting opportunities, even when fun, enriching, and/or fulfilling do not necessarily contribute to the growth of your career.

Jobs provide you with an opportunity to grow new skills and gain new experiences. Over time, an accumulation of related, focused skills can develop into a profession, but the development of jobs into a profession is far from a guaranteed outcome. Disconnected, unfocused skills obtained from an unplanned series of jobs will generate an inferior quality of future opportunities compared to a coherent set of jobs that developed into a profession.

Whether a job contributes to the development of a meaningful profession aligned with your long-term goals is not something any employer can or will consider for you.

This is something that you must assess and may not be obvious just by looking at your North Star.

As you consider new opportunities, remember that opportunities can exist both within and outside your current employer. You can use the same approach for qualifying both internal and external roles.

Select jobs to pursue that support your career

Part of developing a vision for what would qualify a job for your career involves prioritizing the different attributes you would like to see in that job. It is as rare to find the "perfect" job which meets all of your desired criteria as it is for an employer to find a "perfect" candidate, so it is important that you have a plan in place to compromise in a way that still meets enough of your criteria to constitute an improvement in your situation and an advancement of your career. Begin by grouping your desired attributes into the following 4 importance categories:

Importance	Personal Wants	Family Needs	Professional Ambitions
Non-Negotiable	You should not invest any time to pursue an opportunity that cannot fulfill all items		
High Priority	These attributes should consume your focus when seeking future opportunities. Opportunities you pursue may not fulfill all items but should fulfill many		
Differentiating	Satisfying attributes in this section should assist you in choosing between opportunities with similar attractiveness		
Nice to Have	These should not impact your decision, but can be used to "sell" your decision to stakeholders		

When you identify and consider opportunities to pursue, start not by determining whether you are qualified for the job, but instead first determine that the job is qualified for your career. If the job fails on any of your non-negotiables, you should move on. If the job only meets a couple of high priority attributes, it also probably is best to move on.

This change in behavior may briefly be scary: You are, after all, cutting down your choices. But in limiting your choices, you are making it possible to choose from better options. You also are empowering yourself to focus on quality rather than quantity in your jobs search. You liberate yourself to spend more time per opportunity without stretching yourself thinner. This ultimately increases the likelihood of securing an offer.

Only after you determine that a job is a good fit for your career should you start to develop a story for why you would be qualified for that job. In most situations, you are more likely to be a fit for a job if the job is also a fit for your career.

You may not be able to address all items from your list of qualifications, but usually you can at least speculate on all the non-negotiables. Those items you cannot immediately address should become questions to explore during interview and/or conversations you have with current employees during the recruiting process.

Many people find that it is helpful to create a numerical scoring mechanism. Some use their rankings. Others add weights to the calculation. The actual mechanics of creating a quantitative element to the qualification approach need only be sensible to you. What is most important is that you are proactively searching for the elements that will lead to your happiness and fulfillment if you end up in that job.

"Prequalifying" a job for your career makes the whole process smoother

While this process to prequalify a job for your career is added effort for many people who have never thought about interviewing a job for their careers, it generally saves time later in the process. Instead of chasing many opportunities hoping to find one that both fits your needs and extends an offer, you can become focused on specific opportunities that you know will fit your needs and you believe strongly that you can secure.

There are many benefits and time savings which accompany application of this approach:
- Avoiding wasted time on incompatible jobs – Job descriptions are marketed to be appealing to candidates just as candidates use their resumes to appeal to employers. It's easy to become excited about a job that is objectively not a good fit for you unless you are rigorous with an initial vetting. When you do get excited and pursue such a job, it is easy to invest many hours of your time and significant emotional energy into a process that ultimately leads to an outcome that you could have

anticipated with a few minutes of critical thinking at the beginning of the process.
- Knowing when to stop – The perfect job rarely exists, so holding out for it generally is a poor decision. However, a job that is near-perfect should exist and should be the target of your pursuit. The challenge for people, especially when the first job offer they receive during a job search is objectively attractive, is to know how near is close enough to perfect to accept and stop searching. The approach of interviewing jobs for your career allows you to measure the "distance" from perfection of any job. With this information you can make a more informed decisions about whether to accept a job offer or continue to pursue other options.
- Telling a compelling story – A surprisingly low percentage of candidates can tell a compelling, coherent, and authentic story about why the job fits them personally. Consequently, those who can stand out from other candidates and present themselves as much less risky hires. Being able to explain the criteria that justified your interest in the job in a powerful foundation for telling this type of story easily.
- Objective selection between competing offers – In the absence of having specific criteria along which to compare multiple opportunities, the decision of which job to take is emotional and rife with risk. Such a decision commonly leads to buyer's remorse and second guessing, but the prequalification process begins to objectify that decision. Chapter 18 will further empower you to make a well-informed decision, based on data, once you receive offers.
- Communicating and selling a decision to your personal stakeholders – Receiving a job offer does immediately shift the decision-making power entirely to you. Nearly all people have a group of stakeholders (spouse, family, friends, current co-workers) to whom they will have to communicate any job change decisions. While few or none may have veto power on the decision, most people will seek (consciously or subconsciously) to garner support from this group for the decision. Interviewing the job for your career equips you with the specifics you need to persuade these people that your decision is sensible and well justified.
- Considering short-term and long-term implications – It's easy to lose sight of long-term career implications when an opportunity offers exciting short-term benefits. The prequalification approach helps you avoid waiting too long to develop skills and experiences that will ultimately be necessary to enable or justify shifts in profession later in

your career. It does so by forcing you to think about the long-term implications of a job change in addition to the short-term ones.

* * *

After an uncomfortably long pause in their discussion, Mark confided to the headhunter that he had no idea what he was really looking for. After assuring him that this was not a catastrophic challenge, the headhunter walked Mark through a process in which they discussed what motivated Mark personally, what constrained him through family and other commitments, and what he could deliver professionally.

Together they pieced together a list of desired attributes topped by the principle non-negotiable that Mark had to be in the same city as his wife's new job. Furthermore, it emerged that Mark was not as tied to the defense industry as he had assumed based solely on his background. Instead, Mark's passions, interests, and capabilities really oriented him toward project management roles in heavy industries. Mark suddenly became comfortable with the idea of moving outside of his industry of familiarity if he remained close to the functional capabilities that differentiated him and which he enjoyed.

Mark immediately felt more confident about his job search. He no longer was afraid that he would find no relevant positions or that he would have to consider hundreds of jobs just to find one. Mark began seeking jobs that would meet his needs. Effectively, he was making jobs compete for his attention. With work, he built a short list of jobs that he thought were very good fits for his needs and which further developed his profession as a project manager. He developed a compelling story for why he was a fit for those jobs and he reached out to his top three choices. In the end, even though his list of prequalified jobs was longer, he only needed to engage his top three choices. Two of the three gave him offers, and he accepted the one that felt like a better fit than anything in the defense industry could have.

* * *

Opportunities to Apply Chapter Concepts
- Create a scoring mechanism to use in conjunction with your North Star list to quantitatively compare opportunities.
- Create a list of interview questions you could ask a recruiter to confirm the fit of a job to your career.

10. DECIDING TO GO OR STAY

Remember, while you might be able to improve your career situation with a change in companies, leaving isn't always the best option. Listen to both your brain and your gut as you evaluate whether an external move would really be better than an internal one – or not moving at all.

Vikram was an ambitious senior vice president in a large global business. He reported directly to the CEO, enjoyed significant autonomy, and was growing his business unit very successfully even as other parts of the company struggled. On the surface, he was in an enviable position that few would consider leaving without a fight.

However, like most situations, the surface didn't tell the whole story. Vikram was travelling much more than he had hoped to, which was causing not only strain on his family, but creating or at least exacerbating some persistent health issues. Political challenges were growing not only with senior leaders outside of Vikram's business unit, but also with his direct reports. Adding to that, Vikram's career progression within the company was becoming less obvious while opportunities to move outside of the company were becoming more prevalent.

Still, Vikram was enjoying his work. From an intellectual perspective, it was hard to imagine doing something else that would be equally satisfying. But from a practical standpoint, it was easy to imagine many of the more mundane, frustrating day-to-day elements getting better elsewhere.

Though the decision to stay was never overwhelmingly obvious, Vikram allowed himself to remain immersed in his company, counting on the satisfaction of building the business he was so passionate about to overcome the pain points associated with it, and hoping that as time passed, an obvious next step would emerge.

* * *

Many people struggle with timing in managing their careers. People are keenly aware that the grass is not always greener on the other side, but sometimes it is. For you to own your career, you must be willing to make difficult decisions that advance your career in the direction that you want it to go. Still, there will be times where deciding *not* to move is the best decision for your career.

- Do you dread waking up on Mondays knowing you have to go into the office?
- Do you feel like you have reached the ceiling of progression in your current company?
- Do you feel underpaid in your current role? Underappreciated?
- Do you arrive home wondering if you accomplished anything today?

If you answered "Yes" to any of those questions, that does *not* necessarily mean it's a good time for you to enter the job market and seek a new position. An answer of "Yes" to any of those questions is, however, a good indication that it is time to turn off the cruise control of your career and start actively driving your career.

Managing your career often is an exercise in risk management. Best laid plans do not always turn out as expected, and no job is perfect. All jobs involve some level of tedium, frustration and annoyance. There will always be uncertainty and lack of predictability which will only increase with a change in position.

Discord with colleagues is one of the most common reasons for people leaving their jobs. Some people are simply difficult to work with and others just don't mesh well with everybody. And while there is no surefire way to improve working relationships with all people, if stressful relationships are the primary reason for considering changing companies, you should pause before deciding to leave and ensure that you thoroughly explored opportunities to address those challenges within your company before choosing to leave.

Obviously, there are many different strategies and techniques for improving difficult working relationships which fall outside of the scope of this book. Some may solve the issues or at least improve the situation. However, if they do not, there are often still opportunities to transfer within the company, change responsibilities or just change how operations are run which will never get tested unless you have the difficult conversation with leadership that could result in the improvements you need without the burden of a job search.

Many people unintentionally harm their careers by making job moves that while sensible on one dimension, fail to contribute meaningfully to long-term career objectives. Early in a career, this type of move can have limited or no consequence provided that both jobs provided ample opportunity to grow skills and experience. Later in a career, though, making a job move that is not aligned with long-term objectives can derail (or at least slow) career growth. Sometimes, it is difficult to recover from such an error.

It often is a good idea to stay in a job – even if it poses challenges to job satisfaction. You may be tempted to move to a new position that would naturally be free of the challenges that make your current job unsatisfying, but almost every job move increases uncertainty in your career. Often, it is possible to address the challenges that you face within your current role or at least within your current employer. Your job satisfaction may increase, and the risks may decrease. With a new job, however, you always introduce uncertainty and risk. So always consider staying in your current job and addressing the sources of dissatisfaction before you commit to leaving.

Job transitions should increase or be neutral to the balance of personal, family and professional motivations. They should either decrease risks related to achieving long-term career objectives or they should come with substantially greater risk-adjusted upside potential to justify the added risk. Most importantly, they need to "feel" good. Though we seek to help you be objective and data-driven in your career decisions, the emotional element of making a job move cannot and should not be wholly disregarded.

Consider using this simple test to justify looking or staying

As a directional support for making the important decision to leave a job or stay, you can take the following test. On a scale of 1 to 5, where 1 is Complete Disagreement, 5 is Complete Agreement and 3 is Having No Opinion, rank your current level of agreement with these statements.

1. I am excited to go to my job

1	2	3	4	5
Dread going to work		No Opinion		Ecstatic to go to work

2. I am valued and listened to in my job

1	2	3	4	5
Ignored, not valued		No Opinion		Valued and Influential

3. I feel physically energized by the work I do

1	2	3	4	5
Drained by work		No Opinion		Gain energy at work

4. I enjoy the people I work with

1	2	3	4	5
Despise them		No Opinion		Friends outside of work

5. I have an appropriate work-life balance

1	2	3	4	5
Totally unsustainable		No Opinion		Great balance

6. I am building useful new skills

1	2	3	4	5
Stagnant or losing skills		No Opinion		Growing my own market value

7. My pay is commensurate with my contributions and the market

1	2	3	4	5
Grossly underpaid		No Opinion		Fairly or overpaid

8. I have the ability to advance my career

1	2	3	4	5
No upward mobility		No Opinion		Many interesting opportunities

9. I have confidence in the direction the company is moving

1	2	3	4	5
Company is sinking		No Opinion		Excited for the future

10. I am able to excel in my job (both capable of and empowered to)

1	2	3	4	5
Completely Disagree		No Opinion		Completely Agree

Everyone scores their jobs slightly differently, but if you have an average score below 3.5, you should give some consideration to intervening in your job situation (not necessarily leaving the company but at least acting to improve job satisfaction) and if you score above 4.5, you probably should stay where you are. This is an imperfect directional guidance so if your gut suggests the opposite, certainly do not constrain yourself because of this test alone, but if you are struggling to justify either staying or starting to look for other options, this simple test can help.

One of the most difficult aspects of the go/no-go decision can be that even in hindsight it is rarely possible to be 100 percent confident that the decision was the best one. Even trying to choose the least "risky" option is rarely 100 percent clear. In some cases, it is easier to imagine opportunities persisting in the market even if you wait to act on them. In other cases, it may be easier to envision returning to the original employer if the decision proves to have been wrong. But there always is the potential that with any go/no-go decision, a door closes on your career and you must accept the consequences - positive or negative.

Revisit the outcome of that simple test with specific details

Regardless of the decision to look at going or staying, the decision to move or not is never actually made until an offer is made or accepted. An offer will confirm or alter assumptions you made about the job and give you the potential to more objectively anticipate if the move will in fact achieve the objective you expected it to. It is not uncommon for someone to change their mind about leaving their current job after they receive offers to move elsewhere. You should never feel that making the decision to look at leaving commits you to leaving. Often the offers you receive provide the necessary data to justify staying.

Chapter 18 provides more specific guidance for handling your offer and completing this final stay or go analysis.

* * *

As frequently happens, hindsight changed the perspective on events for Vikram. Not long after he first started wrestling with his go/no-go decision, the decision was made for him. A change in CEO changed the dynamic of his situation. What had been a complex equilibrium of positives and negatives that made for challenging decision-making quickly became an untenable situation. He had to leave the company.

Reflecting on the situation, again with the benefit of hindsight, Vikram tried to imagine if he would have done anything differently if he had known how things would turn out. For Vikram, the most important non-negotiables for any job were – and are - being engaged in a topic he was passionate about, felt challenged by, and was empowered to make a material impact on. When he made the decision to stay, no other company offered him the same certainty of meeting his objective.

Furthermore, there was no way for Vikram to know if the decisions that ultimately changed the situation for him would have unfolded in the same way had he had left earlier. If he had gone to a different company, he could have found himself in a state of regret, wondering what could have been had he not gone, and the situation not evolved in the way it did.

* * *

Opportunities to Apply Chapter Concepts
- Take the 10-question test to gauge the likely value in pursuing other opportunities.

LAND YOUR NEXT JOB

11. BUILDING A JOB SEARCH PLAN

Whether the search for a job is an exciting pursuit of new opportunities or a terrifying necessity, most people tend to throw themselves into search activities without first setting up a clear plan. Early planning – before you send off a single resume – takes time at the outset, but ultimately makes for a shorter, more efficient search, and leads to a better destination.

Sofia had decided to pursue a job in the media sector. Despite having never worked in the industry, she had identified powerful alignment between her objectives and opportunities she was confident existed in the industry.

Sofia had spent a time thinking about what was important to her, to her family, and to her career. She was clear that she needed to move to an industry that had more options that would empower her to improve her family life and feed her thirsty ego. She wanted to increase the amount of time she spent with her family by traveling less and by being more present at home when she was not working, and she wanted to work on projects with big values attached to them.

She was a shrewd negotiator. She had an engaging, affable demeanor, but while her personality was disarming, she relished strategy and was very successful at subtly manipulating an audience. With the number of large transactions taking place in the media industry, Sofia was confident that there was a role for her in business development for some lucky company.

Not wanting to waste effort or be ill-prepared for an opportunity, Sofia set out to meticulously plan her job search. She started by prioritizing the things that she wanted from her next role, as well as the constraints she needed to satisfy to improve her family life. She described the responsibilities she thought she would enjoy from her next job as well as the skills she believed differentiated her from others. She prioritized these factors in a list, so she could quickly assess whether an opportunity was worth her time to explore.

She created a list of companies familiar to her in the industry and spent the next two weeks researching each, not only examining whether they were likely to fulfill the items on her list, but also finding competitor companies to investigate.

Armed with a short list of interesting companies, she pulled up her contact list and LinkedIn page on her laptop and started collecting names of people she thought might be able to help her in her job search. She prioritized these too and gave herself some deadlines for connecting with people.

* * *

No matter what, your engagement with potential employers will be more effective if you plan out your activities rather than improvising your way through the recruiting process. That is the case whether you have been terminated by an employer, have decided to improve your career situation, or are simply testing the market to understand your positioning and potential options.

Though the individual recruiting experience is likely to vary with each employer, your approach to finding your next job should follow some predictable steps. Before you engage with an employer, you want to do four things:

- **Developing your personal narrative** involves describing your personal journey to set a direction for your career and the baseline for a story to justify your transitions.
- **Engaging your network** takes an issues-based approach inventorying who can support you in the efforts and reaching out to them to involve them in those efforts.
- **Building your collateral and story** is a matter of synthesizing a message about your ambitions and capabilities into compelling documents and narratives that create interest in companies to explore opportunities with you.
- **Planning for success** involves having a plan for integration and an approach for deciding to accept or reject an offer.

Your job search plan can take any format that is effective for you. Different people benefit from different levels of detail in their job search plans, but nearly all benefit from addressing the topics identified in this chapter.

Especially if it has been years since you went through a job search, expect to go through several iterations of your plan. In an ideal scenario, a plan, once designed, would need only to be executed. In practice, it is much more common for people develop a plan only to revisit and update it regularly as the job search progresses. This is normal and still effective.

If you have an existing career plan (such as the plan we describe in Chapter 2, that document is likely to provide much useful information for the job search plan.

Write your personal narrative to organize your thoughts and story

Your personal narrative is the story of how you got to where you are today. While not every part of your narrative will be relevant to employers, that story has material impact on what motivates you today in addition to describing what you are able to do for an employer. Ultimately, composing this narrative is as much value to you for understanding yourself as it is for employers to understand you.

People who seek jobs that are aligned with their career aspirations are generally happier and more successful than those who simply chase jobs for which they expect to be qualified. Consequently, it is important to present a potential employer a coherent, logical story for your job change. For that story to be successful, it must address both your ability to perform the functions required by the job and the job's ability to fulfill your career objectives.

Your personal narrative need not be a polished literary document, but it should:

- Beginning with high school (or at least as far back as you think is relevant in telling the story of who you are today), capture from the jobs that you held:
    o Why you selected them
    o What you learned about yourself during the job
    o What made you successful or unsuccessful in the job
- Describe the motivating factors and limitations that you will use in determining the best fit opportunity:
    o Personal drivers
    o Family constraints
    o Professional opportunities
- Clarify goals
    o What do you want to do?
    o What are you able to do?
    o What do you need from your next job?

If you are unemployed when you begin this activity, your goal may seem like it is simply to get any job, but even in that situation, it behooves you to be more specific to avoid taking a job that quickly returns to you to the job market to restart the process because that job was poorly aligned with your career needs.

One of the most challenging things for job searchers to do is to say "no" to an opportunity without first thoroughly exploring it. Talented people are a potential fit for many more job opportunities than there are opportunities that fit their careers. Being able to quickly say "no" to jobs which will not benefit your career keeps you from wasting time on jobs that will never fit your career needs.

Most people initiate their jobs searches with the intention of addressing one or more areas of concern in their current employment. Setting the objective to increase wealth creation potential, reduce travel, improve work-life balance, build specific skills necessary for long-term objectives, or any other specific motivation will help you quickly anticipate whether a job opportunity will address your needs.

Job satisfaction is generally enabled by a balance of addressing your personal wants, your familial and social needs and your professional ambitions. Job search planning requires you to understand these different sources of motivation. You need to be able to answer:

- What brings you fulfillment and enjoyment irrespective of how anybody else is impacted?
- What priorities and practical constraints need to be satisfied because of how they impact others in a way that influences you?
- What skills, knowledge, and capabilities do you have and want to utilize in the role, and how do you expect those to evolve?

These pieces of information need to be clearly aligned with your personal narrative (depending how thorough you are in constructing your personal narrative, this information may simply be plucked from that narrative. It also may also come from the North Star exercise described in Chapter 6). If there is a conflict between the personal narrative and your goals, both should be reassessed until they align. Otherwise, you run the risk of either pursuing a job that ultimately will not satisfy you or pursuing a great job but struggling to explain your interest in the job to employers in a way they will relate to.

Establish your criteria for job selection and pre-qualification of opportunities

Your sources of motivation will direct the creation of your criteria for job selection. Collectively, those sources of motivation provide a list of attributes you would like to see in a future job. They also provide insight about attributes you hope to avoid. From the list of motivations you compiled, you should segment the attributes into three lists:

1. Non-Negotiables – What are the attributes that if not satisfied would lead you to not pursue the opportunity at all?
2. High priority - What attributes do you want to see which are most likely to influence your decision?
3. Nice-to-haves – What attributes would you like to see but would only influential your decision if considering otherwise comparable offers?

Though a seemingly simple task, it is important that you generate an accurate and realistic set of lists. A lengthy non-negotiable list will limit the number of opportunities, something which could be helpful or problematic, depending on the scope of your search. Items on the "nice-to-have" list have the possibility of not being realized, so if they are more than just a "nice-to-have," you should be realistic about that.

Ultimately, you want to commit to honoring these lists. They will allow you to pre-qualify jobs for your career as discussed in Chapter 9. Once you determine that an opportunity fails to meet any of your non-negotiable needs, reject it immediately. This is how you use your job search plan to avoid wasting time on predictably futile pursuits.

Develop an activity plan as a tool to keep yourself accountable to making progress

While many people's initial thought is to seek out job boards and begin searching for posted jobs based on what they perceive themselves qualified for, most people find quicker success when they begin their search with an issues-based engagement of their personal network. This concept will be explored in much more detail in the next chapter.

Having developed your personal narrative and criteria for jobs, you want to begin the process of identifying specific opportunities. You could simply launch into calling people in your network, going to target company websites in search of job postings, or scanning large consolidated job boards, but most people find the overall process less frantic and more comfortable if they plan the steps out in advance.

Describing goals at a task level on a week-by-week basis (day-by-day basis if you are currently unemployed) will help you to know that you are making progress in your search even without having interview invitations or offer letters flowing into your inbox. In the activity plan section of job search plan, you should include:

- Engaging with members of your personal board of directors
- Contacting advocates, potential advocates, and new contacts you hope to bring into your network
- Researching target companies

As you progress through the job search process, you will naturally want to update the activity plan with tasks such as:

- Supporting potential advocates through the issues-based advocacy approach described in Chapter 12
- Scheduling/holding meetings with potential advocates
- Updating digital presence
- Creating opportunity-specific collateral such as resumes and cover letters

For some people, building a job search plan in this level of detail feels like overkill, and in some cases, it is. However, many people have a strong tendency to chase the newest or next opportunity without properly preparing for other opportunities. If your pursuit of one opportunity is distracted by a newer, apparently shinier one, your preparation is likely to suffer. When you follow a detailed activity plan, you prepare more thoroughly and are less likely to use a generic rather than customized resume, more likely to have a better understanding of the company during an interview, and less likely to be surprised by interview questions.

Candidates should use their judgment and knowledge of their personal tendencies to optimize the formality with which they plan out activities.

Create a strategy for offer evaluation

The optimal time to decide how you will choose among multiple job offers (including staying where you are if currently employed) is *before* you have competing offers. In the absence of a predefined process, candidates often find themselves conflicted by emotional (gut) responses that differ in outcome from seemingly rational analysis.

Taking a methodical approach to understanding and "valuing" job offers will help you to comfortably reach a decision that you can have confidence in and readily explain and sell to yourself, your spouse, your friends, and other parties who have an interest in your decision. This approach needs to be defined during the planning stages – before companies and/or offers can elicit an emotional response to the situation. Chapter 18 provides detailed guidance on how to effectively manage this.

* * *

As Sofia worked through her list of contacts, she was fortunate to uncover a couple of interesting opportunities. She refined her focus within those opportunities to ones that offered flexible scheduling and allowed occasional remote working. Even as she continued to engage people in her network, she added specific tasks to effectively respond to these emerging opportunities.

She knew she needed to build her understanding of the companies, specifically given her limited industry acumen. She also needed to develop her story now that she had a specific audience in mind. She allotted time to work on her resume and added a few more phone calls to her to-do list to talk through the situation with her mentors and confirm the direction she was going made sense for her before she got too much further.

Even though Sofia was an industry outsider, she impressed prospective employers quickly. The research and preparation she had done had allowed her to benefit from the opportunities she had accessed through her network. She walked in confident, informed, and in control of the situation. Her functional skills spoke for themselves. Focusing her efforts on only a few high-potential opportunities had allowed her to prepare for those interviews so thoroughly that she overcame her lack of industry experience.

* * *

Opportunities to Apply Chapter Concepts
- Compose your personal narrative.
- Create a list of job search activities and develop a timeline for executing them.
- Develop and describe your approach for comparing offers.

12. EXPLORING OPPORTUNITIES THROUGH YOUR NETWORK

The people you know create relationship capital that makes you valuable to potential employers and can help lead you to opportunities you might otherwise never find. It also is a key factor in your success while in any job – not just during transition.

Keisha was a management consultant who for the past 8 months had been questioning whether she wanted to stay in consulting or switch to a corporate role. She loved consulting and by every measure was successful in the craft, but she felt like the travel and long hours were getting in the way of starting a family, something that was important to her.

Every few weeks, Keisha would get frustrated with her job and poke around on job boards looking for something better. This exercise usually made her appreciate her job more because she rarely found exciting jobs, but occasionally she was intrigued enough by one or two of them that she put in an application. Unfortunately, she was never successful in even getting a call for an interview.

Keisha almost had herself convinced to remain in consulting when she learned the small company she worked for had been acquired by a much larger one. Keisha knew the large company well and was not at all excited by the prospect of integrating into their very different culture, which would likely exacerbate the quality of life issues she already was facing in the consulting industry.

After spending four weeks of nights and weekends scouring job boards and applying to postings, she had little to show for her efforts. While she had applied to many jobs, only three opportunities had really excited her. Of those, only one seemed like it had any chance of being better than her pre-acquisition employment. She got a few interviews but had yet to develop any real traction.

For the first time in a long while, she was starting to feel nervous about her career. She unlocked her phone and called a friend who seemed to really like the place she worked. Keisha had wanted to handle her job search herself and not be a burden to any of her friends, but she was seeing desperation on the horizon and decided her friends would understand if she asked for a little help.

After some of the normal small talk, Keisha summarized her situation and asked her friend if the company her friend worked for was hiring. While Keisha's friend was sympathetic and happy to listen, the friend didn't think the company was hiring but offered to double-check with someone in HR. Energized by the friend's willingness to help, Keisha repeated the process a few more times. Unfortunately, the results were consistent: initial call followed by no action to actually get an interview.

Keisha then remembered that a family friend was a senior executive at a company that could be interesting to her. Assuming she was struggling because she was aiming too low in the food chain, she got the friend's email from her mother and reached out to him. Unfortunately, the outcome was the same. He didn't have any open positions that required her qualifications, but he was happy for her to send over her resume in case something come up.

At this point, desperation now appeared to be sprinting towards Keisha. If job boards weren't doing it for her and her network wasn't making anything happen, what options did she have?

* * *

As introduced in the prior chapter, any job search should be aided by your network of contacts and advocates. These people can improve your decision-making, elevate your performance during evaluation, connect you with new, relevant potential advocates, and even create unique access to opportunities you otherwise never would be considered for. In short, they can both make you better for the opportunities you find and provide you with opportunities you wouldn't find on your own.

One of the best ways to reduce stress and constrain the effort required by a job search is to avoid chasing after jobs that are not a good fit for your career. The personal board of directors introduced in Chapter 3 can be instrumental in helping you focus your efforts only on opportunities that fit your career objectives. Before devoting time to exploring opportunities, it is useful to engage some members of your board of directors to confirm that the criteria you will use to screen jobs for their fit to your career objectives are sensible and will keep you from wasting time on jobs that ultimately are not a good fit for your career.

Even as a highly qualified candidate, it is easy to get lost or overlooked amid the noise when pursuing highly competitive positions, making it more attractive to pursue opportunities for which you have advocates and advantaged access. Once you have a clear set of criteria to use in assessing the fit of opportunities to your career, you should avoid some of this noise by starting your search not on job boards, but with your advocates and then others from your extensive list of contacts.

Within your list of contacts are likely ==people working for companies that are or can become target companies.== You also probably know people working for companies not of interest to you, but who are familiar with the company you are interested in and know people who work at those companies. Both can be helpful in the job search.

For each contact, it is useful to think about the company they work for and its issues. Is the company likely to align with and fulfill your job search objectives? Do you have something compelling to offer that company which aligns with its issues and likely needs?

As you work through the list of people you know, you will identify companies that interest you and in which you have potential advocates. Once you complete the review of your network, you should add to the list of targeted companies, additional companies with whom you may not have a connection, but which would enable you to meet your career objectives.

Depending on the size of your network, you may opt to not thoroughly exhaust your network. It is generally only feasible to explore 8-to-12 opportunities at any point in time. People with very extensive networks may pause their review of their network after identifying about 10 opportunities to explore. Those with smaller networks may exhaustively review their network and then begin acting on their 10 most promising prospects.

Not all opportunities that you explore will result in entering a recruiting process. While there are many times where this process creates access to job opportunities, there are some companies that simply are not able to hire people. Even in these situations, there is merit in exploring the opportunity with your advocates. After all, it would be overwhelming to work through 10 recruiting processes at once. However, if the pursuit of 10 different opportunities leads to two or three potential jobs, the efforts have paid off. Remember: ==the objective is not to maximize the number of offers but to maximize the quality of fit.==

Searching job boards for additional opportunities makes sense if you identify fewer than 10 opportunities through your network or once you have pursued all the opportunities available through your network.

Create active support during your job search

This approach is powerful for you as a candidate because of the leverage and support created by your advocates. However, it is important to remember that being an advocate for somebody during a job search process can be a risky albeit rewarding proposition. Assuming you are ultimately hired and successful in a new job, your advocate(s) shares in that success and grows his/her political capital. For most, it also is emotionally rewarding to help others achieve their goals. Depending on how the relationship started, you may wish to develop the relationship and utilize the advocate differently. Note that you can have many advocates. In fact, having more than one increases the likely impact.

How you engage with potential advocates effectively depends largely on how close your initial relationship is with that person. Revisiting the categorization introduced in Chapter 3, the way you approach members of your network to support you in the job search should vary based on closeness of the relationship:

- Preexisting relationships
    o You can often be very transparent about wanting their support and share your vision for ideal support from them. Ask what they would be comfortable doing to help you and work from there.
    o Involving these people early makes them far more useful than engaging them late in the process.
- People you seek out to be advocates
    o Tools like LinkedIn and Hoovers can identify people you can connect with in target companies. It usually is overly ambitious to think they will become supporters, but they are often open to providing contextual information about the company, and might expose you to other connections.
    o You can reach out early in the process, but sometimes it is helpful to get in touch when you are engaged in the recruiting process and have more specific questions to ask.
- People you meet during the process
    o While you do not control whom you meet during the interview process, you do control what you do following that meeting. Developing relationships beyond the minimal transactional engagement necessary for the recruiting process often can inspire somebody to advocate for you.

- Go beyond the minimal thank you email to try and deepen the relationship. You may find that someone you met by chance becomes a great supporter of yours.

Take an issues-based approach to securing advocacy through shared wins

For you to develop your relationships into advocate relationships, it is important to understand the issues facing people within your network. Strong relationships are built on mutual understanding and care for the success of the other person. Understanding their issues will empower you to connect on a deeper level and should expose opportunities to support them and make them successful.

Issues are not necessarily negative. Issues are simply the most pressing concerns of the individual and are as often opportunities as challenges. The hallmark of an issue is its ability to consume effort and emotion from an individual.

There are principally three types of advocates: those inside a target company, those outside a target company, and conscribed advocates.

Advocates within a target business

People, especially when actively pursuing new jobs, strongly value access to advocates who are current employees or closely associated with a target company. Depending on the level of the person within the organization and their closeness to the job being sought, these people can:

- Help you to bypass red tape and/or accelerate your process
- Connect you with opportunities that are not available online
- Sponsor you as a candidate through employee referral programs
- Give you guidance on the company, enhancing your interview quality
- Assist you during your preparation
- Support you during hiring discussion debates
- Provide helpful information that improves your final decision
- Sponsor you during your integration

The willingness of an individual to support you is largely influenced by the closeness of your relationship to them. Their willingness to help also is influenced by personal risk. Providing you opinions and stories about their experience in the company incurs far less personal risk than contacting the hiring manager and providing a positive testimonial on your behalf.

It is important to keep in mind that many people feel bound to a sense of fairness in the process, especially those with formal hiring roles such as people in human resources. You should be deliberate in how you approach them seeking support to avoid the possibility of appearing to seek inappropriate advantage over other candidates. Instead, it is best to keep discussions and requests for support centered around enabling you to present yourself most effectively. Avoid anything that can be interpreted as you are seeking an unfair advantage over other candidates.

It is common for an advocate to potentially benefit personally (and often financially) from your ability to impact business performance if you are hired. They have a vested interest in your success and are therefore people you want to regularly engage.

Advocates outside the target business

It is likely that for some of the jobs you seek, you will not have preexisting relationships with people who can advocate for you within the business. However, many people underestimate the potential for advocates to support them from *outside* the target business.

For this population, there is neither concern about fairness nor significant concern about personal risk. Success for them is fully aligned with your success without being tempered by the success of the target organization. While it is rare for this group to influence the recruiting process of another organization, there are many ways that this group can still support you, including:

- Alerting you to job openings/needs at other companies they are aware of through their network
- Helping establish process expectations (resume review, interviewing, etc.) based their company's/personal approach
- Supplementing your knowledge of a company with their personal experiences (if they work in a same, similar, or related industry)
- Coaching you while you prepare your brand, resume, and/or interview
- Performing mock interviews with you for practice
- Recommending and/or introducing you to their connections

Engaging people not directly associated with a target company often has uncertain impact ranging from no impact to substantial support. Job seekers often find that people within their network of close contacts are connected in surprising ways to contacts they would like to have. This is especially true when engaging with people in a principally social setting (fellow alumni, parents from children's schools, etc.).

Conscribed advocates

Conscribed advocates are people who have a monetary incentive to participate in your process. These relationships are discussed in more detail in Chapter 4 and generally fall into one of three categories:

- **Coaches** are service providers whom you pay to support you in specific aspects of your career management or job search. The services can include writing resumes and preparing you for interviewers to holistic, end-to-end handholding. Coaches carry many different titles depending on the service they provide, but are invested in your success because you are their customer. Generally, their services are fee-based and not tied to a particular outcome.
- **Search firms** are service providers that companies pay to find and initially qualify candidates for the open positions that the company has. When dealing with search firms, you are a valuable commodity, but you are *not* the client. While it is in the best interest of the search firm to get you placed, their priority is filling *their* searches rather than on finding *you* a job. Therefore, while search firms are cost-effective advocates for you (since the hiring company pays their fees), they are not the most reliable advocates.
- **Placement firms** are service providers that candidates pay to market them to relevant companies. Unlike with search firms, *you*, as the candidate, are the client. With these firms, the priority is to get you placed. Success is no more guaranteed, but you have more influence on the level of activity on your behalf. These companies help get you in the door with target companies, often even the absence of a posted job description.

The support that you utilize during a job search should neither be limited to a single person nor be an all-hands-on-deck approach. The people you engage will likely evolve over time during the job search process.

Get organized to make managing engagements with your network easier

For many people, especially those blessed with an extensive network, it is easy to become overwhelmed with the information you compile on your network, even before beginning to reach out to your network for support. Many people find it liberating and helpful to build a spreadsheet and manage their interactions from that spreadsheet.

While the exact format is immaterial and should be whatever works best for you, most people find it helpful to include some or all of the following:

- Company
- First
- Last
- Level / title
- Closeness of relationship
- Priority
- Phone
- Email
- Last contact date
- Target date for next contact
- Location
- Industry
- Function
- Company Issues
- Individual Issues
- Why should they hire me
- Why would I want to work there
- Notes from past discussions

Building this sort of spreadsheet is a significant effort when first created, but keeping it updated requires much less effort and the dividends paid during a job search can be substantial.

Continually grow and refine your network of contacts

It is natural through this process to find that there are gaps in your network or areas where it would be beneficial to have additional or stronger advocacy relationships. While it would be ideal to have been cultivating these relationships for years, beginning the effort to build a relationship out of a practical need during a particular job search is far from a lost cause. While an emerging, new relationship will rarely have the same impact as a lengthy, sustained relationship, a new advocate can still have an important impact on your behalf.

Frequently, one or more of the following types of people would be helpful as an advocate or at least a member of your network during your interview and integration processes, but might not already exist in your network:

- The hiring manager or someone in a similar role
    o Can help you understand the most important attributes for succeeding in the role (and in the recruiting process), enabling you to make a better decision on whether to pursue the position and create a more effective strategy to pursue the role if suitable
- Someone who works for or has worked for the hiring manager
    o Can provide helpful context to decide if the role fits your needs and help you present yourself in an appealing way to the key decision-maker
- Future peers
    o Can give meaningful and unique context for the expected experience if hired, improving the quality of your decision whether to pursue the specific role
- Someone who has been in the company for at least five years
    o Can credibly confirm or refute expectations related to the company, role, and/or hiring manager and provide guidance on what makes people succeed or struggle in the company
- A recruiter or someone in a human resources role
    o Can provide access to comprehensive information and credible expectations for details on the recruiting process and other structural elements (compensation, career advancement, performance management, etc.) in the organization
- Someone who entered the role in a similar way to you (mid-career hire or internal promotion from a similar position/experience level)

- Can offer credible and relevant guidance on what to expect and how best to succeed in your efforts

In addition to being sources of information, any of these people may become supporters of your candidacy or impediments to it. It thus becomes important to develop relationships in an effective way and not only unlock access to useful information but do so in a way that has a higher likelihood of generating a supporter than in creating an obstacle. There are four common ways to reach out to people once you have identified them as those you want to build a relationship with:

1. Connect through an advocate – Seek an introduction by someone who already is close to you and supportive of your efforts
    - Has the highest likelihood of success
    - Does, however, require some relationship capital be spent by the advocate, so choose connections wisely for maximum impact
    - While you want to avoid being transactional, it is appropriate to be transparent about both the origin and rationale for the connection
2. Enhance an existing relationship – Invest time and effort into becoming a closer connection with someone you already know (even if only vaguely) or becoming connected with someone in a different context (such as converting/augmenting a personal relationship to a professional one)
    - This approach has the lowest likelihood of outright rejection
    - Because the person already knows you, you need to present a focused objective and/or purpose and engage in a different dimension/setting
    - Must appeal to sense of mutual interest and/or benefit
3. Social media (LinkedIn, etc.) – Reach out to people you do not know, but believe you would like to, through social media tools
    - It is critical that in your initial contact you establish some element of commonality while also being transparent about why you are making contact
    - Patience and bounded persistence are key as such relationships are generally slow to develop
4. Professional resources (Hoovers, etc.) – Purchase access to such resources to identify and contact people with a specific profile and for a specific purpose
    - These resources enable the most specific targeting, but require you to provide the most compelling story for initial contact
    - Expect inconsistent results

- Need to have a very targeted message, but cast a wide net to have multiple options

During your initial contact, it is typically good to appeal with a sense of unstated mutual benefit and/or appeal to the ego/altruism of the individual. For this purpose, you want to understand and appeal to the individual's unique issues and your ability to help them address those issues. You need these people to want to spend their valuable time with you. To do that, you must find some way to deliver value for them. While there is a subset of the population for which altruism is a sufficient motivator, most people are willing to help you in relative magnitude to the mutual benefit they have received or stand to receive.

A sympathetic ear is a good start. People value those who are willing to supportively listen to them and engage in interesting conversation, but this will rarely be enough to earn an advocate relation. You need to find a way to deliver more value.

Before reaching out to potential supporters, you need think about:

- The challenges facing the businesses they are in
- The personal challenges unique to their position or situation within the business
- The causes or activities the person is passionate about
- How you have supported that person in the past (if applicable) and how you can support that person now

Having something interesting to talk about is the necessary beginning to developing a relationship. However, to achieve a sufficiently deep relationship where the individual is willing to advocate on your behalf typically requires a level of mutual support/benefit that goes beyond good conversation.

Finding ways to support the other person before you seek their support is a good strategy for increasing the likelihood of receiving support later. There are many ways to support somebody that are more meaningful than just offering a sympathetic ear. Some ideas include:

- Sharing interesting articles, podcasts, books, or other knowledge resources
- Connecting people who share related interests or expertise
- Acting as a sounding board for ideas (proposing new ideas or giving feedback)
- Referring candidates or job opportunities
- Mentoring or being mentored

- Recommending high-quality suppliers or giving testimonials to products/services
- Sharing personal learning experiences
- Providing testimonial on behalf of somebody
- Supporting charities or schools
- Volunteering at events organized by or supported by others

There is no predictable formula for developing the type of relationships that result in ready support from others. The opportunity to support somebody often will not emerge except through discussion, and often not on the first conversation. Relationships regularly take time to develop. Those who are most likely to successfully develop a wide network of advocates support others regularly and subconsciously. However, even as an intentional behavior, such activities are impactful – especially if you begin doing them well before you need support yourself.

Always remember to be appreciative of the efforts of your advocates irrespective of the impact they make on your behalf. It is important to not just express gratitude for their support, but to show your gratitude through continued support as an advocate for them whenever feasible. This continued support is crucial to maintaining your network. More important even than this is the fact that repeated consistent interactions with members of your network is a powerful and compelling way to both expand your network and to convert contacts into advocates for the future.

* * *

Keisha's aunt was an executive for a retail company and had offered in the past to be a mentor. Though her aunt's company did not interest her, Keisha did greatly respect her aunt's business acumen, and right now, Keisha needed some guidance. She called her aunt and explained the situation including her current frustrations and fears.

After quietly listening, her aunt offered two pieces of advice that ultimately changed Keisha's job search for the better. First, she asked, "Why didn't you start with your network?" She explained to Keisha that people want to help the people they care about, and especially like to help people who have helped them in the past or might help them in the future. Keisha's aunt shared that in her career, most of her job changes had originated through her network of contacts and not from impersonal job boards or newspaper ads.

Second, she asked, "When you talk to people, why are you asking for a job?" Her aunt went on to point out that Keisha was limiting her contacts' abilities to help her by asking for one thing: a job. If she instead talked about her goals, and sought advice on getting there, her contacts could do all sorts of things to help her. They might be able to introduce her to other people (headhunters, colleagues, friends) who might have job opportunities or at least be the next step in a chain of discussions leading to a job opportunity. They could give advice on how best to present herself in the face of an opportunity. They could suggest companies to pursue. And nothing in any of those interactions would prevent them from offering her a job if one was available.

Keisha's aunt further suggested that Keisha be careful to not let the conversation be just about her. If she could help other people, they would become more likely to help her.

Following that conversation, Keisha felt like she needed to regroup and restart her job search process. She stopped spending time on job boards and instead spent time with her contacts, first those on her phone and later those from her LinkedIn page.

For each person she tried to figure out what they were doing in their career and tried to come up with at least one topic that the person would find interesting. She also gave every contact a score for how relevant their job was to her interests. She wasn't concerned about whether a person might be able to offer her an interesting job, but instead looked at conversations as opportunities for her to learn about people, companies, industries or even (ideally) job opportunities relevant to her.

She made a list of people to contact, focusing first on people who scored highly in relevance and with whom she had an interesting topic to use as an excuse to talk. In some cases, she shared an article or a paper she thought was mutually interesting. In some cases, she asked a question about a current event or industry topic. In one case she even led by sharing a job lead that she unintentionally found when looking for herself, but thought could be perfect for that friend if he was in the job market.

While Keisha felt like she was doing a lot more work following this process, she realized that she was spending only slightly more time than she had been when looking at job boards, yet she felt much more accomplished. This approach was certainly different, but it was more exciting, even if she had no idea if or how it would work.

Some of her conversations were simply pleasant chats resulting in nothing tangible for her job search, but many of her conversations naturally led into follow-ups. Soon, she found herself getting connected to interesting people she had never met. She was exploring jobs through backdoors she was invited to walk through only because of who she knew or had been talking to. Keisha felt like she was privy to opportunities that she never would have known about had she not spoken with her aunt and changed her approach. The path to her next job still was not clear, but she no longer felt like the time spent working toward that job was wasted, as she had felt when relying on job boards.

It took two months from the restart, but Keisha received a call from an executive she had met six weeks prior. A friend had introduced them based on Keisha asking that friend to help her understand the business model for small businesses partnering with large distributors and leveraging the distributor's supply chain. While their initial conversation had nothing to do with finding Keisha a job, when a position opened in that executive's team, he remembered *his conversation with Keisha, reached out to her with the opportunity, and ultimately hired her.*

* * *

Opportunities to Apply Chapter Concepts
- Create list of connections within your network and identify level of closeness, company and issues (personal and company).
- Using your job criteria, assess potential for each company to have interesting opportunities.
- Identify your personal board of directors.
- List any additional companies you would like to pursue, but currently lack connections and describe a plan for seeking potential advocates.

13. RESEARCHING POTENTIAL EMPLOYERS

Researching your potential employer early in the process can pay big dividends and prevent big problems. A little research can help you determine if you actually want to work for a specific company – and can help you figure out how best to sell yourself to that company.

Dale was convinced that it was the right time to move companies. He was further convinced that he knew what he wanted. Already established in the agribusiness sector, he had no ambitions to leave the industry, rather he wanted to find a company that was more progressive than his current employer. Dale was fascinated by the emerging technologies in farming, particularly those related to blockchain and cutting edge "farm to fork" tracking initiatives.

Dale reached out to the network he had built over the years. He shared his ambitions and his ideas about where to go. He identified and developed advocates for himself in the recruiting process, and he secured multiple offers. All signs pointed to him having made a great decision for himself.

Yet after about a year in his new job, Dale was miserable. Although he was delivering revenue that exceeded his targets and his customers were thrilled with the work he did for them, he felt like he was treated as a second-class citizen among his peers and superiors. When he accepted the new company's offer, he had been sold on the idea of building a business in the agribusiness space. Yet now, everyone around was pushing him to expand his scope into new geographies or new industries. He felt isolated and misled. Adding to the frustration, he could not explain how this had happened.

It was not until Dale decided to leave and started interviewing again that he realized how the problem had been created. He had not taken the time to confirm that he and the company were using the same definitions when they spoke. When Dale thought about growing a business, he thought about serving more clients on the same topics or serving the same clients in new ways within the same space. Growth of the top line and bottom line was growth in Dale's mind. However, when the company spoke about growth, it meant expansion across geographies and industry verticals. Expanding up or down the supply chain would work, but simply growing revenue in a small space was not the sort of growth the company was looking for.

When Dale did his original research, he assumed that because he was using the same vocabulary as the company, both had the same definition of "growth." Further, he failed to thoroughly research how the company operated and who succeeded there. Had he looked to find people whose profiles looked like his, he would have realized that hardly anybody at senior levels was specialized. The company valued generalists – not specialists like Dale. While Dale knew what he was looking for, he made the subtle but substantial mistake of only going surface-deep to confirm that he would be getting what he wanted from the move.

As Dale embarked on his new job search, he made a concerted effort to understand not just what his target companies did, but how they did it and what sort of person succeeded at them. That added a set of dimensions which, along with his prior level of diligence and introspection, enabled him to land a new job in a start-up company that proved to be exactly what he wanted.

* * *

Successful candidates increase their influence during their job search processes by effectively collecting and using the right information about target companies. Whether you use this information to confidently expect the job you are considering pursuing will meet your specific criteria and fit into your intended career path or to wow a prospective employer with a focused, polished resume and/or interview, basing your decisions on data is key to achieving your desired outcomes.

Companies come in many different shapes, sizes, ownership structures, and levels of transparency. Public companies are typically easier to research than private companies, and the larger a company becomes and the longer it has been in business, the more likely you are to find the information you would like to know. You are very unlikely to have access to everything you would like to know, so some educated guessing will almost always be necessary. That guessing will be improved by the data you do find.

First and foremost, your preliminary research needs to enable you to test the fit of the job for your career objectives. Chapter 9 discussed how to prequalify a job for its fit with your career objectives. This chapter will help you to find the data you need to complete that process.

Having established that a fit for your career is possible (ideally probable), your preliminary research should guide the way in which you present yourself to the employer. Your resume, cover letter, and personal interactions should all be tailored to fit the needs of the company and justify your ability to address its issues.

Whether trying to decide if a company is right for you, preparing a custom resume, or preparing for an upcoming interview, the tools and sources of information are generally the same:

- Company Website
- Company Investor Documents (Annual Report, 10-Ks)
- Company Social Media
- Job Posting
- Employer Intelligence Websites (Glass Door, Vault)
- LinkedIn
- Personal Network
    o Advocates
    o Professional Networks
    o Alumni Networks

There are many ways to utilize the information contained in these sources. Depending on your individual objectives (e.g. interview preparation vs. testing fit for career) some sources will be more relevant than others. However, it is important to realize that most sources will not directly tell you what you seek to understand, and those that do may do so with questionable credibility. The most effective insights you collect during preliminary research are likely to come from the connections between pieces of information, not from the information directly.

Begin with the company website

Nearly every company has a website, but websites vary widely in purpose and type of information they provide. Still, the website is one of the easier resources to find and is generally credible even if rarely a comprehensive resource.

The utility of a website for job search purposes varies significantly. Companies that do significant direct to consumer business are likely to have websites focused on e-commerce. Consequently, they often offer little information about what you can expect to experience when working for them. Companies that engage in business-to-business services and products may offer more direct insight depending on how closely tied they think company culture and customer experience are.

There are a few commonly useful items to search for on a company website:

- Press Releases – Learning what a company is proud of and/or thinks the market wants to know helps you to understand what the company values. It also empowers you to appear well-informed during an interview by demonstrating your awareness of current company events.
- History of the Company – The origins of a company often provide insight into the corporate culture. Companies with origins as family businesses often place higher value on personal relationships than companies that have been bought, sold and/or sliced up by private equity firms, and are likely more focused on profits than relationships.
- Locations – Many jobs have or could have geographic flexibility built in (either initially or at future stages in your career). The website is often a good source of information on current geographic footprint.
- Corporate Social Responsibility (CSR) – Companies that engage in CSR activities are often proud of these activities and promote them on their websites. These activities can illuminate core values and/or potentially align with your personal interests.
- Careers/Jobs – Larger companies often have dedicating recruiting sections and/or job boards integrated into their websites. When available, these can set very specific expectations for the recruiting process and/or current hiring interests.

Even the language used on a website can be instructive about the company. A company whose language focuses on profitability may have a different culture than one that more prominently speaks about innovation. The pictures of people on a website often suggest their target customer market. Pictures of younger generations suggest that demographic as the target while more senior or varied representations can suggest a different focus area.

Companies with colorful, busy, and engaging websites may suggest an emphasis on creative minds whereas easily navigable, clean sites with practical information may indicate emphasis on structured thinking or business practicality.

Always remember that the website is the company's way of presenting itself as it wants to be known. This is rarely completely different than it would be commonly described, but you should recognize that corporate websites may provide an exaggerated picture rather than what could be objectively considered a fair characterization.

Investor documents require more work to pick through but may have informational gems

Usually available through the company's website, investor documents can be enlightening on many dimensions. Annual and quarterly reports, 10-Qs and 10-Ks, and investor calls and presentations all can provide helpful information. While it is unlikely to be useful to read all the available documents, reading some of the most recent can help to understand:

- Names of individuals in top leadership positions – In addition to being familiar with names in the event they come up in conversation during interviews, understanding the background of key individuals (often through using LinkedIn or other resources in conjunction with the document) can provide insight into what to expect from the company in terms of mission, direction, and/or culture.
  For example, leaders who have a laid-back mentality and approachable demeanor are more likely to inspire a likewise relaxed corporate culture than somebody who is known for long work hours and limited patience. Leaders whose origins are in other industries are more likely to focus on financial outcomes than operational excellence as they were likely brought in for their ability to drive financial results, not their industry acumen.
- Business priorities – Annual and quarterly reports are particularly helpful in understanding what efforts have the greatest backing. This either increases or diminishes the likely internal support/investment in activities supported by the role you would be interviewing for. For example, if product A is identified as a priority for the company and you are being considered for a position related to product B, you can expect less attention and fewer company resources than the person in a similar position, but related to product A.
- Financial performance – Understanding whether a business is growing, contracting or simply harvesting business sets an expectation for the priorities and pressures one will experience after joining. In extreme cases, it can raise concern for stability of the job being offered. For example, a business that has doubled in size over the prior four years is experiencing extreme growth, and you should anticipate some level of

disorganization and focus on immediate issues rather than strategic initiatives – at least while this growth is maintained. You also can predict potential for accelerated career growth within the company assuming growth is sustained at or near the current level. By contrast, a company that has met its revenue targets, but with a modest 5 percent CAGR is more likely to focus on efficient operations and long-term initiatives providing less frantic activity, but also less rapid career growth potential.

- Key competitors – Relevant not only during interviewing to demonstrate that you understand the business landscape, this can also help you to find opportunities within your network to engage people for additional intelligence and perspective on the company.
- For example, recognizing that Company A, where a close friend works, is a direct competitor of the company you are interviewing with provides the opportunity for you to talk to your friend at Company A about her impressions of your potential employer. While perhaps tainted by the competitor mindset, that intelligence often creates great talking points to explore during an interview and can empower you to demonstrate a stronger command of the competitive landscape.
- Key products/offerings – Thoroughly understanding the company's products and offerings allows you to orient your messaging about yourself in the direction of skills, capabilities, and experiences that will be relevant and valuable to the company.
- For example, being able to demonstrate that you understand the history and subtle aspects of the value proposition of the iPhone would be helpful if you were interviewing for a position at Apple. Even if the employer does not expect you to know such information as a prerequisite for the job, you are more likely to stand out from other candidates if you take the time to proactively research the key products or offerings and demonstrate an enhanced level of understanding.
- Competitive advantage – Knowing how a company perceives and pursues competitive advantage provides an opportunity for you to showcase your ability to support those efforts while helping you understand the company's key issues.

For example, knowing that the company views its customer service as its competitive advantage enables you to emphasize your customer-facing skills on your resume and interviews whereas for a company that views its technology as advantage should lead you to emphasize your technical knowledge instead.

Carefully use social media

Access to information through social media is an attractive and natural for many candidates because of the ease with which that information can be accessed. However, in most industries, social media is neither the most prolific nor most credible source of information. Still, it does have some useful applications:

- In exceptional cases, corporate culture can be observed through the postings on social media. Wendy's, for example, regularly banters with competitors, displaying the witty, fun culture it aims to create for its employees.
- Increasingly, companies review *your* social media. Especially if your accounts are public, it is useful to at least follow companies with whom you are pursuing employment to demonstrate your interest in the company. Also, make sense that there is nothing on your social media which you would not want a potential employer to see.
- Often, it is possible to use social media to identify people outside of your current network (or on the periphery) who could be useful additions to your network and even potential advocates. If you see somebody on social media regularly posting about or tagging the company you are interested, they may be worth connecting with. This is discussed in much more detail in Chapter 12.
- With caution, you can get a sense of public opinion of companies through websites such as Glassdoor and Indeed (more on this later in the chapter) as well as comments on social media pages.

Keep in mind that most content on social media is biased in some way. Company-generated content will be curated to serve a company purpose. Unsolicited content from the public, on the other hand, will range from honest and forthright to misleading and propagandist. This should not deter you from using the information, as long as you verify your conclusions through other sources.

Job postings reveal more than you might think at first

The job posting itself can provide far more information about the company than just what is explicitly written. By reading between the lines, you often find interesting indications of more. For example:

- Repeated references to a topic in multiple phrasings and/or contexts could indicate core values of the company. For example, a company that lists many of the tasks with the adverb "safely" likely places a premium on safety and may consider its safety record to be a competitive advantage.
- Unless there is an obvious rationale for sequencing, it is common for companies to list responsibilities in decreasing order of importance to the role. Hence it often is fair to assume that the first three bullet points in a description of responsibilities or skills are more critical than the last three.
- Companies that provide lists of specific skills in the job posting are more likely to be using a computerized applicant tracking system than those that have short or very general job descriptions. Seeing such lists should trigger additional care in optimizing the resume you submit to obviously demonstrate compliance with the job description.
- The relative presence of industry versus functional jargon in the job description can indicate whether the company is more concerned with industry background or depth of functional skill. While most companies would prefer both, most people are inevitably forced to position themselves as stronger in one topic or the other, making it useful to align your positioning to match the company's priority.

You should be careful not to place too much faith in your suppositions based only on the job posting. These sorts of observations are educated guesses and are most valuable when other sources corroborate them.

Employer intelligence websites can be helpful or misleading

Just as crowdsourced review forums revolutionized how people make decisions on a wide range of products and services, many websites seek to provide access to similar reviews for employers. While the spirit of sites such as Glass Door and Vault is certainly supportive of candidate agendas, it is important to utilize information cautiously.

Most job boards and employer intelligence websites offer some or all the following:

- Rankings of current and past employee satisfaction levels
- Company profiles and reviews
- Intelligence on the recruiting process
- Salary expectations for specific roles in specific companies
- Interview support

There is no doubt that information on any of these topics can be helpful to a job searcher; however, the employer/candidate transaction is much more complicated than the purchase of a meal at a restaurant or the decision to use one plumbing company over another one. There is an enormous amount of context that remains opaque to people who use these sites, and that can skew opinions in dangerous directions.

It is difficult to know how rankings and company profiles are developed. Content provided by companies versus content consolidated from a variety of unsolicited volunteers have different levels of credibility and different potentials to mislead. People with strongly negative or strongly positive views on a company are more likely to take the time to provide input while people whose views are in the middle participate less frequently. As a result, the picture is almost always skewed or incomplete.

Salary values (even ranges) are generally delivered with aggregation across one or more of location, highest level of education, years of work experience, unique qualifications, and internal/external hire, the blending of which can reduce the relevance of the numbers. Furthermore, unless there is total clarity between total rewards value, total compensation, legal base salary and the minimum, expected and maximum amounts for each, it is difficult to confidently compare equivalent figures.

Yet, even with these concerns, there is value to be extracted. Reviews that provide specific examples of experiences can be instructive because they allow you to draw your own conclusions about the company and your reaction to similar circumstances.

Salary data may not be credible when it comes to setting expectations for specific numbers but is still useful to compare between employers, allowing you to reasonably expect Company A to be more lucrative than Company B even if you cannot credibly estimate the exact compensation at either.

Even when information seems suspect, the content can lead you to ask meaningful questions to members of your network and/or people you engage with during an interview process. For example, if you read conflicting reports around the rate of career progression in a company, it would be useful to discuss how rate of career progression is determined from a credible source such as the recruiter or hiring manager.

LinkedIn offers data useful for many purposes

LinkedIn has immense value to both employers and candidates. To understand how important the site has become, consider this: Some employers have made a LinkedIn profile review their initial screening device. Instead of seeking resumes and cover letters, they read LinkedIn.

As a candidate, LinkedIn has a few different potential ways to add value:

- It provides a more flexible canvas than a resume to describe work history, skills, and capabilities. You are not constrained by the customary one or two-page format and you can attach files and links.
- People can provide endorsements reinforcing or validating the messages you provide on your page.
- It provides access to profiles of other people and the ability to search for and contact those you do not yet know, but who may be relevant to your job search.
- You can research the backgrounds of people you engage with during the recruiting process and will likely find it helpful to learn about the people who interview you before you meet them. There is more on this later in this chapter.
- LinkedIn lets you search for people who have similar backgrounds to yours and work at your target company. This allows you to test how naturally you fit into the existing organization.

Even as LinkedIn gives you greater flexibility in telling your story by letting you include attachments and longer content than a resume can accommodate, it imposes its own constraints. You cannot, for example, customize content to the unique interests of a specific employer or job in the way you can customize your resume for each opportunity. This forces you to either keep your LinkedIn profile generic and relevant to all your opportunities or pursue opportunities in series allowing you to adjust your LinkedIn profile each time you start pursuing a new opportunity.

The ability to research the backgrounds of interviewers is a unique and an underutilized tool by many people. While not every company broadcasts the identity of interviewers before the interview, many will provide that information if asked. Through LinkedIn, you can walk into an interview knowing something about your interviewer.

One of the many reasons that people typically find interviews uncomfortable is the unequal starting point: One party knows significantly more about the other party due to the resume. Assuming you know the identity of the interviewer in advance and he or she has a populated LinkedIn profile, there may still be a discrepancy in knowledge, but it will be greatly reduced. This knowledge can empower you to have a strategy to appeal to the interviewer's personal agenda, interests and/or background.

This also helps you make a personal connection with the interviewer in addition to a professional one. For example, sharing a common alma mater is a great conversation topic to break the ice and establish a connection. Having same or similar educational degrees, having previous work experience in related or competitive companies, and mutual social or civic interests are among the many things you could find which can enrich the conversation. While you need not disclose that you reviewed the person's profile, you should not avoid doing so, especially if asked. It is arguably a sign of respect that you took the time to research the interviewer in advance of meeting them.

Addressing a very different purpose, LinkedIn can also help you understand how frequently people like you are successful in a target company. There are many forms of talent and many different profiles of skills. While no two people are identical, many people will share commonalities with you. If an organization employs people who share common attributes, interests, skills and/or backgrounds with you, it can be a good indication that the company may be a suitable fit for you culturally. Similarly, if no one in a company's leadership shares common interests with you, it should be cause for concern about the fit.

As you meet and interview with people during the recruiting process, it is important to constantly challenge yourself to assess whether the people you meet are people you would want to work with and/or leaders you would like to emulate. Lack of examples of both should concern you. LinkedIn helps you supplement this type of analysis by seeking out profiles of people you do not interact with during the recruiting process.

Never forget your personal network

As discussed in detail in Chapter 12, your personal network has immense potential to support you in career decisions and job pursuits. You should engage this community early in your job search, so you can benefit from existing relationships and begin forging new ones based on specific purposes or objectives.

Depending on their relationship to the target opportunity, advocates within your personal network can give you inside advice on how the company operates and help you assess the fit of the opportunity for your career objectives. They may be able to connect you with people outside of your personal network who can provide useful intelligence on the opportunity and/or company.

Alumni and professional networks also should be tapped. Even when your existing relationships through these channels are not especially strong or even nonexistent, people in these networks often are willing to help. Their support will likely be less valuable than the support of an advocate, but the cost to explore these channels is generally very low and can lead to a valuable new relationship regardless of the outcome of that particular opportunity.

Your primary concern should be to qualify the job for your career

Companies can get included in your job search in many ways. Whether the company (or a search firm delegate) finds you, you actively pursue the company, you are referred to the company by a connection, or you simply stumble onto them during your general research, you must quickly assess that company's potential fit for your career. Ultimately, if the company is not a fit for you, *there is no value* in devoting time to exploring opportunities – regardless of how good a fit you may be for them.

As introduced more thoroughly in Chapter 9, understanding the fit of a job to your career begins with understanding:

- Can the company meet all your non-negotiables?
- Which high priority items is the company likely to fulfill?
- Are there nice-to-haves that they obviously provide?

It is unlikely that you can confidently answer all these affirmatively, but during preliminary research, assume a company can meet your criteria until proven otherwise. Once proven otherwise, end all pursuits of the opportunity.

For example, it may not be possible to confirm that salary expectations can be met using preliminary research, but if a company does not have an office in your non-negotiable location, you can quickly determine this and move on.

Even if you cannot address all your core concerns, it is likely that you can develop enough understanding of company culture, priorities, market positioning, and potential to contribute to future job opportunities to effectively prioritize the opportunity in relation to other opportunities.

Assuming you have developed a story that addresses why the opportunity fits your career, you then want to make sure you are able to craft a story that addresses why the company should hire you.

Only if the company fits your needs, should you worry about fitting their needs

Research alone is unlikely to confirm that a company meets your needs or that you meet theirs, but it can help you determine whether you meet the needs of the company. Exploring this topic thoroughly not only prevents you from wasting time on opportunities for which you are not qualified, but also enables you to better focus your personal story and collateral (resume, cover letter, etc.) to have the greatest impact on an employer.

There are three key questions to answer as you engage with a company about a specific opportunity:

- **Why is the company hiring for the job?** - Replacing an employee often leads to an emphasis on finding specific technical or domain knowledge, whereas hiring for growth often focuses on general skills and cultural fit. Is the company hiring to grow in response to a new market opportunity or a mandate from the board, to replace somebody who left, to change the skill set of the person in the position, or some other reason?
- **What makes the company (and/or role within the company) unique?** - A company's culture is typically heavily influenced by what makes it unique. Understanding that can lead you to highlight aspects of yourself which promote strong cultural alignment. Is the company a leader in a particular aspect of its industry? Is it the largest, oldest, most innovative, least reckless, or somehow otherwise unique?
- **What differentiates high and low performance in** the role you are applying for? - Demonstrating that your expectations for the role are aligned with those of the company reduces risk for them and empowers you to proactively demonstrate that you possess the necessary skills. For example, does the company look for innovators, hard workers, leaders, intelligent followers, loyalty, self-motivators or other predictable attributes?

Answering these questions, even if only as an unconfirmed hypothesis, enables you to emphasize elements of your background that fit your expectations of the company. Doing so at this point is a calculated but safe gamble. At this point in the process, the company has no reason to expect you to understand these nuances (even if the data to reach that conclusion may be available if you pull from the right sources). This generates a high potential upside if your hypothesis is correct because your submitted profile will accurately match their target.

Fortunately, there is limited downside risk to this approach. Because the company could not assume you would understand these unstated nuances from the job profile, they cannot expect you to address them immediately. As you understand the opportunity more accurately, you may choose to pivot based on the confirmed needs of the company.

Do not go overboard on research

Ultimately, your preliminary research involves significant educated guessing. There is an immense amount of work that can be done during this preliminary research stage. The amount that you do is a calculated trade-off that you should make considering the urgency of your move (Are you currently employed? Do you have already identified opportunities to which you need to respond?), the number of opportunities you have identified (or want to explore before making a move), and your general confidence with the recruiting process (confidence grows with research but added research usually has diminishing returns beyond a certain point).

Most people benefit from doing at least some preliminary research into each opportunity, and many opt to research opportunities in two stages. They first capture just enough information to craft an effective resume and submit their application for an opportunity. If invited to interview, they will do additional research, particularly into specific people and in the context of the scheduled interview.

However, preliminary research should not be constrained to what you know. Poking around the edges of your targets also can be a good idea. Research that looks at the industry at large, geography, or some other broader attribute instead of narrowly researching a specific company can uncover opportunities you did not know you were missing. Furthermore, as in Kate's situation, you might find that the company was not as great a fit as you expected (or is an even better fit).

Be sure to step back from your focus on specific company research to be sure you have the right companies on your list. An external validating conversation with a research firm or an experienced search consultant can help head off the blinder effect.

* * *

Opportunities to Apply Chapter Concepts

- Build a profile for a company (one of your target companies if you are actively searching for a job or just an interesting company if not) and ensure you can describe:
    o 3-5 top-level issues facing the company.
    o The competitive advantage the company believes it has in the market
    o 2-3 specific attributes that would make the company's culture (operating behavior) attractive or unattractive to you.
    o 3-5 employees who would be useful to know if you were to pursue an opportunity with the company.

14. WRITING A COMPELLING RESUME

Your resume is a strategically written marketing document customized to each specific audience and demonstrating your unique and thorough fit for the position you are seeking – not a static, comprehensive chronology of every job you have held.

Through no fault of her own, Lina had been laid off. She had been a solid performer in the finance department of a small medical device company, and she had enjoyed the work – especially as demand for one of the company's products took off. The company became so successful, in fact, it was acquired by a larger organization that had no place for Lina.

Lina received a healthy severance package, but that did little to calm her nerves as she re-entered the job market. She had worked for the medical device company for more than six years. It was her second "real" job after college, and despite three years of meaningful work experience, she was still very much a junior hire at the time. She fully expected her job search experience this time to be different. She had accomplished a lot in the past 6+ years and knew that had to mean something and create access to different opportunities.

After taking two weeks to decompress, she pulled up her old resume from six years earlier and began to add to it. She populated the old resume with new information about project after project. She described new skills and described completing two interesting continuing education classes – all to make things look as attractive as possible. Then she sent the resume off to her brother, her old boss, and two friends, asking for their advice.

When she received only a couple of comments on formatting and identifying a few typos, she assumed the resume was ready to go. Energized, she began scrolling through job postings on online job boards looking for opportunities. Despite having worked in the medical field most recently, Lina felt no strong tie to the industry (she had worked for a software company previously) so she searched quite broadly.

Happily, she found many jobs that looked interesting and which she felt she was well qualified for. Lina began firing off resumes, worrying more that she might have trouble scheduling too many interviews than not having enough opportunities.

Unfortunately, her excitement quickly dissipated as the interviews she expected failed to materialize. The few companies she heard back from contacted her with generic "Thank you for your interest" rejection emails. She found herself unsure whether to be optimistic that the companies she had not heard from were just slow in reaching out to her, or to be frustrated that they did not even take the time to officially reject her.

* * *

When people begin a job search, their first thought frequently is, "It's time to dust off my resume" – as if wiping the dust off a stuck-in-time document is a good idea. Frequently, your resume and cover letter are your introductions to employers. And while a well-crafted, customized resume can open doors, one that still has evidence of dust can keep those doors closed.

Unfortunately, applicants frequently are unaware of what is wrong with their resumes. Unlike in an interview, where body language, intonation, and even direct feedback can help a candidate understand what worked well and what did not, resumes often are reviewed without the candidate knowing who looked at them, much less getting some indication of what the reviewer liked and did not like.

Candidates recognize that a resume is almost always required to earn the opportunity to interview for a position. Consequently, most job-seekers spend a significant amount of effort preparing these documents. However, the resume serves only a few specific purposes and often is misunderstood. Before discussing the do's and don'ts of resumes, it is important to understand what resumes are and how they are used.

Resumes and Curriculum Vitae (CVs) are similar documents. Both tell a story about your qualifications, but they have different purposes.

Resumes	CVs
• Summary of your education, work history, credentials, and other accomplishments and skills • Sometimes include objectives and career summary statement • Commonly 1-2 pages • Most frequently used in the US	• Provides a summary of your experience and skills, and typically includes information on your academic background, including teaching experience, degrees, research, awards, publications, presentations, and other achievements • Commonly 2-4 pages • Used regularly outside of the US or for academic or research positions in the US

For simplicity, this book will focus on resumes. Most of the guidance, however, applies equally well to constructing a curriculum vitae.

Employers have a variety of uses for resumes. Different people within an organization may use the same resume document for different purposes, and larger companies may utilize resumes differently than smaller companies. However, a well-crafted resume should be able to serve many applications.

Companies regularly use the resume to do one more of the following:

- Confirm if a candidate meets the minimum qualifications for a job
- Identify "nice-to-haves" in a candidate's background that make that candidate a particularly good fit for a job
- Assess the relevance of past positions to the role in question
- Confirm position/level to consider for the individual
- Build a case for hiring the individual
    o Determine conditions that would deliver a return on investment
    o Estimate upside potential and sources of risk if hired
- Develop a list of questions/topics to explore during an interview
- Estimate the likelihood that an individual will be retained if hired
- Understand the likely risks associated with hiring the candidate

No candidate is offered a job based solely on his or her resume, but many people are rejected from potential jobs based only on the resume. Your goal is to use your resume to inspire a potential employer to offer you an interview and continue the recruiting process.

Unsuccessful candidates frequently commit one or more of the following resumes missteps in their individual approach:

- Letting the resume lead the process
- Delivering data rather than a story
- Giving an autobiography instead of a commercial
- Lacking purpose
- Shotgun delivery of the resume

Committing one or more of these errors does not doom a candidate, but often makes it difficult to move forward with a potential employer.

Construct your resume to meet specific needs, not to find your direction

Your resume is not a matter of public record. Its contents are not predetermined. While employers may have expectations about what they will see on your resume, it is not like a disclosure form when selling a property. You get to decide what story to tell, what facts to use in telling the story, and how to tell it.

Candidates who start their job search by constructing a resume generally do so either because they have never thought critically about the purpose for the resume, or because they are looking for the resume to direct their job search by enabling them to seek out jobs based on what they believe they are qualified to do.

While this approach can result in a job, it is akin to driving a car by looking at the rearview mirror instead of through the windshield. Looking at what is behind you to steer yourself can work if the road is straight, but navigating becomes very tricky if you need to make turns to reach your destination.

A resume developed with only an eye on the past – not a focus on the future – will steer your job search toward jobs that are very close to what you have done in the past. For some people, this will result in positive job moves, but all people will drive their careers more safely toward their ideal destination by looking forward as they compile a resume.

Building a good resume should start by understanding:

- Your individual wants, needs, and ambitions
- The needs and objectives of the specific employer
- The case for the job fitting your career objectives
- The argument for you being positioned for success in the job

It should become obvious from this list that creating your resume should happen *after* you have identified what you want and found some opportunities that you believe could meet those needs. For some people, this will feel like a significant and uncomfortable shift in approach, but it consistently empowers you to both avoid jobs that would ultimately leave you unfulfilled or unhappy while preparing you to present yourself as a compelling candidate to the employers who can offer you a great path forward.

Tell a story, do not just deliver facts

Humans are predisposed to emotionally connect with stories. Attaching purpose to facts makes those facts not only more memorable, but also more meaningful. Your resume *must tell an interesting story.* A collection of facts is not interesting without an underlying story. This story does not need to be told explicitly, but your resume should have a story which not only makes logical sense, but also naturally leads toward a future chapter that justifies your move into the job you are seeking.

Resumes may be collections of short facts, but when composed carefully, they can be remembered as if they had been part of a story. For example, if your resume simply describes you working as ballet dancer then an interior designer and most recently an accountant, the reader is unlikely to understand the connections between the three jobs. Worse, the reader is likely to struggle to understand why you are applying for the job of production assistant on a film.

However, imagine instead a resume that conveys that experience in ballet developing an interest in the theater manifesting the dream of one day running a set design company. If the resume explains that you entered into interior design to master the artistic side of design and studied accounting in college and took the accounting position to understand the financial side to the business, then it becomes feasible to imagine how, before you attempt to branch off on your own, you want to add film experience to understand the unique mindset and demands of directors and producers, particularly as they interact with set designer.

By exposing elements of *why you took the jobs* you did not just *what* you did to earn money, you help the reader understand your story and more importantly imagine the job you for which you are applying as a natural, obvious next step. You need not dispense with the standard formatting of a resume, but you should incorporate enough contextual detail to clarify your story. Some of this will more naturally fit into a cover letter, but it is certainly beneficial is the story also comes across clearly from the resume alone.

Make your resume a commercial – not an autobiography

Your resume is a *marketing document*. Its job is to inspire an employer to want more information about you. If your goal was to write an autobiography, you would instead be aiming to answer all questions the reader has about you in one lengthy document. Since you instead hope to start more conversations with your marketing document, you need only introduce a few of the most exciting and relevant points.

Resumes that are unnecessarily packed with information lose impact for many reasons:

- They take a long time to read, making it less likely that an employer will fully review them. As a result, the potential employer is only exposed to part of your story.
- Too much information can either duplicate pieces of your story or risk creating conflicting messages within it.
- All additional information requires effort by the reader to fit into the story. As the story becomes more complex, the likelihood that the reader will understand it comprehensively and in the desired way decreases.

As you construct your resume, try to make every piece of information serve a specific purpose. Make each entry meaningfully contribute to your story and/or demonstrate that you meet the qualifications required for the job. Irrelevant content – even when it is objectively impressive – does not help you advance in the process.

You should not expect that a prospective employer will read everything on your resume. You need your resume to be interesting if skimmed for only 30 seconds, but also have the depth to hold a reader's attention when his/her skimming identifies a specific topic of interest and initiates a closer read.

You do not want to comprehensively describe yourself or prove your depth on topics using the resume alone. A little bit of intrigue and mystery can incentivize readers to seek more from you and move you forward in the recruiting process.

Give your resume specific goals

While the high-level objective of your resume may be to get you a job, having a more specific purpose will enhance the impact of the resume.

When crafting the resume, think about goals associated with your story and what will make you unique as a candidate. For example:

- Demonstrate that you have a mastery of a specific skill.
- Qualify yourself as an accomplished leader.
- Differentiate yourself from other candidates by a specific attribute or experience.
- Alleviate anticipated employer concerns related to an atypical background for the role.
- Explain why the job is a natural and compelling fit the next step in your career.

Having a clear purpose and telling a compelling story are closely related. Whether you start by telling your story and molding it to your purpose or begin with your purpose and write your story to meet those needs, the two must work together to generate impact.

Shoot with a rifle – not a shotgun

Internet job boards offer easy access to many job openings and allow you to circulate one generic version of your resume to many employers quickly. While this may seem efficient, it is rarely effective.

When a shotgun is fired, many pellets blast into a general vicinity. The idea is that by shooting many projectiles, at least one is likely to hit its target. A rifle, by contrast, fires a single bullet. These weapons rely on accuracy, rather than volume to successfully hit their targets.

When candidates take a "shotgun" approach, they build a single resume and share it with many employers. They hope that the general vicinity of the resume will be close enough to fit one of the employers and materialize into a real opportunity. When a candidate takes a rifle approach, he or she must create a unique resume for each employer. This approach offers candidates the opportunity to focus each resume on each potential employer's needs counting on accuracy to increase the likelihood of materializing the opportunity.

Experience shows that the rifle approach is more effective at getting results for candidates quickly. Because recruiting processes more favorably respond to the rifle approach, candidates using the shotgun approach often end up with longer search efforts and many rushed efforts to prepare for the few employers who do invite them to continue the process.

Think of a candidate as a car and the company as a potential car-buyer. Using the shotgun approach, the candidate ends up presenting herself as a base-model white sedan because anybody who needs to commute can benefit from that vehicle. A sports car enthusiast, family man, and off-road junkie all can use a sedan for their commutes. For the sports car enthusiast to be excited, he or she needs a faster car than the sedan. The family man wants more space for the children. The off-road enthusiast could commute in the sedan but would need a different vehicle to enjoy going off-road. Had candidate chosen to be a Jeep, a minivan, or sports car, she could predict that she would be wrong for 2/3 of the buyers. But by trying to be functional for all three, she ended up appealing to none.

Candidates who take the time to understand what they want in a job find the rifle approach easier because they only pursue a subset of jobs – the ones suitable for their career goals. This both creates focus and makes it easier for the candidate to present a compelling story about why they are pursuing the opportunity.

Candidates who choose the shotgun approach should ask themselves if they have thoroughly thought through what they want in a job. A resume that is not tailored to a potential employer's needs is by nature not optimally crafted for the opportunity.

Start building your resume based on purpose, key messages, and audience

To develop a resume anchored by a specific purpose, start by answering a few simple questions:

Suggested Considerations	Examples
What is the purpose for the resume?	- Inspire the interest of a specific company - Provide generic context (e.g. for headhunter or posting to job website such as Indeed)
What are the three most important things you want a reader to retain about you?	- Highly experienced in X skill - Unique among similarly skilled people because of Y - Specific impressive achievement
What is most important to your intended audience?	- Fit into culture defined by A, B, and C - Have expertise in specific technical or industry skill - Experience in addressing specific situation or challenge

Remember that your resume needs to define and promote your personal *brand* (discussed in Chapter 7). An effective resume will not only demonstrate that you are qualified for the job in question, but will present you as memorable, unique, and positively differentiated from other candidates. It also will confirm you as fitting the level of the position for which you are applying.

For example, if you are fluent in Spanish or MCSE certified, you should state so explicitly. However, if you have a strong attention to detail, you are better off including an example of how your attention to detail captured an error in a valuation model that saved a client from overpaying for an acquisition by $10 million rather than simply stating you have strong attention to detail[2]. If a skill or qualification can be objectively measured, it can be stated; if it is subjectively measured, it is better demonstrated.

Be careful to focus on attributes that are both relevant to the role you are seeking and appropriate for the level of seniority you intend to pursue. Including your skills

---

[2] Vague statements such as "strong attention to detail" should only be used for managing risks associated with ATS. We will address these directly later in this chapter

with Microsoft Office might be appropriate for an entry-level position, but even though such skills are necessary in senior executive positions, they are not differentiating for that level and should be assumed instead not stated on the resume.

Also, be wary of listing skills that you do not want to use in the role. If your brand comes across as strongly global, yet you do not want to travel, you may have a challenge getting hired.

As you pull together information that supports your objectives for the resume and conveys your personal brand, begin compiling that information in a meaningful and relatable story. Do not expect it to read elegantly like a novel but do aim to have things appear in a sequence that aligns with a compelling story.

Whenever feasible, target your audience(s)

As you tailor your resume to each opportunity, remember that you may have multiple audiences within a company. It is best to provide a resume that addresses the needs of all probable readers. This is easy if you know exactly who will see your resume and what their backgrounds are, but because you rarely will have that information, you must speculate.

Common Reviewer	Typical Concerns
Human resources	<ul><li>Wants to confirm that you meet minimum qualifications for the job</li><li>Looks for consistency and logic in the "story;" May research some aspects of the resume to confirm validity</li><li>Often lacks deep technical/industry background, so it is important that the resume is understandable to a layperson as well as an expert</li></ul>
Hiring manager	<ul><li>Concerned with technical/industry skills and ability to deliver on the job</li><li>Wants to be convinced that you can do the job with limited oversight, training and/or intervention</li></ul>
Hiring manager's boss	<ul><li>Wants to be impressed with delivery potential and past accolades</li><li>Typically wants to see proven results</li></ul>

| Future peers | • Want to see a similar or relatable background
• Want to know if you can integrate with the team culturally and whether you will alleviate rather than add to their workload |

You can and should produce unique resumes for each employer (and ideally for each job within an organization if you are applying for multiple jobs). You will rarely, however, be able to give each stakeholder a customized resume. Even if possible, it would not necessarily be productive. However, you should do your best to ensure that the resume you provide gives enough information to address the unique needs and interests of all probable stakeholders.

Select an appropriate organizational framework for your resume

There are theoretically limitless ways to convey your work history and employment value on a page or two, but there are a few conventional frameworks that are familiar to nearly all employers. It is advisable to use one of those conventional frameworks. You should assume that prospective employers will not read your entire resume, so you should aim to convey the most compelling information early in the resume, maximizing the chances of that material being read.

The basic organization of the resume should support the story that the resume is intended to sell. Most people naturally organize their story in chronological order. However, some stories are easier to tell and to understand when organized by topic, rather than time.

Type	Description	Typical Application
Chronological	Describes activities and accomplishments in the order in which they happened. Generally beginning with the most recent and moving backward in time.	Default for most people. Works well when pursuing a job that is easy to see as a natural next step or when career to date has remained within a narrow industry or job function.
Functional	Describes experience organized by industry, capability, or achievement	Generally, only applicable for people with a career history of 20 years or more, or those who have gone through one or more significant changes in profession. In some cases, this design may be used to avoid drawing attention to recent activities or gaps in timeline.
Combination	Has elements of both chronological and functional resumes	This format enables people to highlight specific experiences while still telling a chronological story and is common for people with project-based roles

    There are situations in which it makes sense to take a very different approach. People in certain creative occupations such as graphic design regularly opt to use the resume as both a tool for sharing their story and qualifications and as a vehicle for demonstrating their craft. If you opt to do this, you have the potential to significantly stand out from other candidates. However, this can be risky if you are not confident that the employer will appreciate the innovation and still obtain the full breadth of needed information.

    There are many examples of sample resumes online. Blindly copying one is a dangerous exercise, but it is a worthwhile practice to benefit from the ideas of others. Seek out a variety of samples and take inspiration from elements you like and do not like on these samples. Because your resume is meant to reflect you, you should organize your resume in a way that you like and that you think will be effective in catching the eye of your desired employer.

Develop the right content for *your* resume

It is difficult to distill the entirety of one's career and capabilities into a story that fits on one or two sheets of paper. There are no universal rules for what to include in your resume, but what you do include has a significant impact on your likelihood of securing a job. Resumes must strike a delicate balance. They must be unique enough to stand out from other resumes while not distracting the reader from the content or obscuring the desired message. The following suggestions will apply in *most* situations:

- Compose the resume with your target audience in mind.
- Try to incorporate some of the language used by the job description to describe yourself on the resume. For example, if the job description calls for "procurement" experience avoid referring to your related experience as "purchasing" experience and instead call it "procurement."
- Ensure that if someone were to use the job description as a checklist, your resume would enable that person to *easily* determine that you meet all minimum requirements. If the job description calls for 15+ years in a manufacturing environment, make sure that you give a description for each company contributing to your 15+ years of experience so that it is obvious each was a manufacturing environment. Often an employer will not be familiar with all the employers on your resume and could incorrectly assume you fail to meet that criteria unless you are explicit.
- Sell yourself with your potential to create value. As much as possible, include *quantifications* showing the monetized (or at least quantified) value you have produced in the past, as this suggests what you can produce if hired. For example, stating that you led a project to reduce operating costs significantly is not nearly as powerful as stating that you were able to reduce operating costs by 15 percent, resulting in a net annual savings of $1.3 million.
- Describe content in way that is impressive, but without embellishment or exaggeration and explain *how* you made things happen. In that prior example, the $1.3 million in savings can be made even more helpful to the employer by explaining that you designed a Six Sigma program that was executed by others, brought in specialized consultants, or did the process re-engineering yourself. These are all potential drivers of the savings, but suggest different approaches and skills. Employers like that added level

of understanding to envision how you would make change happen in their company.
- Focus on recent activities. Include older content only when it illuminates aspects of your qualifications not otherwise evident or when uniquely impressive and differentiating (awards and/or accolades, for example).
- Avoid utilizing significant space to discuss experience or skills not relevant to the position being sought, even if objectively impressive; Eliminate them if possible without derailing the story.
- In addition to describing your role at past employers, provide a small amount of contextual information about those employers. This helps potential employers understand the businesses of past employers and frees them from having to research and as noted above, can help to demonstrate you meet the minimum requirements of the job.
- Avoid using complete sentences.
- Be consistent in your formatting (whatever formatting you use) and use a single, consistent font (varying size is okay and often useful).
- Ensure that the document is legible when printed on standard 8.5"x11" or A4 paper.

The process of building a resume should always be iterative. Even when starting from an existing resume, you should expect to make multiple revisions before confidently submitting it.

Regardless of how you opt to format your resume, include the following elements of content:

Context – There are many ways and different levels of transparency in which you can explain why you are interested in the position. A cover letter is a much better vehicle for describing your context in detail, but if the resume is viewed without the cover letter, you want to equip the reader with some level of context. Objective statements, goal statements, introductions/overviews, or even just a summary tagline statement all are ways to provide context. Most people would not use all these tools but using at least one is advisable.

Skills – Be sure to highlight distinct individual skills. Some people opt to create an independent section for skills while others simply use formatting (such as italicizing text) to draw attention to the words that describe skills within other parts of the resume. Making skills easy to find is important when considering that many readers may initially scan the resume in search of specific skills.

Experience – Potential employers want to know how you might contribute to their organizations, so your resume must explain the ways that you have been employed, made money and/or contributed to your previous employers. While employment history is the obvious source of content, you may also include business ownerships (of any size), political offices or involvement, board memberships, significant volunteer experience, or other material time investments which could indicate useful skills, capabilities, or experiences relevant to the employer.

Additionally, some people choose to include one or more of the following components:

Element	Typical Context for Use	Pros	Cons
Introduction	Enables you to provide a short overview of the most salient points about yourself; An opportunity to explicitly articulate your brand	Increases your control over what somebody remembers from your resume	If not done well, can lead prospective employers to discard your resume without thorough review
Objective Statement	Explains the rationale for your interest in the job and provides some insight in your career path. Differs from an introduction only in the need for a specific, targeted outcome.	Enables the resume to explain why the job is a good fit for you, alleviating potential concerns about retention risk	Difficult to do well as such statements must be both relevant to the company and on brand with rest of the resume
Skills Section	Asserts that you have specific skills relevant to the position	Highly effective in keyword searches used by some large companies' computer systems and by people when scanning	Does not demonstrate proficiency level and could cause employer to position you for a role leveraging skills that you have but may not prefer

Accomplishments Section	Demonstrates achievements relevant to the role being applied for	Shows actual achievements in terms of size, scale, scope, impact value, role and relevance	Can appear to be sales-like if not formatted correctly.
Work Authorization	Confirms for employer in which countries you can legally work	If not obvious that you can legally work in a relevant country, this can avoid an unwarranted dismissal	If apparent from other content (on resume or provided separately) this becomes wasted redundancy
List of Publications	List of compositions that have been published for which you were the/an author *Usually only on CV – not resume*	Shows ability to write and be published (relevant for some jobs) and confirms credibility on topics with external sources	Unnecessary use of space if not relevant to job; Can undermine credibility if quality of publications is not appropriate for role
Link to Digital Presence	Link to LinkedIn page or individual website, enabling reader access to additional information about you	Effectively enables you to provide access to limitless detail about yourself without making the resume overly dense or lengthy	Requires you to take equal care in curating the linked materials and ensuring consistency in message and content
Personal Interests	List of non-professional interests and/or activities in which you are involved	Humanizes you, making you more relatable as a person; Can lead to conversation in an interview that better bonds you with the interviewer	Uses space to discuss content that you know is not related to the position and could appear trivial or frivolous

As you compile content for your resume, it is important to remember that how you state something can have as much – or more – impact than what you say. Your resume should be brief, memorable, and impactful all at once. ==Specific quantifications almost always are preferable to generalizations.==

Avoid: Was part of a team that updated the marketing strategy for the southwest region of the business to grow the business significantly after years of poor performance

Instead try: Provided the competitive landscape expertise that empowered the team I was working with to develop a new marketing strategy, penetrate two key clients in a previously stagnant region, and deliver 12% revenue growth with a $25M book of business

The second phrasing strengthens your resume:

- By describing your specific contributions, you offer greater insight into how you would fit into a future team, eliminating the guesswork around what you (not your team) contributed.
- Specific, quantitative results ascribe an appropriate level of gravity to the outcome, making the results more impressive.
- Making yourself, rather than the team, the focal point of the statement suggests a high level of importance to your contributions that is less obvious in the original description without implying that you updated the strategy on your own.

With resumes, context is important, but details do not always add value. Because your reader may not have an extended attention span, brevity is important. It is best to give just enough to make the content understandable and inspire interest/questions without giving more.

Avoid: After customer satisfaction scores dropped for the third quarter in a row, determined that inconsistent delivery times were causing the poor feedback and isolated the root cause to be suboptimal inventory levels; Identified a flaw in the safety stock calculation process and an inefficiency in the reorder process which once addressed resulted in improvements to the delivery time and improvements in customer satisfaction.

Instead try: ==Led a diagnostic that resulted in the redesign== of the supply chain process, enabling improvements to inventory management resulting in a 15% reduction in restocking time and 20% decrease in negative customer feedback.

The second phrasing strengthens your resume:

- It removes unnecessary detail while still allowing the reader to infer the eliminated information

- Adds quantitative elements that increase the perception of material impact
- Helps the reader understand the situation, and suggests natural, positive questions to ask during an interview
- Releases space on the resume for additional content

You will almost certainly compile more content than can fit on your resume. This is a positive sign, and a reminder that you can repurpose content. You may determine that some of the information you gather is unnecessary in the context of one job, it could be useful if you apply for a different position.

Veterans have some additional things to think about

It is common for employers to struggle with understanding the qualifications of people who seek to switch industries. Even when the fundamental skills required to be successful in two industries overlap significantly, the unique vocabulary and/or jargon that one industry associates with those skills can be significantly different from the terminology another industry uses for the same basic activities and skills.

This challenge is especially acute for people who have military service in their background. In many ways, veterans have the same challenges as civilians who are moving from one industry to another and must ensure potential employers understand their merits and qualifications. Veterans must carefully describe their military experience in terms relatable to civilians to achieve this understanding.

For example, a resume entry of "qualified underway officer of the deck on a nuclear-powered aircraft carrier as junior officer; safely navigated and operated a capital warship in waters of a war zone" likely makes sense to others with a Naval background but is likely to sound impressive but irrelevant to somebody who lacks military experience.

One strategy to help your reader understand that your experience is relevant is to explain what you learned from the experience. This way, you explain to audiences *why* they should care about your experience For example, "As underway officer of the deck on a nuclear-powered aircraft carrier, evaluated and compartmentalized large volumes of data quickly to address critical risks while navigating the confined waters of a war zone without being distracted by secondary concerns" provides context that is relatable in a civilian business context.

Veterans also should be aware that some of their more impressive military accomplishments can sound like embellished to a civilian mind. While few civilian roles allow a 25-year-old to oversee hundreds of people, this sort of responsibility is not uncommon in the military. However, this responsibility is often localized to a specific topic – the 25-year-old may be responsible for the training curriculum for 300 people but not have full executive oversight of them. Veterans should not be shy about sharing these accomplishments but should provide enough detail that civilian readers do not doubt the authenticity of the claims.

Don't fear applicant tracking systems but do be prepared for them

Anyone who plans to apply to job postings at large companies or through online job boards should pay careful attention to word choice. Large companies and those that recruit online frequently automate initial screening of candidate resumes through applicant tracking systems (ATS). These systems prescreen resumes before any human even sees them. As fallible as humans are during the recruiting process, the limitations of ATS programs are even more fallible. If you ever are asked to submit your resume in Microsoft Word form, you can be almost certain an ATS is involved.

ATS are not inherently bad, but a resume that would wow any human reader could be rejected by an ATS if the resume was composed without consideration for the system. However, a resume that most humans would not be wowed by will almost always also be disappointing to the ATS.

Avoiding issues with an ATS is not a matter of fooling the system. Instead it is about *reducing the chance the system could exclude your resume for objectively invalid reasons*. It is not possible to avoid this potential entirely, but the following actions will reduce the chance of a "false negative" from the ATS:

- Borrow precise language from the job description. If the job description calls for project management experience, include "project management" on your resume (assuming you have such experience) and avoid calling it "project leadership" or "program management" or even "project-management".

- Only abbreviate terms if abbreviated in the job description. For example, reference an MBA or Master of Business Administration based on how the company describes it on the job description.
- Avoid including distinctions such as Ph.D. or CPA with your name unless they also appear later in the resume as they can be mistaken for part of your name instead of as qualifications.
- Write out months and years rather than using numerical shorthand.
- Avoid headers, footers, complex formatting or other potentially distracting formatting elements which might challenge the ATS in recognizing content.
- Use plain language. Many people vary word choice to avoid repetition or to be very precise in messaging. While this is important in some contexts, it can lead to dismissal by ATS. For example, if a job description for a consulting position required 10 years of experience, which the candidate had, but identified as three years of consulting, five years of advisory work and four years of consulting management, the ATS might mistakenly determine that requirement was not satisfied.
- Consider including a standalone "Skills" section, and include relevant skills, particularly those included in the job description.

Though ATS often seem like a black box which disappointed candidates are quick to blame when they don't get a job, it is rare for an ATS to discard strong candidates. Still, there is no downside to being cautious and making efforts to avoid being one of the outlier cases where the ATS *does* discard a strong candidate.

Do not be overzealous in trying to optimize your resume for ATS. Any resume that passes the ATS is likely to be reviewed by at least one, if not many, humans before the candidate moves forward in the process. If the resume is stuffed full of keywords that do not contribute to the resume's overall story (and, in fact, were clearly added simply to pass all the ATS tests), it is unlikely to excite the human despite passing the ATS test.

Most people find it best to produce a high-quality resume first and then review it for possible ATS weaknesses. Initial designs focused on the ATS are less likely to have the same level of compelling content and coherent story. If you find that you are spending a lot of time worrying about an ATS review and/or making drastic changes to your resume for this purpose, you are probably doing more than you should.

Start thinking about the future influence of artificial intelligence (AI)

While use of ATS is mainstream, the use of artificial intelligence to aid in the recruiting process remains mostly on the horizon, though some pioneering companies are starting to incorporate AI into their recruiting processes. Though candidates probably should be more concerned with optimizing the resume for ATS than for AI, many of the optimizations that candidates can make to improve their attractiveness are generally good practices with or without AI.

One of the principle reasons that companies are drawn to using AI is the perception of greater ability to identify candidates who have attractive credentials but are weak on soft skills, culture, or motivation. These performance factors typically require critical thinking to assess and have traditionally been left to humans to manage. In many cases, mismatches are so obvious that candidates can be identified as a poor fit within the first few minutes of an interview, suggesting that the time to interview was really wasted time for both parties.

AI seeks to build on the screening capabilities of ATS and look not just for the presence of key hard skills and experiences, but also gauge soft skills, motivation, and cultural fit. While wholesale reconstruction of your resume should not be your response to the potential of AI review, you may wish to rethink decisions to exclude contextual information from your resume. If you opted not to include an objective or introduction statement that gives some explanation for your interest in the job, you may choose to include such information in the context of AI seeking to test your motivation. This underscores the importance of including a well-constructed cover letter with your resume. We discuss cover letters in the next chapter.

AI systems often draw from many data sources. It is therefore important that you curate as many of these sources as you can. AI systems will review social media sites, making it important that your social media presence reflects the same personal brand that you project with your resume. For example, if your resume and LinkedIn page disagree or present you in vastly different ways, AI systems may misinterpret you or consider the authenticity of the data to be suspect.

Additionally, you should consider the impact of social media. Unless you want more personal parts of your social media (Facebook or Instagram, for instance) to be influential on your job search, consider making some or all content private. However, if you have interesting content such as blogs that demonstrate your interests, thoughtfulness, and skills as a content creator, you may want to draw attention to them and ensure that they are both public, and widely shared.

Avoid hurting your candidacy with trivial but impactful errors

A good resume alone won't earn you your dream job, but even a great candidate can be hurt by a poor resume. A few very avoidable things could drastically reduce the impact of your resume, so you want to avoid these common flaws:

- Typos, poor grammar, slang, unattractive formatting, and anything that detracts from the professionalism of the resume becomes a distraction. Even if not material to the content of the resume, these errors can send a signal that you are not serious about the position (or not a serious person).
- Excessive use of passive voice and/or use of tired phrases such as "responsible for," and "key contributor of" that say little about your specific actions or involvement lose the reader's interest. Instead use active voice and speak in specifics. Tell your reader that you "pioneered," "accelerated," "benchmarked," "incentivized," or "orchestrated" activities or outcome, not as a mechanism to use fancy buzzwords, but to offer greater precision in the way that you describe your role and contributions.
- Avoid employing buzzwords or "resume speak" that do not differentiate you, especially if they speak to attributes that should be a given for the role. Phrases such as "results-oriented," "compelling leader," "proven track record of success," and "strong communicator" are ubiquitous but clichéd. Only use these words if specifically referenced in the job description.
- Densely packed, excessive information makes the resume difficult to read. Your resume should be readable on a smartphone and should hold reader attention with concise, value-focused statements. It is far more useful to leave a little mystery and create a reason for the reader to discuss the resume with you than to tell try and tell an exhaustive story in only two pages. Do not attempt to be comprehensive. Instead include only the most relevant and impressive content.

- If you are submitting your resume as a Microsoft Word file, remove all tracked changes, comments, unintentional formatting (e.g. highlighting things as a personal reminder during editing), and irrelevant property information from the file. These items can distract and detract from the resume. You want the employer to see only the finished product.

Candidates generally have a much higher tolerance for mediocrity in resumes than employers do, so if there is an aspect of your resume that you do not think is compelling or is poorly constructed, the odds are good that you are correct. However, there may be aspects of your resume which you are fond of but do not impress others. Therefore, it is advisable to get outside support to polish your resume.

Get help to polish your resume

Numerous services specialize in writing and editing resumes, at a wide variety of price points. Whether you use paid services or your network of family, peers, mentors and friends to give your resume a second and third look, getting an unbiased review is a good idea. You may not need to do this for every job you apply for, but certainly consider doing it for your first submission and for any jobs you are especially excited about.

In seeking outside support and input, you should never simply ask for feedback. "Let me know what you think" is not actually a request for useful, actionable feedback. It is a request to have your ego stroked. Without specific questions, the reviewer can only give generic responses that likely will sound good but offer little information for you to act on. Instead, be specific about what you want your resume to do.

You will receive better feedback if you instead approach somebody with:

"I am trying to have my resume demonstrate that I have deep experience in X, Y, and Z and show that my knowledge of A and B will set me up for success as a [insert job]. Do you think this resume conveys that message?"
Or
"I believe that Company A finds X skill and Y experience to be really important for this position. I haven't had the opportunity to work thoroughly with either, but I think I have done enough similar things in the past to be qualified. Do you think the resume shows that?"

By asking questions such as these, you give your reviewers the context they need to properly help you. Without context, you end up subject to their personal preferences and are more likely to get guidance on aesthetics rather than on content that is materially meaningful to your job search.

As you iterate to reach a final product, go through the following steps:

- Test to see that you are achieving your goals. We suggested starting the process by defining specific goals for your resume. Revisit that list of goals and then reread your resume. If you cannot point to parts of your resume that accomplish those gorals you set out to address, then a significant revision in content may still be necessary.
- Verify that the story your resume tells is coherent with both your personal brand and the job description. Read your resume and try to create a personal brand statement just based on the resume content. If that personal brand statement is significantly different than your intended personal brand statement, you may need to further revise the resume. Similarly, you should be able to use your resume to clearly show that you meet the needs in the job description.
- Confirm that it is compelling. If the resume serves its purpose but doesn't describe somebody you would want to hire if it were your choice, you may still need significant revisions. Imagine that you had to justify hiring you to somebody just based off the resume. Would your resume do more than prove that you are qualified and provide at least one specific reason to be very excited by the prospect of hiring you?
- Review each entry to make sure each adds unique and relevant value. If it duplicates information or is irrelevant to the company, job, or resume purpose, remove it.
- Review each entry for brevity. If the statement can be made more succinctly without losing clarity, make the change.
- Look for qualitative statements. If a quantification can be provided, make the change to provide it. If it cannot, try to substantiate the claim in some objectively defendable way. For example, if you claim to be a compelling leader, you may include that three people not in your direct chain of command sought you out as a mentor due to your reputation.
- Review for ATS compliance. If you are not using the same language as the job description and can adjust certain words without harming your message, do so.
- Modify to maximize visual appeal. Your very last step should be to adjust the formatting to have an attractive appearance that is easily read and fits on 1 or 2 pages.
- Confirm that the resume prints as attractively as it appears on the screen.

* * *

Laura's roommate came home one day approximately two weeks after Laura had excitedly begun applying to positions through job boards and found Laura dejectedly hunched over a couple of job description printouts and a copy of her resume. Peaking over Laura's shoulder, the roommate was surprised by the first job description she saw.

"Are you applying for a position at a technology company?" she asked Laura. "I thought you were a medical person. At least that's what your resume showed me, and that's all I have ever known you to do." Laura's roommate was unintentionally pointing out two key points that Laura had handled poorly in her job search to date: First, she did not set clear objectives for the story her resume should tell. Second, when she sought feedback on her resume, she did not tell her reviewers what to look for. Consequently, they unintentionally gave her a false sense of confidence regarding her resume.

Laura's roommate put Laura's resume next to the job description and challenged her to show where her resume showed that she met each of the qualifications. For some of the qualifications, it was obvious, but while Laura could explain her qualification to her roommate, she could not point to anything on her resume that did.

At that point, Laura understood that she had not been approaching her job search as effectively as she needed to – especially if she wanted to make a shift in industry.

While Laura still had no way to know exactly why each of her applications had been rejected, she now had a clear path forward to improve her chances in her next submissions.

She realized that her resume only needed to tell the story that would matter to each employer – not her whole story. She also realized that she would need to tell a slightly different story to each employer. While that struck her as a lot of work, how could she expect an employer to find her qualified for a job if even her roommate couldn't tell, based on the resume, that she was qualified for it.

* * *

Opportunities to Apply Chapter Concepts
- If actively pursuing opportunities:
    o Define the needs to be met by your resume.
    o Describe the purpose, key messages, and audience for your resume.
- If outside of an active job search, review previous resumes to:
    o Assess the alignment to intended brand.
    o Review the quality of the encompassed story.
    o Look for phrasing and/or word choice that could be improved.

15. LEADING WITH A COVER LETTER

Cover letters are your first opportunity to create a great first impression. Use your cover letter to tell a story that draws employers in and makes them want to get to know you better.

Christa was a 5th grade teacher who loved her job and had a promising career in a highly regarded school district. After seven years of teaching, she opted to step away and become a full-time mom. While she loved spending time with her two children, she regularly found herself missing the classroom. She vowed to herself that she would return to the classroom once her youngest was able to enter school full-time.

Christa believed she had a strong resume. She had a master's degree and seven years of teaching experience. She was well-liked and had been honored with recognition and awards. She was confident that former colleagues and supervisors alike would speak highly of her if contacted to provide a reference.

A few months before the next school year began, Christa went online, found a few open positions at nearby schools, and submitted her resume through a job board. She was confident that she would soon be able to work on lesson plans and decorations for her classroom. After 10 days, however, she hadn't received a call from any school. Her confidence faded.

* * *

Job-seekers must achieve many small milestones before they receive an offer. Unless a potential employer actively recruits them, the process starts when they make the employer aware of their interest. Christa, for example, applied for the job through an online submission. At that point, the process often becomes opaque – and sometimes frustrating – for the candidate. Candidates don't know if they inspired the company to take an interest in them until the company either invites them to be evaluated (usually via interview) or informs them of the decision not to move forward. Not only is the timeline for contact often unclear, but some companies never respond.

The first milestone occurs when a potential employer moves you from the group of all interested candidates to the group of all interesting candidates. More candidates exit the process at this stage than in any other stage of the process. Yet many candidates do not properly prepare to succeed at this crucial stage.

All companies have a process for becoming interested or disinterested in applicants before a formal evaluation process. These processes are specific to each company, but almost all cover four principle questions, typically in the following order:

1. Does the candidate have the minimum requirements for the job?
2. Does the candidate have enough of the targeted/ideal requirements for the job?
3. Does the candidate stand out in some interesting way?
4. Does the candidate pass the "sniff" test for potential fit?

While the first two questions are generally objectively measured for most requirements, the latter two are subjective. Even elements of minimum and/or desired requirements which are tied to level of skill in a qualification can be subjective. Candidates should view these subjective questions as opportunities to increase the likelihood of the positive outcomes and benefit from them accordingly.

Don't argue about it, just write a cover letter

Many people believe that with the digitalization of recruiting and the mainstream nature of online tools for recruiting processes, the cover letter has become an unnecessary relic. While it is true that the role of cover letters has changed, their utility has increased – not decreased – and candidates ought to pay more attention to them, not less.

Here are several common misconceptions about cover letters:

- Cover letters provide the same information as resumes, but with less detail and in prose form.
    - The most effective cover letters augment your resume with context and storyline that do not fit within the structure of the resume. They sometimes include some of the same information

- for clarity, but they are meant to provide different and complementary information.
- Most companies do not read cover letters.
  - It is true that not all companies read cover letters. However, there also are companies read resumes *only after* a cover letter has first captured their attention. Whether they read the cover letter during the screening process or not, the cover letter is very regularly read by those who interview and evaluate candidates.
- Candidates can only submit a cover letter if the company asks for one.
  - Some web-based application processes do not obviously request or accept a cover letter. Often, with some ingenuity there still is a way to include a cover letter (for example, as an attachment in a single file that includes a resume).
- When applying to a job via reference from a friend/colleague/headhunter, there is no need for a cover letter.
  - Cover letters not only are useful as documents of reference for potential employers, but they also function as preparation tools for candidates, forcing them to organize their story coherently before talking to a potential employer. There are many situations in which you may be contacted by an employer unexpectedly. In these situations, having previously organized your thoughts helps you to perform well during short-notice interactions.

Cover letters have two principle purposes:

- Provide an employer with information not included on the resume, but which the candidate believes could materially influence the employer's perception of potential fit
- Help the employer understand why the candidate is pursuing the job and on what basis the applicant believes he or she is a good fit who will meet the employer's needs

As noted many times in this book, humans have a unique affinity for and reaction to stories. People internalize stories better than individual facts, and remember them better than facts alone. Well-constructed resumes present a series of facts in a way that empowers a reader to imagine a story associated with the subject. Cover letters allow candidates to tell the story without assuming the reader will connect the facts as intended. They share the story *as a story*.

Furthermore, cover letters are blank canvases for job applicants. Resumes carry certain expectations for what content will and will not be included. Cover letters have fewer limitations. Furthermore, cover letters are often perceived as optional. In a competitive market where the key to success is positive differentiation, the ability to do something that others are not doing should be immediately attractive.

When considering whether to write a cover letter, the question should really be why wouldn't you? Even in a hypothetical scenario in which an employer explicitly says not to provide one, the organization of thoughts that goes into writing a cover letter will help you be focused, succinct, and compelling in your interactions with the employer – even if you never send it.

Start by collecting the basic content

There are several preparation steps that when done prior to composing the cover letter makes the process of writing it simpler and the results more compelling. Cover letters should include:

- A demonstration that you understand the role and company enough to be credibly interested in the role and potentially qualified for it
- An explanation of why the job is a fit for your personal needs
- (optional) Context that enhances an employer's understanding of your situation and motivations
- (optional) Comment related to the employer's unique issues and how hiring you will address them productively

To start the process of writing a cover letter, identify and capture the messages you would like to convey to the employer. Compile three lists, aligned with the objectives above, before composing content for the actual cover letter:

1. What do you want from a job – If you have completed the exercises in Chapter 6, you already have this available to you. If you skipped that chapter, either go back and work through it, or simply compose a list of the criteria you are using to identify potential jobs that fit your career objectives.
2. What does the employer want from a candidate – Hypothesize what the employer is hoping to find. To be clear, this is not a restatement of the job posting. This should involve a bit of research and critical thinking to identify the skills and capabilities (technical and non-technical, soft and

hard) that will differentiate candidates from one another. Your objective in crafting the list is not to identify the checkboxes the employer will use to determine if a candidate is qualified, but to identify what will make you stand out from the crowd of applicants. Focusing on issues critical to the employer will help determine what an employer needs from a candidate. For example, in a technical sales job, experience in the industry and a certain amount of education and experience may be requirements, but the differentiating feature may be the size and quality of your network. Your network of contacts may not be addressed on the job description but might be an attribute you can anticipate being valuable to the employer.

3. What do you want the employer to know about your situation – Some people can anticipate the questions or concerns an employer may have regarding their candidacy. If you have a gap in your resume, are changing professions, are seeking a more junior position than your current role, or expect that an employer might struggle to envision the role as a coherent and logical next step in your career, you should capture those elements.

Having created these lists, prioritize the elements and select a subset to include in the cover letter based on your desire to:

- Generate interest in yourself as a candidate
- Supplement, not duplicate, information on your resume
- Proactively address weaknesses in your fit as a candidate, ideally converting them from weaknesses to strengths

Once you have prioritized content for your cover letter, you can begin stitching together a narrative. Remember that your cover letter must tell a story. With the core content already identified from your prioritized lists, composing your cover letter should be an exercise in connecting ideas with words and context – not generating a masterpiece of literature.

Make yourself compelling

The only thing better than a big win is a big win-win. Recruiting should not be viewed as a zero-sum game where there are winners and losers. In hiring, if one side "loses," both sides "lose." If an employee feels that he accepted a job that is a less than great fit for his or her career, that employee is likely to have low motivation, leave the company relatively quickly, or both. Sure, the company was able to "win" by filling a vacant position, but one could argue that they really lost because they got an unmotivated employee and/or the gap that was filled will soon become a gap again.

Help the employer feel confident that hiring you is a win-win:

1) Show that this role is a great fit for your career - One of the easiest ways to make yourself compelling is to show that the position being sought fits for your ambitions and goals. When employers are uncertain about your rationale for applying for a role, they will attach high risk to your motivation and retention.

While no candidate is hired without some risk, risks associated with skill set and/or experience are easier for employers to manage. If your mastery of a programming language is not quite strong enough, you can be sent to a training class to boost it. If your communication skills are not up to par, you can be given a mentor or a coach to help with them. However, if the job does not contribute to your career aspirations, there is nothing the employer can do to fix that.

Furthermore, employers are not suited to assess how the job fits your career aspirations. Employers are well-qualified to assess your ability to do the job they want you to do. Since only you can assess whether any particular job is the right fit for your career, you need to communicate the positive outcome of that assessment convincingly.

Thus, it is extremely valuable for you to thoroughly assess this fit (Chapters 6 and 9 are especially helpful for this) and be able to clearly tell a convincing story. You need not tell the whole story in the cover letter, but you certainly need to include enough highlights for the outcome to seem reasonable.

2) Don't just tell your story, demonstrate it – There is a subtle but compelling difference between telling something about yourself and demonstrating it.

For example, anybody can claim to be a philanthropist. However, if philanthropy were a requirement for a job and one candidate had donated $20,000 to charities and another had never donated a penny, the first would seem much more qualified. However, if the second candidate had worked full-time for a charitable organization for two years and refused to take any salary during that time, the second candidate might objectively have a case for being more philanthropic. However, if Candidate 2 only puts in his cover letter that he is philanthropic, and Candidate 1 notes his monetary donations in his cover letter and/or resume, Candidate 1 will likely stand out positively from Candidate 2.

In a more realistic example, imagine that fluency in a specific second language is either a necessity or a differentiating feature for a role. Candidate 1 states he is fluent in Spanish at a native speaker level and is eager to use that ability on the job. Candidate 2 states that she is fluent in Spanish and regularly presented to clients in Spanish at her previous job. Even though Candidate 2 never claims native speaker quality to her fluency and Candidate 1 does, by providing the example that she has successfully operated in Spanish in a business context, her assertion of fluency is more credible. On that specific point, she would clearly be the more compelling candidate.

3) Use the opportunity to explain non-obvious connections – Unlike with the resume, which relies on the reader to connect facts in the desired way, the cover letter allows the author to lead the reader to make non-obvious connections.

One common example is a disconnect between university degree and work history. An engineer who isn't working as an engineer or an architect with a work history that does not – or does not *seem* to – involve architecture are likely still benefiting significantly from their university educations. In fact, they often benefit in novel, valuable ways that replace or improve upon traditional educations for the role in question. Cover letters give people like this an opportunity to position what otherwise looks like a disconnect as an asset.

Explaining how the problem-solving and analytical skills learned during the pursuit of your engineering degree have helped you in your non-engineering jobs and how you expect those skills to help you in the job you are pursuing can move your resume from looking out-of-place to appearing as a natural fit.

Show you understand the company and role

Often, candidates apply to many jobs without specific interest in any of them. This "shotgun" approach is ineffective for both candidate and employer, but because it is common, employers become sensitive to it, and find ways to quickly confirm that applicants are serious and educated in their interest in the job.

Presenting yourself as a win-win hire requires that the job is a good fit for your ambitions. However, if you do not accurately and thoroughly understand the company and role, your premise for deciding that the job is a good fit will be fundamentally flawed. Thus, employers are comforted when they learn that you thoroughly understand what you will be getting into if you are hired.

For many job-seekers this concept is easy to grasp but difficult to execute. You need to:

- Demonstrate your understanding without just stating facts that the reader undoubtedly knows better than you

- Not appear like you just copy-and-pasted something from the website or job description
- Avoid making "insightful" conjectures that are inaccurate

The following techniques can help you to demonstrate your knowledge of a company subtly and safely:

Avoid making the company the focus of a sentence

Instead of saying "ABC is the market leader in its competitive space", integrate that statement into a sentence that is fundamentally about a different topic. For example, "Having worked for a small company and struggling to gain the attention of suppliers, I expect ABC's position as market leader garners much greater supplier attention which would enable me to focus on creative and optimal solutions, rather than persistent communications."

Draw parallels or comparisons

Using comparisons can accomplish multiple objectives. In addition to showing that you understand the company, comparisons let you expose attributes or ideas that could separate you from other candidates. For example, "I have always valued companies that establish a strong brand and remain true to it. Unlike Company X[3], which seems to chase every new fad, ABC has built a strength around its core product and brand. Though it continues to optimize and improve that product, it does so without recklessly pursuing trends that could erode value."

Involve a personal story

Explaining your connection with the company not only personalizes the association between you and the employer, but allows you to introduce an understanding of the company and/or role. For example, "I first learned about ABC from a business school colleague. Her description of it as a company that allows employees extensive freedom to focus on the topics most interesting to them and a company that is more focused on getting good business results than following complex processes really appealed to my interest in working in an environment that promotes taking personal ownership of the product."

Keep in mind that however you expose your understanding of the company and/or role, your goal should not be to demonstrate a comprehensive understanding of the company's history or current behavior. No company expects that of you. Instead, you want to demonstrate that you understand the company well enough to 1) know what

---

[3] You generally want to avoid using a current or former employer to fill the role of Company X in the example. Sharing negative opinions about current or past employers frequency creates a bad impression so if your parallels or comparisons could be seen as casting a company in a negative light, make sure that company is not one also on your resume.

you are getting into if you are hired and 2) confirm that the job fits with your career ambitions.

Preemptively address the concerns of employers if you can anticipate them

Many people correctly or unnecessarily worry that without additional context, their resume will raise questions or create concerns that discount them as candidates. Often candidates worry about issues that prove immaterial, but either way, the cover letter becomes a tool to preempt such negative outcomes.

Nothing you say in a cover letter will make up for failing to meet any of the basic requirements of the job description. Proactively addressing certain "risk factors," however, can reduce a potential employer's level of concern. The following attributes, when present on a resume, frequently trigger concern by the employer but can be mitigated using a well-written cover letter:

- Extended gap in employment
- Switch in profession
- Incoherence in level (promotion or repositioning)
- Short tenure(s) in previous employer(s)

Whenever you can share a credible story that positions your risk factor as an asset rather than a concern, you should do so in your cover letter. This is not a suggestion that you make up a fictional story. Your cover letter needs to be factual. However, there are many situations where such stories exist and just need to be told.

There are cases where you can only reduce the risk, not convert it to an asset. In these situations, you may choose not to address the risk in case the employer does not perceive your situation as a risk. A common example of this is in promotion situations. You may expect the employer to see the job for which you are applying as a promotion, and therefore question your readiness. Addressing this in the cover letter could reduce those concerns, but if the employer was not initially concerned, raising the issue in the cover letter could inspire the employer to become concerned.

Each situation should be addressed uniquely and genuinely. Following are a few generic examples of ways that these situations have been effectively addressed. Note that context is important, and these are designed to be used for inspiration not as templates.

Extended gap in employment

After taking a brief break from the workplace to focus on supporting a family member through a difficult medical issue, I am happy to reenter the workforce and resume pursuing my career objectives.

Switch in profession

Having effectively captured a key career objective with my last role, I am excited to shift my focus to pursuing this different but equally important objective through this new role.

Incoherence in level

(Promotion) Having excelled in my current role, my responsibilities have gradually increased to the point that I have been operating at the next level for some time. I am excited by the prospect of continuing my career development and high performance in a company that recognizes my current contributions at the appropriate level and provides an exciting path for continued career progression.

(Repositioning) Having proven my capabilities in many different capacities, I have been fortunate to understand through experience the range of ways I can contribute to companies. Considering this in the context of my family and personal needs, I have determined that this role affords me the optimal balance of contributing to a company while honoring my personal and family commitments in a fulfilling way.

Short tenure(s) at previous employer(s)

As I entered a new phase in my career a few years ago, my focus was on developing as broad a set of experiences as possible. I was fortunate to have had the opportunity to grow in a variety of contexts and organizations. Now, as I transition into the next phase of my career, I am seeking a position where I can sustainably grow within a single organization. My experiences have demonstrated to me that the attributes I most value in my next sustained role are present in your company and key to my intended career progression.

Consider this hypothetical example if you are struggling to get started

If you are struggling to get started or to imagine how all of this comes together, the following basic narrative is a good starting point for many (not all) job search contexts.

> Dear Employer,
> As [insert adjective(s) to describe yourself that are also attributes from list 2 (what the employer wants)], I was excited by the opportunity encompassed by [identify the job you are seeking]. This position would [insert points from list 1 (what you want) in the context of how the job would satisfy them].
> [Describe something interesting and unique about the company.] Having [describe an interesting personal experience and relate it to the attributes of the company you just discussed.] My [insert qualification(s) from list 2] will set me apart as I [highlight specific relevant components of the job description].
> [Insert additional relevant context]
> [Express interest in continued discussion]
> Thanks,
> Name

As a practical, but hypothetical example:

Excerpt from List 1[4] – What the candidate wants
- Work requires solving problems, not just executing a process
- Enables me to work with progressive, new technologies
- Work style involves a collaborative environment
- Engage regularly with people
- Greater than $85k total annual income
- Have line of sight to at least two growth positions in the company
- Does not require relocation

Excerpt from List 2[5] – What the employer wants
- Meets minimum requirements of job posting

---

[4] For simplicity, a shortened list is depicted in the book. It is more common for lists like this to include at least 10-15 entries
[5] All the requirements on a posted job description are obviously relevant as employer wants; however, the purpose of this list is to try to anticipate the wants of the employer that are not explicitly defined in the job description

- Is social and easy to communicate with: Want somebody whom others won't avoid talking to
- Communicates technical topics well: Want somebody who can make complex topics seems simple and interesting while still communicating the important pieces of information
- Understands manufacturing well enough to be credible with floor staff: Want this specific audience to listen to, not dismiss the candidate as lacking the background to be credible
- Has enough gravitas and composure to present to senior leadership: Want to avoid having a "middle person" communicate with senior leaders
- Is curious and innovative: Want somebody who will take initiative and come up with ideas rather than waiting for others to do so
- General understanding of computer programming: Even though the job doesn't require programming, want somebody who understands the limitations and challenges of programming, so they don't have crazy or unrealistic expectations or make unrealistic requests

Could result in the following cover letter:

Dear hiring manager at Widgets, Inc.

As a creative problem-solver and an unapologetically social person, I was excited by the opportunity encompassed by your manufacturing liaison position. The idea of a job that marries solving complex logistical puzzles with the social necessity to engage a wide variety of stakeholders beautifully suits my analytical mind and high emotional intelligence.

When Widgets, Inc. began using artificial intelligence to improve demand forecasting last year, it moved in a direction that I had been advocating for in my previous role at ABC Company. Having dabbled in artificial intelligence during an elective course at university, I have long been convinced of its value in supply chain optimization. Being part of an organization that shares that vision with me would be incredibly exciting.

As you consider candidates to fill this position, I hope that you will see my engineering background as a tool empowering me to rapidly digest and communicate technical jargon. I hope you will be impressed by my past success reducing safety stock levels by 12 percent while concurrently improving customer deliver times by seven percent, and see that as an indication of my potential to deliver material performance improvements to Widgets, Inc.

Please also know that my motivation in applying is not to get out of a bad situation, but out of admiration for Widgets, Inc. and my firm conviction that this *opportunity would be an outstanding next step for my career. I look forward to discussing the opportunity with you soon.*

Thank you,

Future employee name

Test your letter before sending it

Few people can sit down and write a brilliant cover letter in a single pass, so expect to write several iterations of your letter. The research you have done and lists you have prepared accelerate the composition process, but you should expect to iterate a few times.

If you followed the process described in this chapter, you already have compiled two lists of wants and selected a few priority wants to address in the cover letter. The first step in reviewing your cover letter should be to reread it and ask yourself if you achieved each of those objectives. If you do not think you did, but have ideas for other ways to achieve them, do so. You may want to save multiple versions so you don't lose ideas as you experiment with them.

If you went through the process in Chapter 7 to develop your personal brand, you should test your cover letter to make sure it aligns with your personal brand statement. You also should test the cover letter for consistency with your resume. While your cover letter and resume should largely include different content, you do not want them to contradict one another on any points.

Once your cover letter achieves your objectives or you have exhausted your ability to improve it, ask a third party (spouse, friend, coach, colleague, etc.) for feedback. It is most effective if you tell them what you want to achieve from the letter before they read it, and then ask them how they think you might better achieve those goals. Simply asking for feedback rarely results in actionable feedback, but asking specific questions turns almost anybody into a useful resource.

Depending on the length of your lists, you may have enough material to compose multiple versions of the cover letter, each focusing on different element. It is often very effective to ask a third party to read multiple versions of your cover letter. Ask them which one they found most compelling and why. This is another way to get high-quality, actionable feedback.

Also use your cover letter as a preparation tool

As we mentioned above, even if you do not you send a cover letter, merely writing one is helpful. In many ways, you can think of your cover letter as your elevator pitch. When confronted with questions like "Why should we hire you?" or "Why do you want to work here?" (questions that come up in some format in almost every recruiting process), you have a well-constructed answer if you have written a strong cover letter.

Additionally, if you followed this process, you have a list of relevant topics to discuss during interviews. Whether you included a point from one of those lists in your cover letter or not, it becomes something potentially relevant in subsequent interviews. Items on your list of personal wants become things to confirm during your discussions, and items on the list of business wants become topics to consider when preparing for interviews.

* * *

Becoming anxious and fearful of not getting a job for the coming school year, Christa reached out to a neighbor who taught at one of the schools that Christa had applied to. She asked the neighbor to look at her resume and give her some ideas for why her applications might not be attracting more attention.

The neighbor obliged and asked Christa why she was not returning to her original school district. The neighbor perceived that district, which paid higher salaries and offered better amenities, as a more attractive place to work. It seemed odd to the neighbor (and perhaps the administrators reviewing Christa's resume) that Christa would be in good standing with that district and not return there. The neighbor also mentioned that there might be concern over the gap in time since her last employment.

Christa realized that administrators might be assuming that she hadn't been welcomed back to her original district and might think she had a performance issue that they should steer clear of. Christa thanked the neighbor for her guidance and realized that if either of these concerns were reducing her attractiveness as a candidate, there was little that could be done on the resume. Christa still had two schools on her list, and she decided that she needed to write a cover letter with each subsequent application to address these potential concerns proactively.

In her letter, she explained that family, not professional constraints, had driven her to take time away from the classroom. She further explained that during her time away from the classroom, she had moved from one suburb to another and was seeking a position close to her current home, so she could spend more time in the classroom without diminishing her time at home. She further positioned this move as an opportunity to bring some of the techniques she learned and utilized in her prior school district to the one with whom she hoped to interview.

Additionally, she incorporated details about the time that she spent working with her nephew, who has a learning disability, into her personal story in the cover letter. This sort of experience was not something she had done professionally, and she had struggled to fit it onto her resume. However, she believed it could help her stand out from other candidates.

Christa shared the cover letter with her neighbor and a few friends, collecting a few additional points of feedback, and made some final tweaks before sending it to the school. Within three days, she received an invitation to interview for the job.

* * *

Opportunities to Apply Chapter Concepts
- If you are actively engaged in a job search, compose a cover letter to one of the companies you are pursuing.
- Otherwise, compose a cover letter to your existing company as if you were seeking the position you currently occupy.

16. PLANNING FOR INTEGRATION

As difficult as getting a job is, *keeping* that job is sometimes a more significant challenge. Your goal is to do more than get a job – it's to get a *fulfilling* job where you will be successful. So it's a good idea to begin integrating into the company as early as your first interview. By taking integration and success into consideration before you join a company, you increase your chances for sustained success and improve your decision-making during the recruiting process.

Regina was an engineer with an MBA and a promising management consulting job. Like many consultants, Regina had her eyes set on making partner. When after two years of being considered for promotion, she still wasn't promoted at the firm she had joined just after getting her MBA, she started to look for opportunities elsewhere where she might be able to get to partner quickly.

Discussions with one firm advanced rapidly. The firm liked Regina's educational background and loved her ability to lead and deliver projects. Her personality was everything the company looked for, and she was even involved in the right things socially to create access to the right people. From Regina's perspective, the firm was active in her industry space and offered more than enough opportunity for her to build a book of her own business and justify a promotion to partner. The people she met were great and the projects the company was engaging in sounded fun and exciting.

However, what she thought was a brilliant move for her career hit stumbling blocks almost immediately. Regina realized that both the clients and the coworkers most focused on her industry were in a different city. Location was an easy fix. She was willing to move, and the company supported the idea. The path to partner, however, was no clearer at her new firm than her last.

Her ability to show her commercial value at the prior firm had been constrained by that company's lack of commitment to her industry. The new firm focused on her industry but presented its own challenges. The way that revenue was credited to partners was different than her previous firm's method. Regina found herself in a situation where other partners already had claimed all the natural clients for Regina to serve. There was plenty of work for her to do, but little potential for her to claim revenue as her own, creating a significant barrier to making partner.

Every box had gotten checked on both sides during the hiring process except for one critical area: integration. Regina and the company never talked about how this perfect fit would remain a perfect fit once she joined. Regina had innocently assumed the path would look the same as in her previous firm, and the company, exuberant to find somebody like Regina, who could fill a delivery need, never thought about how they could offer her a compelling long-term career.

* * *

For many people, accepting a job offer is the culmination and completion of the job search process. However, the persistent reality is that half of the experienced hires made by companies are gone after only two years. Having the right skills, capabilities, and experience for a job does not alone ensure that an employee will succeed in that role. Functioning effectively in an organization requires much more than just that.

Integration involves not only success in the organization, but outside it, as well. Frequently, accepting a new job means moving to a new city, which affects an entire family. Even if your job move keeps you in the same location, it is not uncommon for integration to succeed in the office and fail outside the office.

Ultimately, you do not want to end up in a job you do not want or one in which you cannot be successful. While some surprises are unavoidable, many of the challenges that drive people to leave jobs soon after taking them can be anticipated, enabling you to either make a different decision about accepting the job or have a plan to avoid or address the issue and set yourself up for success.

While quick departures are neither lethal to the careers of the employee nor catastrophic to the company, there is significant cost to both sides. Instead of risking incurring that cost, make sure to plan for your integration before you accept a new job.

There are six principal areas of integration to address in preparation for a new position:

- Family – Ensure you can manage any significant impacts on your personal life well enough to allow you to focus on creating early success in the new job.
- "100 Day Plan" – Prepare a set of actions to quickly deliver impact in the new role and establish a basis for longer term success while confirming to the company that you were the right hire.

- Organization/Stakeholder Map – Identify, to the best of your ability, who you will interact with in the new organization and how they connect with and influence others.
- Political Capital – Recognize how to establish and develop influence within the organization.
- Intellectual Capital – Plan to use your knowledge base to move the needle for the company and establish your position and performance.
- Social Capital – Plan to enhance your engagement outside of the office through hobbies, interests, social functions, clubs, associations, boards, etc.

Have a plan for addressing the needs of your family

Your family's contentment affects your job success. If a job move causes discord in your family, your professional success can suffer. But few people actively plan actions to help their families adapt to new professional situations.

This is typically an easier process for unmarried people without children, but consideration for the impact on parents, grandparents, siblings, and others can be substantial and deserves attention.

For moves that do not involve geographic relocation, planning for family integration often is simple. However, even without a change in physical location, changes in travel, working hours, flexible working, and even commute times can impact others in your family. Successful people anticipate and proactively address these impacts within the family.

Common concerns to address include:

With and Without Geographic Relocation	With Geographic Relocation
• Ability to be present (and/or prepare) family meals • Ability to be present for and/or provide transportation to children's school and extracurricular activities • Changes in child-care approach • Commitment to social groups (e.g. religious, civic, community organizations) • Impacts to discretionary spending • Changes in energy level after work • Alterations to weekend and/or holiday behavioral norms	• Changes in school • Changes in cultural norms • Weather-related changes • Language differences • Proximity to family • Connectedness with friends and social circles • Holiday travel

How you address these concerns (or others that you identify) will be specific to your family, but having a plan in place before you start your new job will significantly reduce the risk of major issues that could jeopardize successful integration. Furthermore, developing your integration plan before accepting an offer can prevent you from putting yourself in an unhealthy situation in the first place.

Create a 100-day plan

While integrating your family is the most important – and most commonly overlooked – aspect of integration for newly hired employees, your new employer wants to quickly confirm that they made a good decision. It is important to not only reaffirm that decision, but to establish a reputation that you want to keep. Having a plan from the beginning gives you purpose and direction, increasing the likelihood of success during this transition period.

Many people incorrectly assume that the company is responsible for integrating a new employee into the organization. While it is sensible for a company to want to protect and maximize its investment in a new employee, there is no guarantee that the company will effectively integrate the employee. Successful employees take an active role in – or even lead – their integration.

Building a formal plan for the first 100 days of your employment is a good way to create a successful integration. The job description provides a good starting point for building your plan but is hardly an exhaustive resource. New employees should enter their new role with an understanding of the following:

- What targets will you set?
- How are you going to personally measure your performance?
- How do you expect to be measured by others?
- How will you establish credibility with your team members?
- What support will you need?
- What support are you best positioned to give to others?

Your answers to these questions create the groundwork for a plan. If you cannot answer any of these questions in advance, be certain to develop answers once you have joined the company. Whether you define this plan over a 100-day horizon or a shorter (or longer) period is less important than having a set of specific actions to take and explicit outcomes to pursue.

Try to understand how people are connected in the new organization

Regardless of the industry, your success will, to some degree, be influenced by your relationships and interactions with others. It may not be possible to understand or fully map the organization and your specific stakeholders before entering your role, but you should make a point of doing so once inside the organization.

As you prepare for your new role, seek to answer the following questions:

- Whom do you want to meet?
- Whom will you interact with on a regular or at least predictable basis?
- How are decisions made and communicated through the organization?
- Which roles wield decision authority on which topics?
- If you have multiple reporting lines, where does the "real" power lie?
- Who would make an attractive advocate to have outside of your immediate reporting line?
- How will you test for gaps in the business that present an opportunity for you to establish a unique identify and add meaningful value?

Initially at least, you will answer those questions with job titles and roles rather than names. This is still helpful. Attaching names to the roles/descriptions will become an early task once you start working.

Plan to build influence through the creation of political capital

Beyond just figuring out the lay of the land, you want to begin understanding the ways to move around within that land. Moving into a new job, especially if at a new company, will naturally change the spheres of influence and the mechanisms and individuals through which you establish and advance your agendas.

Part of your research during the interview process should be to understand how decisions are made and how influence is generated. While you will not have a complete understanding until you have been in the role for some time, you should start to build your political capital as soon as possible.

Ask yourself:

- Who are the people I will most regularly interact with?
- What is the "currency" of power/influence in the organization?
- How do people obtain that currency?
- Who will most frequently be affected by my actions and decisions?
- Whose actions and decisions will most affect me?
- Whom do I need to meet? Which meetings are likely to happen naturally, and which do I need to initiate?
- Whom do I believe I can begin to empower and/or support in their objectives? How will I do so?
- Who are my likely supporters and blockers? How can I connect with each of them to build political capital?

Many of these questions will be difficult or impossible to answer before joining the company and operating in your role for a while, but asking them can nonetheless inspire certain actions and objectives to add to your 100-day plan.

Find ways to benefit from your intellectual capital

As you prepare to move into a new job, your intellectual capital should be one of the more straightforward tools you use to establish yourself for success. It is likely that your knowledge played a significant role in the company's decision to hire you. Still, answering the following questions can ensure you maximize the impact of your intellectual capital and position yourself to develop new capital.

- Why did they hire me? How do I ensure I demonstrate my knowledge and *visibly* meet/exceed those expectations?
- What knowledge differentiates me now? Is that differentiation sustainable as a long-term platform, or should I seek to evolve?
- What issues are most pressing for the company? What knowledge do I have, or could I develop to make an impact on the company?
- Within the spectrum of knowledge topics, where can I establish myself as unique within the company and provide something not already supplied by others? Which topics could I move into without compromising my personal brand?

Before you start your new job, many of the answers will only be educated guesses. Even without having confirmed answers, having a plan to cultivate and utilize your intellectual capital is helpful. Without a preset plan, you are likely to face one of the following challenges:

- You become so busy with the day-to-day responsibilities of your role that you lose sight of the pursuits of long-term growth, and your intellectual capital remains stagnant.
- The company unexpectedly pushes you in a direction that does not align with where you would like to move, but you cannot push back and redirect in a more optimal way because you do not have a credible alternative in mind.

Having a plan does not prevent business priorities from pushing you in a different direction, but at least you are able push in the direction most interesting and beneficial to you.

Do not forget to start early on generating social capital

Social capital takes the longest to establish and can be the most rewarding to have. It may be difficult to plan for developing social capital before you start in your new job, but it is generally useful to plan for developing it once in the organization.

There are many pieces of information to capture as you are integrating into the new company. The information you learn when meeting people initially can inspire specific actions that develop into very meaningful social capital. For example, it will be helpful for you to keep track of:

- Who has children?
    - How old are they?
    - What schools do they attend?
    - What activities are they involved in?
- What hobbies do people have?
    - Do people golf, bowl, ski?
    - What sports teams are favorites?
    - Are people foodies, wine connoisseurs, whisky collectors?
- Where do people invest time and non-work energy?
    - What charities are they passionate about?
    - Do people sit on boards?
    - Which churches do they belong to?

This knowledge can lead you to create opportunities to develop social capital:

- Invite to dinner with spouse and/or family
- Invite to social lunch/happy hour
- Introduce to friends with mutual interests
- Hold playdates for children
- Attend children's school events
- Volunteer to coach a child's sports team
- Participate in fundraisers
- Invite to play golf or other sports
- Invite to attend sporting events
- Attend charity events
- Volunteer to support charities
- Become active in civic or charity groups
- Attend church and related functions

Building social capital is a long effort. Fortunately, most of the foundational activities are themselves naturally enjoyable and/or fulfilling. You may not include many specific actions in your 100-day plan, but as you join an organization, you have a unique opportunity to learn about people and collect information that leads directly to social capital in the future.

Many more details on political, intellectual and social capital exist in Chapter 8.

Use integration planning as a competitive advantage during recruiting

While integration planning seems like a topic that becomes relevant only after you have accepted an offer, there are a few compelling reasons to integrate it into the earlier stages of your recruiting efforts.

First, being able to discuss your plan for integration (even when based on imperfect or inaccurate assumptions) with interviewers during the recruiting process shows a level of commitment to generating results that most candidates do not demonstrate. Showing that your goals and thoughts extend well beyond a job offer demonstrates to employers that you are looking at the big picture of what it will take for both you and the company to be successful. This will differentiate you from most candidates, who focus solely on getting to an offer.

Second, this sort of planning helps you decide whether to accept or decline a company's job offer. If you do not integrate well, you are likely to leave quickly. This does not help your career and can, in fact, harm it.

Remember that one of your responsibilities as a candidate is to interview the job for your career. Part of that is confirming that you believe you will be successful at that company which requires effective integration. If you cannot convince yourself that you can successfully integrate into the company, you should strongly consider not taking the job.

Third, knowing how easy – or difficult – integration into a new company will be should help you to better risk-adjust your opportunities so that you make the best decision when choosing between competing options.

Finally, when done well, the integration process can begin with recruiting. There are cases where employers even extend their recruiting process to allow candidates to begin the integration process before even receiving an offer. The relationships you will want to develop as you integrate could be relationships you started building while recruiting.

Don't forget to apply your plan when you join

As useful as your integration plan is during your recruiting process, its principal value remains in helping you integrate. Be sure that once you accept an offer you do not forget to revisit, update and then apply your integration plan.

* * *

Sanjay had a Ph.D. in chemistry and a lucrative job in R&D at a large pharmaceutical company. He was performing well at this job, but the long approval timelines and low success rate for projects that are native to the pharmaceutical industry was diminishing his interest in the sector. Ever since a friend from his university chemistry program took a position in the food industry, Sanjay had fantasized about joining an organization that had shorter product development timelines and generated results more easily discussed at cocktail parties.

With the encouragement of his wife, Sanjay reached out to a major food company and applied for a product developer position in the company's R&D group. Sanjay had all the qualifications to be a great fit for the role except for never having worked in the industry. Sanjay suspected this would concern some people during the recruiting process, but he also thought the outside, fresh perspective he would bring could be valuable.

Sanjay had a few extended conversations with his friend in the food industry. With his friend's help, he pieced together a clear vision for the role he was trying to earn. These conversations also led him to ask additional questions early in the recruiting process.

Sanjay used this information to map out a plan for what he would do if hired. He took an honest inventory of what he did not know and developed a plan for filling those gaps. He also looked at the company's performance in the niche industry addressed by the role and surmised the issues he would need to tackle. He built a plan for addressing these concerns and even used LinkedIn to learn about the people who he would work closely with, identifying topics of mutual interest.

As expected, the hiring manager for the position was concerned by Sanjay's effort to switch industries. He questioned little of Sanjay's technical knowledge but appeared doubtful of his commitment or fit until Sanjay offered to walk him through the integration plan Sanjay had drafted. Sanjay talked his potential future boss through the steps he had imagined for closing knowledge gaps and for building relationships with his new co-workers. He shared his vision for his agenda and the steps he would take to achieve business objectives. By the end of the conversation, the hiring manager's tone had completely changed. It seemed to him that Sanjay was more prepared for this role as an outsider than any of the insiders he had interviewed. He decided to take a chance on Sanjay.

* * *

Opportunities to Apply Chapter Concepts
- Think about the early days in your current position. What would you do differently if you were to join again?
- Build an integration plan either for an opportunity you are pursuing or for your current job as if you were able to rejoin the company under the original context, but with your current knowledge.

17. IMPRESSING DURING YOUR INTERVIEW

Look at interviews as an opportunity to shine. But to shine your brightest, know that you need to prepare effectively – and know how.

Diane had spent 20 years growing her career in telecom, and had her eyes set on a senior management position. She excelled in her jobs, demonstrating an impressive work ethic and extensive technical knowledge. She actively cultivated a professional network and developed a deep knowledge of digital transformation, which seemed to be one of the hottest topics in her industry at the time. Though Diane liked her company, there was no room for her to move up in the foreseeable future, so she decided to seek senior management opportunities in other telecom companies.

Diane's resume was impressive, and her skills relevant and in demand, so it was no surprise that she quickly lined up interviews with three companies. She thoroughly and expertly answered the questions asked of her and walked out of each interview feeling like things had gone well, which made it difficult for Diane to understand why she did not get invited for a single second-round interview. Oddly, one company passed on the opportunity to hire her as an employee but asked if she would be interested in working as a consultant to them on a project to select and leverage the best technologies.

Diane reached out to the recruiters asking for feedback, which came back very consistent. Her knowledge was extensive, but none of the companies saw her as fitting in. The disconnect seemed to be behavioral rather than related to knowledge or capabilities. Unsatisfied, but unable to learn more from the recruiters, Diane reached out to a trusted advisor and recounted the interview experience as best she could. Diane's advisor hypothesized that Diane might have been answering the questions in a way that addressed Diane's agenda and interests without addressing the intentions of the interviewer or the needs of the company. She suggested that Diane work with a coach to get some expert advice.

Diane took that recommendation and did a mock interview with a coach. The coach recorded the interview, and as Diane listened to the recording, a few things became clear. First, Diane treated every question like a technical question. She realized that even as the interviewer sought to understand why or how Diane would do something, she responded by explaining what she would do and when.

Reflecting further on prior interviews, Diane realized that companies already believed in her command of technical issues. Interviewers instead wanted to address her ability to implement change, which involves a different, less technical skill set. While Diane had been effective implementing change in her current role, she was so focused on displaying her technical skills that she missed the opportunity to address the real concern in the interview.

Furthermore, while she displayed high intelligence, her emotional intelligence came across low. She had not engaged effectively with the interviewer. If she couldn't listen thoroughly and respond directly and accurately to an interviewer, how could she manage such a significant change in the organization? The coach suggested that while Diane's lengthy tenure promoted loyalty and longevity as positives, it probably also was calling into question her ability to integrate into a new culture. The coach suggested that during interviews, Diane should ask questions which demonstrated her awareness of the possible issue and suggest she also had the ability to manage it.

In summary, Diane needed to pay more attention to the interviewer and respond more precisely to the questions asked. She needed to set aside her desire to demonstrate the full breadth of her unique knowledge and provide the information that would impress the interviewer – not what would impress herself.

* * *

Interviewing is one of the most interactive aspects of the job search process, but it often is misunderstood and is burdened with many misconceptions.

Many people fail to recognize that the candidate and the interviewer have aligned goals. Both want the interview to lead to a successful hire. Interviewers gain nothing when a candidate does poorly in an interview. An interviewer's goal is not to trick the candidate or cause the candidate to look bad. Instead, interviewers endeavor to see the best that a candidate has to offer. This effort often leads to challenging questions that create an opportunity for candidates to stand out in a crowd – or to fail miserably.

Other candidates fail to realize that not being offered the job is not always a negative. More challenges arise from being in a job that does not fully suit you than from being declined for such a position. Candidates should not seek to land a job which they do not have the skills, attributes, or motivation required to succeed in, and consequently will face a daily struggle. When a company passes on you, the decision generally benefits you because you do not end up in situation that could do more harm than help to your career.

Lack of preparation can tank an interview even for the most qualified candidate. However, even thorough, effective preparation does not guarantee you will be hired. At your best, you may still not possess the right skills and knowledge to effectively deliver in the role you are interviewing for. However, if you are not prepared to demonstrate your best, the interviewer will assume they have seen your best, and it is less than you or they want.

Accurately understand the context for the interview

Interviewing well is a skill that improves with practice and preparation. Even people who have a natural ability to interview well improve their performance with some practice and targeted preparation. Chapter 13 provides detailed suggestions for improving your understanding of the company and context for hiring which can help to prepare you for interviews.

While there are many different formats for interviews, the goals for the company are generally consistent and can be summarized as an attempt to answer the following basic questions:

1. If given the opportunity, can we reasonably expect this individual to perform the activities required by the job at the quality level required to meet business objectives?
2. Will the individual integrate well into the organization, ideally improving output beyond his/her own responsibilities and without harming existing operations?
3. Can we reasonably expect that the individual will remain committed to his/her role in the business long enough that the company generates a meaningful return on the hiring investment?
4. Assuming a "yes" answer to each of the preceding questions, is this the strongest of the candidates who have been interviewed and received three "yes" answers to the above questions?

As a candidate, you want to provide credible answers that demonstrate that you satisfy each of those criteria.

Do not reduce your chances by failing to address the basics

While the contents of an interview will vary, adhering to the following basic guidelines should be a given for any situation:

- Determine your plans for getting to the interview the night before and allot ample time to reach the location at least five minutes ahead of your scheduled appointment. If traffic is a concern, being very early is always preferable to being even a little late.
- Dress at least as formally as you expect is the norm for the job (in other words, how you expect your interviewer to be dressed). Being overdressed will not reflect poorly on you but being underdressed could. If you have any doubts, dress in business formal.
- Have impeccable hygiene. Be showered, with clean and pressed clothing. If you wear cologne or makeup, ensure neither is overpowering. Ensure that your hair is neither unkempt nor distracting, and that it reflects a professional demeanor.
- Bring a portfolio or binder which includes printed copies of your resume and any supporting documents you may want to discuss in the interview (such as a client contact list). Ensure you have blank paper for notes and two working pens.
- Silence your phone (including keeping it from vibrating), watch, and any other devices which could make distracting noises.
- Treat all people you interact with at the office or interview location with respect, positivity, and friendliness. You never know who will provide input on their interactions with you.

For video interviews, such as those conducted via Skype, the same guidelines apply. Unless you know the interview will be audio only, you should maintain the same dress standards even in a video interview.

While there could be situations in which the following guiding principles can be broken, in most situations you should:

- **Concentrate on listening to the interviewer.** Do not try to anticipate what they want to know (or should want to know). Instead listen carefully and respond specifically and thoughtfully to the exact questions asked to you.

- Do not interrupt the interviewer, even if you think you can finish his or her sentence.
- Keep your answers short and to the specific point introduced by the interviewer. Avoid "wandering" or "waffling" with your answers. You may be inclined to provide additional information that you think is relevant, even if it is the interviewer hasn't asked about it. Before embarking on a new topic, ask the interviewer if he or she would like you to continue in that new direction.
- Be authentic. Do not give answers that you think the interviewer wants to hear unless your authentic answer happens to be that "preferred" answer. Remember that how you present yourself during the interview will set the expectations for you if hired, so you want to set realistic expectations.
- Demonstrate engagement during the interview: Maintain eye contact. Take occasional written notes (if it feels appropriate). Ask meaningful questions, but don't ask questions just for the sake of asking questions.
- Treat the interview like a conversation, not an interrogation. The best interviews will involve natural and enjoyable dialogue in addition to an exchange of useful information.

Nervousness happens, but the best way to avoid it is to be well-prepared. Even so, be aware of your personal tendencies when nervous. Each person behaves differently under pressure, but displaying any of the following behaviors can sidetrack an interview or detract from your professionalism or gravitas:

- Giving excessive or unnecessary details (too much information for the question or audience)
- Artificially buying time – Starting an answer with "That's a great question" or "Let me see" can imply a lack of preparation and diminishes the credibility of the answer you do eventually give. Do not be afraid to have a little silence in the conversation instead.
- Fighting for control of the conversation – Steering the conversation to your agenda and topics of your choice signals discomfort with or inability to converse on the topics chosen by the interviewer
- "Bird walking" – moving from one topic to another without specific purpose
- Engaging in a transactional manner – While an interview necessarily involves questions and answers, these should flow in a conversation – not devolve into an interrogation. Answering in ways that curtail rather

than open the conversation displays discomfort and/or lack of preparation.
- Repetition – When you repeat yourself, you are giving the impression that you are either not paying attention to the conversation or that you lack enough depth to introduce new content into the discussion
- Lack of eye contact – Suggests disinterest in the conversation
- Fidgeting – Shows your nervousness and can distract an interviewer to the point of disengagement
- Excessive and/or large gesturing – Some gesturing can be useful to illustrate or enhance a point, but a little goes a long way and too much can be distracting

Always prepare for an interview

Drafting responses to possible interview questions in advance of the interview is one of the best ways to be confident during the interview and deliver concise, compelling responses to questions. While it is impossible to know exactly what you'll be asked and impractical to memorize answers even if you did know, having prepared answers to some questions in advance will help you quickly deliver strong answers without rambling or stalling to think.

Being able to closely predict some of the lines of conversation in an interview requires you to have a reasonably correct understanding of the motivations of the company in hiring you. You want to understand:

- Why is the company hiring for the job?
- What makes the company (and/or role within the company) unique?
- What differentiates high and low performance in the role?

When you understand these questions, you may be able to foresee certain questions. For example, a company that is hiring to expand its product offering may value cross-functional experience more than a company hiring to replace somebody who left, because the role in the latter scenario is more established and job description more certain than when hiring in a new space. Knowing this, you could anticipate questions to assess your skills in areas outside of your stated specialization. In a leadership role, the ability to inspire and influence people could be more valuable than deep technical knowledge, so you could expect more questions that relate to how you interact with people than questions which assess your technical knowledge.

In addition to understanding the motivations of the company, it is important to clearly understand your own motivations. You should be able to clearly explain:

- Why are you interested in the job?
- What do you expect would differentiate you from other candidates?
- What is going to make you successful?

Companies want to hire people who will stay with them for many years. People are less likely to leave a job that fits their career and personal aspirations than a position that is simply a job. They also are less likely to leave a place where they are successful.

Just about everybody has a boss, and the people interviewing you will most likely have to sell their decision to hire you to a superior. Thus, they will need to justify their belief that you are qualified for the position, a better fit than other candidates, have a low risk of underperforming, and are likely to remain with the company for a reasonable amount of time.

While it always is good to be prepared for any question, if you know who your audience will be during an interview, you are can better anticipate the likely types of questions and optimize your preparation effort:

Common Reviewer	Typical Concerns
Human resources	• Background/Skill/Competency questions will typically be limited to confirming that minimum qualifications are met for the job • Likely to see many motivational questions as HR seeks to hire people who will stay with the company for an extended time • Likely to have many behavioral questions and emotional intelligence questions as they look for cultural fit
Hiring manager	• Wants to be convinced that you can do the job with limited oversight, training and/or intervention so will likely focus on technical/industry skills and experience to determine ability to deliver on the job • Likely to see some behavioral questions to set expectations for working dynamic
Hiring manager's boss	• Is concerned with cultural fit and potential business impact • Typically wants to discuss past results and may ask behavioral and emotional intelligence questions to gauge cultural fit
Future peers	• Will typically ask more social questions as they seek to assess cultural fit and determine if they would enjoy working with you • Will often explore background and technical/industry skills that confirm that you would alleviate rather than add to their workload

Know that not all interview questions are designed equally

Companies ask a variety of questions to capture information on diverse topics and test different dimensions of fit. Most questions fit in one of four categories:

1) Behavioral questions - assume that best predictor of future behavior is past behavior. Interviewers using behavioral questions are typically more interested in the *why* and *how* of the situation described than understanding *what* the situation entailed or the outcome. Questions of this category often have a similar construction to:

- Give an example of a goal you reached and tell me how you achieved it
- Give an example of a goal you didn't meet and how you handled it
- Describe a stressful situation at work and how you addressed it

It is rare for an employer to expect or want a specific answer from a behavioral question. These questions typically serve the purpose of understanding how the candidate's mind works. In general, the most impressive answers are those that show a high level of introspection (i.e. shows the candidate understands how his/her mind works) and intention (i.e. shows that the candidate is thoughtful and purposeful).

One of the most troublesome questions for people to answer is when they are asked about their weaknesses. There is no "best" way to answer this, but there are a few things to keep in mind:

- Everybody has a weakness. Weaknesses are not necessarily problems, they are simply a reflection of nobody having perfectly consistent levels of strength across their collections of skills. A weakness is simply your least strong strength. Do not fear talking about it.
- If you avoid talking about your weakness by changing the subject or by trying to present your weakness as a strength, you are more likely to look like you are covering something way worse than the reality that you are trying to somehow bypass answering a difficult, awkward question.
- Be prepared to give examples and justify your claims, especially if you choose to claim a weakness that is really a positive dressed up as a weakness such as "I am too diligent", "I work too hard," or "I am a perfectionist." To most interviewers, these sound like attempts to avoid an honest answer, showing either limited introspection or an attempt to hide a big skeleton in your closet. However, if you truly believe one is a weakness for you, then you should be able to give examples of how it has been a barrier to your success in your past and what you are doing to improve on those weaknesses. Faced with the choice between saying you have identified a weakness but choose to do nothing about it, that you are intentionally trying to make mistakes, or choosing a different weakness than being too diligent, the last option is probably the most attractive.

- Companies assume you have a weakness, they just don't want it to be core to the job. If you are weak in your ability to influence others and you are applying for a sales role, then the company should be concerned. If instead you are applying for a role processing invoices, this weakness, while not ideal, is essentially immaterial to your future performance in *that* job.
- Companies like to know that you will get better with time, but people who lack introspection require significant oversight and support to improve, whereas introspective people can identify the need for change themselves and act on it. If you can show that you not only are able to identify your weaker areas but also proactively address them, you show a company that they can expect you to improve over time with limited management burden.
- Egos can lead people to excel in their work or to be counterproductive in their behavior. Companies know that it is inevitable that your ego will become burdened at some point and they want to know how you will respond. Weaknesses also are a burden to the ego. If when talking about your weakness it becomes apparent that your ego drove you to address issues in an effective way (such as you seeking help from others) rather than creating counterproductive behaviors (such as hiding from your issues or deflecting them to others), the company can build confidence that you will perform well even when you inevitably run into adversity.

This line of questioning is one of the more difficult approaches for learning about a candidate that an interviewer can take, and it is often as uncomfortable for them as it is for the candidate. So while it is important to have thought through this question in advance in case you receive it in some format, you should not agonize over it. As long as you do not break down entirely when answering this question, it is likely that other questions will carry much more influence on the outcome.

2) Motivation questions - are a subset of behavioral questions that aim to expose passions and attitude. These questions seek to understand why you behave the way you do and expose how your behaviors are influenced. As with other behavioral questions, there is no universally optimal way to answer these questions. Different companies may prefer different traits depending on their culture and the needs of the role.

While there is no universally optimal way to answer these questions, it is almost always a bad strategy to be dishonest or misleading with them. It is difficult to force yourself to be motivated unnaturally, so if you set the expectation that you are naturally motivated in an inaccurate way and the company hires you expecting that to motivate you, expect that the company will try to motivate you in that way. This can leave you unmotivated and unfulfilled.

Interviewers often listen to questions seeking to understand the natural tendencies of a candidate along the following dimensions:

- Internal vs. external responses:
    - Internal: "Let me tell you all the things I tried first before finally coming up with an idea that worked."
    - External: "Let me tell you what got in my way and why it wasn't my fault that I couldn't do it."
- Action vs. Plan:
    - Action: "I immediately took action and continued acting until it was resolved."
    - Plan: "I considered the following options and weighed them on these dimensions before picking the right one and acted."
- Individual vs. Team:
    - Individual: "It was my responsibility, so I did these things to make it work."
    - Team: "I consulted with the affected people and weighed their advice in reaching my final conclusion."

Many people feel an obligation to be "politically correct" in their answers to such questions. Candidates often assume it is taboo to be motivated by wealth, influence, or recognition. If such "taboo" motivators are in play for you, it is possible that your interviewer could have an adverse reaction to hearing that. But you are more likely to benefit from an honest answer than by trying to promote something of secondary importance to avoid bringing up a taboo topic.

Remember that not getting a job is a better outcome if the job is a poor fit for your personality, ambitions, and needs. Furthermore, some topics that may have a certain social political correctness have a different corporate political correctness. For example, companies might want to hire people who are motivated by wealth. It is easier for a company to offer an employee money than the promise of solving world hunger (or any other social concern that may not be related to the core business of the company). Companies find it reassuring to know that an employee will be motivated by the rewards they offer.

Savvy interviewers also seek to gain intelligence on how to "sell" you the job. While the compensation and benefits for some positions sometimes are fixed, there often is room for employers to craft an offer to specifically attract a person. How you answer motivational questions can influence how the company courts you if they decide to attempt to bring you on.

3) Questions about skills and competency - are usually the most familiar to candidates. These questions are particularly comfortable because they call for more objective answers than other types of questions do. Skills and competency questions typically invite candidates to share things about themselves that they are proud of.

There is no need to be modest about skills or accomplishments, but you should not embellish or exaggerate them. You want maximum "credit" for what you can and/or have done without setting unrealistic expectations for your future delivery.

Avoid going into unnecessary detail. In most situations, you could say far more about yourself than an interviewer cares to hear about. Listen carefully to the specific questions and give concise, focused answers without trying to be comprehensive.

You are better off piquing an interviewer's interest on a topic, leading them to ask follow-up questions than filling your first answer with too much information. The latter approach could give the impression that you don't listen well. Also, when you talk too much, you run the risk of losing your message in extraneous information.

To the extent that it is possible, it is helpful to understand the background of your interviewer before the interview. That way, you can tailor the level and type of detail you provide to their level of knowledge and likely interest. For example, you may want to provide simpler answers with less jargon to an HR interviewer than to your potential boss.

4) Emotional intelligence questions - are often the most uncomfortable and unexpected.

Questions about emotional intelligence are designed to reveal whether an individual is aware of how his or her actions affect other people. By their nature, these questions have no "right" or "wrong" answers, and often candidates feel like any answer will reflect poorly on them. For this reason, it is especially helpful to prepare for such questions so that you can convey a positive tone and not wish you could invoke the 5th Amendment.

In the modern workplace, collaboration is critical to business success. There are many ways to be successful when working with others, but some styles work better in certain environments than others. Emotional intelligence questions help employers assess the quality of the fit between your natural tendencies and the way their business operates.

As with behavioral questions, the interviewer typically learns more from you explaining the *why* and *how* of the situation than the *what*, *when*, or *who*. It is to your advantage to explain your thought process in greater detail than the actions and outcomes that resulted from that thought process.

Expect to discuss imperfect situations. Interviewers know that mistakes happen on the job. While some questions may seem like they are intended to trick you into making yourself look bad, they are more likely focused on understanding how you persevere through adversity. It would be unrealistic to think that any candidate will execute his/her role without ever running into hardship. The employer needs to know that when that inevitably happens, the employee will be able to effectively handle the situation.

Interview Preparation

During the actual interview, you should focus only on your answer – not on thinking through other nuances of the question. However, as you develop practice questions and answers during your pre-interview preparation, you should consider the following:

- Think about your responses from the perspective of the interviewer/company. Things you believe are interesting about yourself may not be materially interesting to them.
- What do you believe the interviewer wants to learn from each question? Make sure you answer the question in a way that clearly addresses the purpose.
- Crisp, targeted answers are more effective than lengthy, comprehensive answers. You would rather an interviewer seek further information through additional follow-up questions than lose the answer they needed during your long-winded response.
- Never feel like you must get everything out at once. You will likely want to share many things with the interviewer. Instead of trying to force information into topics that are only loosely related, trust that natural opportunities to share those pieces of information will arise.
- Recognize that interviewers use different types of questions to elicit different types of information. Try to craft answers that make it easy for the interviewer to learn what he/she wants to understand (see more on this in subsequent pages).

While it may seem silly at first, it is best to answer practice questions aloud. The pace at which you convert thoughts to words is different than when your answers remain only in your mind. Practicing speaking your answers helps you to avoid long-winded answers because you hear the actual pace of the answer – not just the pace at which you can conjure the content.

In addition to practicing at least a few questions of each of the four types, you should specifically focus on questions relevant to your upcoming interview(s). You may also want to practice some questions that you find difficult or uncomfortable to answer, even if do not expect those questions to be asked. Becoming comfortable answering difficult questions reduces the potential that you will be surprised in an interview and builds your confidence and poise.

Many people also find it helpful to physically write or at least type out the answers to questions. Not only does this force you to spend more time thinking about the answer because of the slower pace of writing than thinking, but the action of writing helps commit the ideas to memory. Rote memorization of answers is rarely effective because of the time required and the low chance of any specific question being asked. Committing key concepts and general response ideas to memory, on the other hand, can be quite valuable.

The appendix contains a list of potential questions that is a useful starting point to inspire you to develop a list of questions to support your preparation efforts. While it is difficult to overprepare, there is a point where answering additional questions and/or doing additional research begins to provide diminishing returns. That point will be different for each person.

Between smart phones and laptops, it is very easy to record yourself. Instead of merely answering practice questions for your own ears, record yourself asking the question, then stating your answer, and listen to it. Just as most people derive great benefits by speaking their answers out loud rather than just thinking about them, they gain additional insight by listening to their recorded answer.

Mock interviews are the next step to intensify preparations. Instead of rehearsing questions in isolation, enlist the support of another person. You can provide your mock interviewer with a script of questions (unless they are qualified to actually interview you for the role) and answer them as if it were a real interview.

Mock interviews ought to be video recorded so that you can review not only the answers you provided, but the body language you exhibited during the interview. If possible, have your mock interviewer review the recording with you so he/she can provide feedback to you in the context of the interview. Depending on how familiar your mock interviewer is with the role, feedback can cover style, such as body language and delivery or also can address content.

Candidates should not feel like they must find a mock interviewer who can credibly replicate the actual interviewer's behavior. While that is preferred, nearly any friend, family member, or colleague willing to help you can do an effective job.

However, candidates who really want to maximize the impact of their preparations should hire a professional coach to assist in interview preparation. These individuals can provide specific insight and practical guidance for improving. There are services and individuals with extensive hiring backgrounds who can not only better simulate the specific interviewers you anticipate speaking with but can give you credible expert advice on how an interviewer is likely to react to your responses and behaviors. These professionals also will coach you on how to better achieve the objectives you want from the interview.

More candidates underprepare than overprepare, so if in doubt, prepare as thoroughly as your schedule allows you to. Appendix C provides a broad sampling of example questions in each category.

Be prepared to ask questions during the interview

Though it would be odd if you asked more questions during an interview than your interviewer, it is rare that you would not be given any opportunity to ask some questions. It is therefore important that you are ready to ask questions that are meaningful for your process. There are fundamentally two reasons candidates receive the "Do you have any questions for me?" query near the end of an interview.

First, interviewers want to provide candidates the opportunity to convince themselves that they want to work for the company. Addressing concerns that candidates have about the company can do this. Going through the assessment process and deciding to hire somebody who decides they do not want to work for that company is not a successful outcome for either side.

Second, interviewers continue to learn about the candidate through the questions that they ask. Savvy interviewers can learn as much about candidates from the questions the candidate asks as the questions asked of the candidate. For example:

- Asking no questions – This shows a lack of interest and/or preparation. Asking no questions despite being offered the opportunity to do so is a less polite way of saying, "I appreciate the opportunity to speak with you, but I do not think this opportunity is right for me."
- Asking about the interviewer's experience – Unless you have a specific curiosity and you believe a first-hand example will be more enlightening than a direct answer to your underlying concern, this question screams a lack of preparation. It shows that you are aware that not asking a question would reflect poorly on you and you are interested enough in the job to want to avoid this, but not interested enough to have prepared in advance for the interview.

Asking, "Can you tell me your favorite part of working for this company?" or "What do you think makes working for this company better than another company?" keeps the interviewer talking and consumes time in the interview, but any answers are unlikely to materially improve your decision-making process. Thus, asking these questions makes you look like are just filling time. If you are genuinely interested in the experience of the interviewer, there are ways to ask about their experience which are positive and do not reflect lack of preparation. We will address those shortly.

- Confirming a hypothesis about a job – This shows that you have invested the time to thoroughly research the job and/or company and are taking the opportunity seriously. For example, "Your recent acquisition of ABC company seems to suggest that you are moving in the direction of a more virtual customer experience. Is this correct or is the company trying to tap into a new market without shifting its principle focus?" shows that you have done research (which implies genuine interest), have business acumen to understand why a company might take those actions, and reflects your interest to capture information which could make the opportunity more or less attractive. All of these reflect positively on you.
- Testing the fit of the job for your needs – This shows a genuine interest in the company and a high degree of self-awareness. It also shows concern for long-term fit indicating a lower risk of you leaving unexpectedly and quickly if you join. Engaging the interviewer with, "Having a sustainable work-life balance that doesn't force a significant trade-off between career advancement and reasonable time with my family is important to me. Can you tell me what the company does to support work-life balance and what sort of hours would be commonly necessary to perform well in this job?" helps to improve your decision making while reassuring the company that you will not become an early flight risk if hired. This is a context in which you could ask about the experience of your interviewer in a safe way. In a context like this, you could ask the interviewer to use his or her experience as an example in answering the question.
- Revisiting a point from earlier in the discussion – This shows that you were listening, paying attention and engaged in the conversation. It reflects well on your personal communication skills and suggests you would engage well with other employees and customers. "I would like to go back to when we were talking about the project you were a part of to accomplish X. Could you tell me more about Y?" is obviously a question that would be specific to the discussion and could not be anticipated in

advance but could reflect positively on *you if* it has relevance to your decision-making process. If you ask a question like this, do not be afraid to also explain why you are asking the question. Doing so should demonstrate your thoughtfulness and intelligence while also increasing the precision and value of the answer you ultimately receive to the question.

Even if you do not end up asking the questions, it is a good practice to enter every interview with at least three questions ready to ask if given the opportunity to ask questions. Never pass up the opportunity to ask a question when invited to do so.

You should be cognizant of an interviewer's time. Do not expect an indefinite amount of time to ask questions, but let the interviewer be the one to cut off the interview. If you are aware that you have passed the allotted time, it is courteous to acknowledge that you are past time and offer to continue another time. However, you should only close the interview if you do not have any more legitimate, high-quality questions. Do not ask questions just for the sake of asking questions, but also try to get as many legitimate questions answered as the interviewer is willing to answer.

Follow-ups to interviews are a low-risk, low-cost way to occasionally improve your situation

While not all employers expect candidates to send a thank you or follow-up correspondence, there is little downside to doing so. It requires only a minimal effort, has almost no downside, and does have upside potential.

Sending a follow-up message ensures that your interviewer will think of you at least once more after the interview. More importantly, it creates a natural opportunity for additional dialogue irrespective of the outcome of the interview. If you do elect to send an email or handwritten letter, consider:

- While handwritten letters are more likely to differentiate you from other candidates, they take longer to arrive, and many companies make hiring decisions rapidly
- Do not presume any outcome, but do be positive in your tone

- There is limited value to sending a follow-up email that simply thanks the interviewer for his or her time. Consider including one of more of the following:
    o Reference to a specific, interesting line of conversation covered during the interview introducing new thoughts on that topic
    o Attachment or link to an article related to something discussed in the interview
    o Reflection on the conversation related to how the job fits well with your aspirations (not why you are a fit for the job) if – and only if – you are introducing something new. A recap of the completed conversation is not beneficial
- The email/letter should be more than one or two lines, but should be brief enough to be read easily on a mobile device

Even if you do not end up joining the company, the people with whom you interview can become useful members of your network. You should not hesitate to engage with people with whom you felt a connection during the process. You never know when they might be helpful to you in the future, or when you might be helpful to them.

* * *

A friend of Diane's had introduced her to the CIO of the telecom company he worked for knowing that one of the CIO's direct reports had just left the company and suspecting that the CIO would need to replace this person. After a brief chat on the phone, the CIO requested Diane's resume and later that week Diane received a call from a recruiter at the company inviting her to come in the following week for two interviews.

Diane was determined to have these interviews go better than the last series of interviews, and committed to being much better prepared. During the brief call with the recruiter, she was able to ask who she would be speaking to and found that she would be interviewing with the VP of HR and with the CIO. Diane began her preparation by calling the friend who made the original introduction. She asked him if he could tell her anything about these two people, ideally hoping to understand what issues were most important to them.

Her friend barely knew the VP of HR, who was fairly new to the company, but he did know the CIO well. Diane's friend shared that the CIO had been with the company for many years. He was promoted two years ago to the CIO spot when the prior CIO retired, leaving the new CIO with a series of projects aimed at modernizing the company. Her friend explained that the company had been slow to adapt to change. When services started moving online and competitors started releasing apps and marketing through social media, this company had incorrectly treated those activities as fads or gimmicks. Now it was stuck playing catch-up.

Diane downloaded the company annual report which seemed to confirm what her friend had told her and equipped her with the names of some of the modernization and digitalization projects that were likely top of mind for the CIO.

She felt like she was starting to understand the issues of the company and the CIO and began drafting the questions she would want to ask a candidate if she was in the CIO's position. Diane wrote 10 questions and answers that she imagined might come up in the interview with the CIO. Next, she thought back to her recent interviews and added questions that she remembered being asked in those interviews which she thought might come up again.

One of her most recent interviews was also with somebody from human resources, and she guessed the questions might be similar. Those questions had not been technical, and some seemed irrelevant to Diane, but she assumed that tripping up on those would be just as problematic as tripping up on the questions that she found more useful, so she decided to prepare for all.

Diane asked her husband to join her in the room. She propped her cell phone up against a book on a shelf and asked her husband to ask her a couple of questions from the list she had just drafted while she recorded the interaction. Later, as she watched the recording, Diane again heard what the coach had told her was going on. Her husband had unintentionally ad-libbed a few of the questions changing from asking "what" to "why" or "how". At the time, Diane had been so focused on her answers that she hadn't noticed the change, but when she listened to the recording, the conversation seemed nonsensical. Her answers were sort of related to those ad-libbed questions, but she was really answering the question in her own head – not the question that was asked.

She also noticed that she stumbled over the questions she had added based on the HR interview. Diane realized she had been trying to answer those questions by remembering what she had written down earlier – and that she was not actually listening to and responding to the questions.

She brought her husband back into the room and asked him to do the exercise again, but this time asking questions that he made up, not ones she gave him. Watching that recording was a very different experience. Diane was clearly focused on listening to the questions and responding directly this time. She was surprised to find that even though there were a few ideas she wished she had included, her answers still sounded pretty good even though her focus had been on listening, not answering. She still floundered a little on the behavioral (HR inspired) questions, but things were improving.

Diane realized that she needed more practice. She reached back out to the coach who had given her the original mock interview asking to do a few more sessions. With some more practice and a lot more feedback, Diane found herself able to both give short, focused answers and not feel like she was missing out on the chance to sell herself better by giving more.

* * *

Opportunities to Apply Chapter Concepts
- Answer the questions in Appendix B in the context of the job you are currently in.
- Pick five questions at random from Appendix C and record yourself answering them.

18. HANDLING YOUR OFFERS

Once you've been offered a job, emotions can take over, and even the smartest job-seekers can struggle to make good decisions about their job offer. Preparing an objective process to consider your options will help you make a confident decision. When you organize your approach before getting your offers, you have a better chance of bringing your gut and your head into alignment.

Mo got an offer from his ideal company and was given a week to accept. He understood the offer was meant to reward long-term performance. While Mo was confident in his ability to perform and realize this long-term potential, there was a short-term issue: Mo had just added a third child to his family, and his partner was planning to quit her lucrative job to stay home for at least four years. Mo felt good about his overall prospects at the company, but the initial transition year would be a problem. His cash flow needs were changing dramatically, and from the looks of the offer, it seemed like Mo's dream job conflicted with his family's needs.

Like many senior executives, Mo's compensation package was a complex mix of guaranteed and variable pay as well as equity. Each component had an earning and delivery schedule, and equity had a vesting period. The timing of the initial offer meant that Mo would have to forfeit all variable pay from his current employer and that he would not have enough time to earn much, if any, variable pay from the new employer by the end of the year. He also would forfeit a significant amount of equity, which meant he wouldn't be able to use that equity to solve the cash flow issue.

Mo built a spreadsheet to compare cash flow and total expected and potential wealth creation in both the leave and stay scenarios. While Mo did not want to make the decision based exclusively on money, his family was his top priority.

The spreadsheet was helpful: It showed that if Mo could delay his start date long enough to receive the variable compensation from his current employer, he would be in a much better cash situation. But because of the timing of the variable pay cycles of the two companies, he wouldn't quite get to where he needed to be. However, if the new employer were to give him a reasonable signing bonus, Mo's transition year would be covered, and he would happily accept the offer without having to worry about his family.

Mo was not sure how the new employer would react to a counteroffer, but he was confident that providing a well-thought-out proposal demonstrating a willingness for some give-and-take would be the best approach. He also decided to be transparent with the employer about the family situation motivating his concerns. Mo proposed a three-month delay in the start date and the addition of a sign-on bonus equal to 25 percent of the typical estimated variable pay for a year. In exchange, Mo would accept a reduced first-year total bonus or take less vacation during the first year.

As it turned out, his new employer was not willing to delay the start, but instead offered to cover the incremental family cash flow needs through a sign-on bonus. It wasn't a gift: The company would reduce Mo's first-year year bonus by the amount of the sign-on bonus, but guaranteed the first-year bonus to be at least as much as the sign-on. In return, Mo would have to repay the full sign-on bonus if he left sooner than two years after his start date.

* * *

You've received an offer. Take a moment to celebrate, or at least feel good.

Now that you've had a smile (or possibly a sip of champagne), there's work to be done. You get to decide whether to accept the offer – and that can involve some complicated dynamics. Your decision affects you as well as your family, friends, coworkers, and others.

During the interview process, you and the company had the same goal: You both wanted to determine whether the job was a good mutual fit. Now, at the offer stage, your agenda diverges from the company's. In many situations, there is plenty of room for mutual win, but there also is ample room for one side to feel underappreciated by the other.

Your responsibility to yourself and your family is to make a decision that is sensible for your career. You have no responsibility to think on behalf of the company (even if you will be expected to begin doing that once hired). With an offer in hand, most people naturally compare the offer with competing offers and with their current situation. So how do you make a good decision?

For most people, choosing among job options is based on the following six dimensions:

- Level – Where will you be positioned within the organization?
- Function – What type of work will you be doing?
- Industry – In which industry will you be working?
- Location – Where will you need to live for the position?
- Fit – How well do you align culturally with the company? How well does the company align with your career ambitions?
- Compensation – How much will you be paid? How will it be structured?

Within each dimension, you likely have a minimum and a target. You already should have determined your minimums when you identified your non-negotiable boundaries earlier in your job search process. If an offer falls below your minimum on any dimension, that should worry you.

For offers that exceed all minimums but fall short of some target or targets, you should be pleased, but not without concern. Consider the offer and carefully think through how much value you are losing because of that shortcoming. If the shortcoming is not monetary, the easiest way to do that is to think about how much money you would be willing to forgo from the compensation aspect of the offer if you were able to exchange cash for reaching the target on that dimension. Removing this amount from the monetary value of the offer will give you an objective way to compare multiple offers even when shortcomings are not monetary in nature. We will explore this more as we continue in the chapter.

Think of compensation in terms of total rewards – not just cash

Modern compensation packages are complex for many reasons. Employers sometimes construct packages to look more attractive than competing offers, even when not as lucrative. In other cases, employers try to optimize the compensation for tax purposes, which may not be immediately obvious but often is for the benefit of the employee. Consequently, it is prudent to avoid thinking about compensation as merely base salary and bonus.

Always include variable compensation, but "risk-adjust" that element for the most likely case. If your offer specifies an annual 20 percent bonus target, only include the potential that is commonly achieved. Though it is uncommon for employers to include the historical earning level of people in the role in an offer letter, most will share that information if asked.

Only include rewards that would benefit you in your current context. Always include cash allowances because cash is useful whether called salary, bonus, or allowance. However, some allowances are not paid to you in cash. For example, if the company offers a company-paid car (as opposed to a cash allowance for a car), this is only valuable to you if you want a car. If you do not have a car or need for a car, this becomes a cost incurred by the company but not something you should consider as valuable to you.

However, if you currently have a car that would get replaced by the company car or would like a car despite not currently having one, the company-provided car is valuable and should add to the total value you ascribe to the offer. However, you should include only the value you would otherwise spend on a car *only if you no longer incur those costs*. If the company car becomes your additional car, include only the differential costs in maintenance on the original car.

Other common examples include schooling allowances which are of no value to you if you do not have or plan to have children, and education reimbursements (or allowances) if you have no ambitions to continue your education. When these rewards apply to your personal situation, they can be compelling components of the offer, and should be included in your calculation of value. But when they do not apply, you need not give the company credit for paying for something irrelevant to you.

Remember to adjust for taxes if any of these allowances are taxable in your location. Also, include singing bonuses and retention bonuses if applicable, but do not include possible severance.

When equity is involved in the offer, be sure to gain clarity on the commonly achieved amount if the awards are variable, as well as the common historical payout from the equity and vesting schedule.

While perks such as subsidized parking and company-provided lunches could be included, we recommend you only include perks if they are greater than 1 percent of total compensation.

Review compensation over the long-term

The timing and distribution of compensation can vary significantly. It is important that you not allow early access to cash to lead you to accept an offer that reduces your total earnings over time. For this reason, it is best to model complex offers for at least five years (unless you plan to leave the new job before reaching the 5-year mark). Because job moves can impact current year earnings, is important to include some historical earnings and model at least your current year if not the full prior year, to account for loss of income based on the timing of your exit. You may want to model multiple lengths of time to see if the situation changes depending on the length of time you look at. This is especially useful when there are significant equity elements involved in offers.

Be careful to understand any signing bonuses thoroughly. These one-time payments are generally attractive because they create quick access to often sizeable amounts of cash, but since they do not recur, they can be misleading. Though in some cases they are meant to "sweeten" the deal and encourage you to take an offer, they more frequently are offered to "keep you whole" and replace some loss of compensation versus your current situation:

- Employers often use a signing bonus to "make up" for "lost" compensation such as missed bonuses or unvested equity that you lose when you switch jobs.
- Upfront bonuses are sometimes used to reduce the impact of a lower salary and/or lower total potential cash compensation. This generally addresses short-term discrepancies, but it is important to understand how that lower starting salary will grow over time before deciding to accept.
- Signing bonuses can have negative tax implications. These rarely make the bonus not worth accepting but do reduce the overall attractiveness.
- Generally, if you think about a signing bonus as serving multiple purposes, you overvalue it, and if you think it is just a gesture of goodwill to make you want to join, you are missing a gap it is meant to cover.

Just as receiving allowances that do not apply to your situation should not be considered valuable to you, you should not include potential earnings which are unrealistic to achieve in your quantification of the total value in the offer. High upside with high risk (low likelihood of achievement) on variable pay schemes such as bonuses, commissions, and equity offerings can lead to very attractive potential earnings. But remember that just having that potential when you are unlikely to achieve it offers little more value than a lottery ticket. It is best to include only the realistically possible potential earnings. If you are unsure how to differentiate between possible and realistic, ask the employer before accepting the offer.

Similarly, substantial equity grants such as shares of stock, RSUs, options, and phantom equity are only as attractive as they are achievable and should only be considered as valuable once vested. The value of these grants may change with time, increasing the importance of analyzing your offer over many years.

Finally, you need to have a reasonable sense of how quickly and substantially your salary will grow. A high starting salary with small raises can be less lucrative over time than a low starting salary with rapid promotion and/or generous raises. Always try to understand the historic precedent – not potential – for such growth. Again, this likely requires a discussion with the employer.

Include the intangible elements of your job offer

Some of the most important elements of a job offer are not immediately associated with a financial value. The amount of vacation, travel, and flexible working arrangements are very real motivators for people and can add to – or reduce – the overall value of an offer. The level of intellectual stimulation, interest, and personal gratification that comes from both the subject matter and the people associated with each role need to be considered.

Assigning intangible elements values based on a hypothetical financial trade-off enables you to continue to be quantitative in your approach to your valuing a job offer even when considering non-monetary aspects. For example:

- Vacation – In a salaried role, you are paid the same wage for vacation days as for working days, but most people would accept a slightly smaller salary in exchange for additional vacation days or would expect additional compensation for fewer days off. This amount is usually more than the daily wage and can be treated as a premium that you add to the total "real" financial value of the offer.
- Travel – Whether you look at travel as a benefit or a burden, you have an ideal level of travel. By considering how much compensation you would be willing to forgo to achieve your ideal level of travel – more travel or less – you can include the impact of travel on the offer's overall value.
- Satisfaction factors – These factors can be a little more difficult to quantify, but they are important. Whether it is a sense of doing good for society or getting a shorter commute time, you should assign values to any aspects of a job that materially impact its attractiveness. In some cases, you will be willing to give up a certain amount compensation in exchange for feeling that your new job allows you to do contribute to a

cause you believe in. Conversely, you might require additional compensation to "feel whole" if that aspect were removed.

The people you work with daily have a significant impact on your happiness. If you know that you are easily frustrated by bureaucracy and you know the company has many bureaucratic processes or if you prefer to work independently, but during the recruiting process you learned your potential new boss is a micromanager, then you should account for these issues in your analysis. More money doesn't always make up for issues, but for minor issues it can help. When you start to think in terms of how much somebody would have to pay you to put up with a painful working environment, you may find that it is easy to justify walking away from an otherwise lucrative offer because you would not be happy in the environment.

Build a quantitative model to support decision-making

Because of the sheer numbers of variables (reward elements) present in an offer, many people find it liberating to build a spreadsheet model to handle the quantitative aspect of comparing offers. Not only does a quantitative model help you keep track of all these different elements and aggregate them, it offers guidance without emotion. It also frequently exposes offer elements which may not be explicitly expressed in an offer letter, leading you to have important relevant questions to ask the employer before accepting the job.

After deciding to make you an offer, the company will usually identify a few features which it believes are most attractive to you – or at least beats other options you may have. The company will emphasize these features, hoping they will grab you emotionally and entice you to accept, whether the offer is objectively best for you or not. Your emotions may steer you in a good direction, but they also can mislead you. It is best to prove or disprove your emotional response with an objective analysis before making any final decisions.

Developing an objective, quantitatively grounded comparison of your options will help you avoid your subconscious emotional response sending you in a dangerous direction. There is no single right way to design such a model, but regardless of the model you build, you should do the following:

1. Define your list of non-negotiables
   - Most people will already have defined this list earlier in the process, but if you have not, now is the time to do so.
   - You want this to be a short but honest list because you should walk away from any opportunity that cannot provide everything on this list.
   - You should discuss this list early in the recruiting process with each potential employer to avoid wasting each other's time if the position cannot fulfill your needs.
2. Define the principle criteria for evaluation
   - Determine the duration of the amount of time into the past and future for which you will calculate value of the offer.
   - Decide how you will value intangibles.
   - Define targets for what you need (part of non-negotiables) and for what you want.
3. Define whom you will consult on your offer
   - Identify if you want to give veto power to anybody.
   - Decide whom you will share information with and what type of feedback you want from them.

You can design and build this spreadsheet at any time in your process. Doing it well in advance of having an offer can be helpful to give you more time after you receive the offer, but often once receiving an offer, you will realize you missed some elements in the model and want to update it. That is normal and appropriate.

The spreadsheet you make should produce objective valuations of multiple opportunities in a comparable format. You can make it as complex as you'd like. Some people create a thorough, discounted cash flow model. Others prefer to simply extrapolate earnings over time. The complexity of the model you employ is up to you and is largely influenced by the level of diversity of your different opportunities.

Adjust your evaluation for risk

All offers come with an inherent risk that A) you and the company are not 100 percent aligned in your understanding of each other's expectations or B) despite best efforts (on both sides), things simply do not work out as planned. Add to that the C) unpredictable family component and D) unpredictable markets, and it becomes important that you assess the potential for any of the following:

- Change in immediate supervisor
- Loss of key advocate(s)
- Incompatibility with supervisor
- Early change in scope of role
- Misunderstanding of expectations
- Lack of resources provided to achieve agenda
- Loss of solvency in company
- Change in corporate strategy
- Mismatch of culture
- Lack of translation of relationships
- Long time to create commercial traction
- Underperformance of supporting team
- Market underperformance
- Discord in family due to location creating distraction
- Other discord in family creating distraction
- Family drives departure from company
- Other risks

It is sensible to adjust your model to represent lower value in the presence of high risk. This is not an exhaustive list of possible risks, so think critically about the risks you are facing. Note that your current situation is not always less risky than a move would be even though there is also risk associated with moving to a situation with more unknowns.

Listen to your ego, but do so carefully

The gut reaction that warns you to keep away from an opportunity may be a useful subconscious response to a risk you haven't quantified. But it might be a detrimental reaction originated by your ego. It's human and helpful to have ego. After all, your ego is a key element in motivating you to excel in your job and to cultivate a great career. However, it is important to understand what your ego craves at a fundamental level so that you objectively, not emotionally, consider offers.

When it comes to compensation, the concept of "fair" is almost always emotional rather than objective. Compensation may be consistent by level or it may be performance-driven, tenure-based, or indexed. But concepts like "fair," "equitable," and "unbiased" are impossible to apply in a meaningful, consistent way. The only way for you to *feel* like your offer is fair is to understand what "fair" means emotionally to you.

If the concept of "fair" is important to your ego, you may want to place a significant value on the philosophical approach to compensation employed by the company – not just the real (financial) compensation of the offer.

If it would upset you that somebody...	...Then you should seek companies that
In the same role as you has higher guaranteed or potential earnings	Have consistent compensation by role/level
With less experience but similar responsibilities has higher guaranteed or potential earnings	Strongly consider tenure in compensation decisions
In a similar role at a competitor has higher guaranteed or potential earnings	Actively benchmark compensation against competitors and adjust regularly to benchmarks/indices
Who, by your estimate, contributed less than you receives similar compensation	Issue rewards based more on individual performance than on business outcomes

Not many job-seekers think to ask a company about their compensation philosophy, but this is not a taboo subject. Especially at the stage of having received an offer, it is appropriate to ask about the general compensation philosophy to more accurately set your expectations for the experience you will have if you accept the offer.

Additionally, it is important to recognize that you cannot assume other people will value you at the same level you have valued yourself. Remember that you have a more complete data set for what you are capable of than anyone else does. You also have an ego which will usually bias your opinion toward a more favorable outcome.

Employers typically restrict themselves to proven and/or objective data in their possession. This means they value you based on your current skills and experiences and on a risk-adjusted expectation for what you might be able to do in the future. You are unlikely to do the same risk adjustment on yourself. And while you have access to some data, you and the employer are almost always working from different data sets. We will get into this in more detail later in this chapter.

The only truly objective measure of your value in the market is a currently valid, written offer from another employer to you.

Make smart decisions from the moment you receive an offer

While each situation is unique, how you handle an offer initially can set the tone for your negotiation, if needed, so we recommend handling the offer with a clear strategy in mind. Fortunately, a few standard practices are effective in most situations.

Employers often ask for a response in a short period of time. If the initial timeframe does not include a weekend, you should request a period that does. This is reasonable, and most will oblige. You need to use that time effectively.

Request the offer in writing before responding. While companies rarely state something verbally that they do not intend to follow through, requesting the offer in writing can buy you some time and simplify your process for considering the offer because you are not forced to capture small details from a conversation.

Be certain to discuss the offer with a company representative by telephone or in person *after* you have reviewed the written offer and *before* accepting it. You should confirm that you fully understand the offer and its elements, and you should ask the company to address any questions you have. Most people find some ambiguity in any offer and it is always better to confirm an answer than assume one.

You also want to have time to put the data from your offer letter into the spreadsheet model you designed for comparing options. This activity usually helps you identify questions you should be asking about your offer. This action will also confirm that all your non-negotiables are satisfied. If they are not, these become points to clarify and later negotiate if they are not satisfied (as opposed to their being a misunderstanding of the offer).

If the output of your spreadsheet model feels "wrong," revisit your assumptions and adjust until your gut and your objective, quantitative model align. Most of the time, disharmony between emotional feeling and objective analysis comes from an intangible not being properly considered or a risk not being incorporated. You should assume neither your gut nor the model is wrong, but instead work to understand why they are different, and then adjust until you feel good about the decision.

After taking these steps, you should reach a decision that is congruent with your emotional response and your objective analysis. Next, test that outcome with members of your personal board of directors, particularly those like your spouse, who are directly affected by the decision. Your ability to sell them on the decision you have reached is a final safety check to ensure the decision will move your career in a good direction.

Decide whether to negotiate

Because you have the most leverage to negotiate before you join a company, there is often little to lose from appropriately and professionally testing the boundaries of your offer. In most cases, the worst that will happen is the company saying "no." However, it is possible for a company to rescind its initial offer, so never negotiate recklessly.

If you have discussed your non-negotiables during the recruiting process, there is a very low likelihood that the offer fails to meet those non-negotiables. If, however, any of your non-negotiables were not met, you have only two choices: negotiate or walk away. If the offer covers your non-negotiables but misses some "nice-to-haves," then you have the choice to negotiate or accept the offer as-is.

Requesting and receiving exceptional consideration costs you relationship capital. If the holistic, aggregate offer already meets your target and would allow you to accept the offer with confidence, you should consider retaining that relationship capital for use later, even if some individual components fall short of your targets. Asking for something but getting a "no" still consumes relationship capital.

Sometimes, however, negotiating is worthwhile. If, for example, you have a competing offer that is currently more attractive, you should negotiate. In that situation, the relationship capital is well spent because either it will improve your position, or it will expire anyway when you accept a different offer.

If you have a compelling reason, it may be sensible to negotiate. But make sure your reason is compelling – not that you simply want more. For example, if your family is accustomed to you having five weeks of vacation at your current job and your offer included only three, this would be a reasonable point to negotiate on. However, if you currently have three weeks of vacation and the offer includes three weeks of vacation, you should only negotiate if more vacation was a non-negotiable that you shared with the company earlier in the process.

You do not want to brand yourself as "high maintenance" by asking for significant exceptional treatment before you even start at a company, but you also do not want to start a new job frustrated because the offer was in some way lacking and you did not even attempt to address that shortcoming.

Before you decide to negotiate, determine if the possible outcome is worth the potential risk: While it is rare for a company to rescind an offer because you tried to negotiate it, it does occasionally happen. If you do not have promising alternative opportunity and cannot remain in your current position, you may want to limit your risk and accept the offer as-is.

If you are going to negotiate, have a plan before negotiating

When you decide to negotiate your offer, it is important to have a strategy that includes multiple different acceptable outcomes. It is not reasonable to expect to receive everything that you want (though in rare cases that can happen). You should be willing to compromise, especially if you want the company to compromise.

You are most likely to be happy with the results of your negotiations if you have a variety of proposals and are prepared to make substitutions in case the company is unable or unwilling to be flexible on your proposed changes.

For example, an employee who considers leaving a role where she had four weeks of annual vacation and is presented with three weeks of annual vacation could reasonably ask for an adjustment upwards. If the company is not willing to add those five days, it may be advantageous for the employee offer a substitution rather than simply moving down from five more days to three. The employee might have more success if she suggests being allowed to work from home on Fridays to have more access to her children, or an additional $2000 in salary to enable a more elaborate vacation that would compensate her family for the additional time spent away from them.

Every company (and context) is different, but in general you can expect employers to be more flexible on certain aspects of an offer than on others:

More Difficult	Less Difficult
• Base compensation • Variable pay potential • Commission percentages • Equity vesting cycles • Level/grade • Anything within the benefits package • Amount of allowances (e.g. housing, car)	• Number of vacation days • Recognized seniority • Title • Sign-on bonus • Start date • Performance targets (as related to variable pay and/or commission) • Work location/flexible working • Relocation support (if applicable)

Your strategy will need to be very specific to your situation, but there is a common flow to effective negotiation that can be a useful starting point. If you want your prospective employer to take your suggested changes seriously, you need to justify them with a compelling reason. What you suggest and how you justify that suggestion will influence your negotiation plan. This chapter is not a template for negotiation but should help you to consider the right questions as you plan your own unique negotiation strategy.

If you have multiple offers, you should negotiate in serial – not in parallel – because *you need to be willing to accept the offer if the company accommodates your request.* Most attempts to create a bidding war fail and can result in the loss of one or more offers. Furthermore, it can sour relationships within your current employer if you put them in a bidding war even if you ultimately stay.

While you cannot be certain you a negotiation will follow your plan, you can start by imaging four distinct components to the discussion:

1. Review Expectations
   - Discuss the expectations that you have for your job search
   - These need to explain your hesitancy to accept the offer
   - They must be consistent with information you provided throughout the interviewing process
2. Establish Expectations as Reasonable
   - Provide justification for why you believe yours is a reasonable request with facts where possible and requests, but not opinions (see chart on next page)
   - Having a written competitor offer is the most compelling rationale

- Your offer comparison model can sometimes help

3. Suggest Changes
    - Make a specific proposal for what you would like to see the employer modify in the offer
    - Be clear that if the company accepts your proposal, you will accept the offer
4. Consider Substitutions
    - Have alternative solutions in mind if your initial proposed changes are not acceptable to the company
    - Be open to considering other options from employer
    - Be willing to provide an answer as soon as you receive the revised written offer or within 48 hours (e.g. if you need to confer with spouse), whichever is later

As you plan for your negotiation, acknowledge the difference among opinions, facts, and requests within the context of your situation and within the changes you are proposing.

In most countries, compensation information is not a matter of public record, but some salary information is readily available. As we noted earlier, websites such as Glass Door and Vault, as well as many job posting sites, provide salary information on a wide range of roles and employers. While usually directionally correct and useful for gross estimation, it is important to note that this information is incomplete and is sourced from individuals and businesses who volunteer it. The reported figures are generally unverified and are subject to the timeliness of update and accuracy of submission.

Family members, friends, and colleagues also may provide data points. These are more likely to be accurate but are often even less current and can be more difficult to establish as contextually relevant. Frequently in a situation like this, the person will know what his/her salary was/is but cannot credibly say why it is that value making it difficult to translate the information accurately to your context. Benchmarking surveys are the most credible and accurate sources, but they cost money and rarely have enough specificity to singular employers to be extremely useful.

Any source will inherently lack contextual information but can still be useful if you carefully utilize the data only in appropriate ways. When considering how to use the information available to you to support your negotiation, think about the information in the following three classifications:

Type	Description	Example of effective use
Opinion	Any statement that includes undescribed context, unverified data or is forward-looking	A compilation of online data about peer companies suggests that the market is typically paying [ ] for similar positions
Fact	A statement which you are willing and able to back up with an objective reference	I have been presented with an offer for [ ] from company [ ]
Request	A personal statement requiring no justification or backup	It is important for me to have a minimum total compensation of [ ] to meet the lifestyle requirements of my family

In arguing for your proposed adjustments, facts are generally the most powerful, but also most difficult pieces of information to collect. It is often advantageous to frame elements of your negotiation as requests rather than to incorporate them as opinions because of the potential for opinions to be challenged or debated.

For example, you have been presented with offers from two competitor companies. One has a base salary of $150,000 and the other has a salary of $140,000. If the rest of the offer was comparable, but you preferred the culture of company making the lower offer, you could reasonably present the other offer as a factual justification for why $150,000 is a reasonable salary.

If instead, you only had the offer of $140,000 but had found online resources that list competitors as paying $150,000, you could either use those online resources as opinions to support your argument or you could explain the desire for $150,000 as important to your family's financial objectives. Many people assume it is more effective to introduce the online resources because it establishes a story about your request simply being for market relevant compensation – something that most companies naturally endeavor to offer. However, the weakness is that the company can dispute the accuracy and/or relevance of the data underpinning those opinions you provided. The conversation shifts from being about you to being about the credibility of the data behind those opinions.

However, a company can neither understand nor dispute your personal or family financial objectives. They may be no more inclined to offer you additional compensation simply because you have these expectations, but the conversation remains about you, increasing the likelihood that you have a dialogue about substitution compensation rather than a conversation about the credibility of conflicting opinions or data.

Remember the negotiation starts a new relationship

It is easy to get wrapped up in the excitement of negotiations and lose sight of the fact that this negotiation marks the beginning of a relationship – not the end. When buying a car, a house, or even a company, the buyer and seller rarely have a credible expectation of maintaining an ongoing relationship after the sale. Thus, it is not unreasonable for either or both parties to be aggressive and self-focused during the negotiation. However, when negotiating a job offer, you are beginning a long relationship. Taking an overly aggressive approach can sour a relationship from the very start.

Ultimately, you should look at this as an effort to achieve mutual benefit. You and the employer both want to reach an agreement that excites you to join the company and motivates you to perform at your top potential – and makes financial sense to the company. The goal should not be for you to squeeze every dime possible out of the company any more than it should be for the company to spend as little on you as possible. Both sides should feel good about the agreement in the end.

Counteroffers are a powerful option if you manage them appropriately

Finally, do not forget about your current employer. If you have been a strong performer in your current role, there is a realistic possibility that your current employer will want to retain you and may be willing to incentivize you to stay with a counteroffer.

While regularly renegotiating or threatening to leave the company is not a sustainable strategy for your long-term career, when you do come close to making the decision to leave your current position, it is usually valuable to discuss the situation with your current employer before leaving. In addition to being a professional courtesy, it can have a practical benefit. Faced with the potential of losing a good employee, many companies will respond to concerns in a way that addresses that employee's needs. In such situations, the employer's needs are met, the employee's needs are met, and the employee avoids the hassles associated with moving to a new company.

In some cases, your current situation may be untenable, and the changes required to make it acceptable would be too dramatic for a company to offer, such as a fundamental cultural shift or opening an office in new location. Even in those situations it is worthwhile to discuss your planned departure with the company before deciding. Companies often are willing to do more to retain employees than those employees expect. There also is little downside to giving your current employer an opportunity to counter. If the conversation sours the relationship (something you hope does not happen), at least you intend to leave anyway. However, do note that you are likely to burn a bridge with your current employer if they accommodate your needs and you still choose to leave. Therefore, only solicit a counteroffer if you are prepared to stay if the company accommodates your needs.

However, timing is delicate. Once you accept an offer, you are likely to destroy the relationship with that other employer if you rescind your acceptance because your company surprised you and was able to offer a compelling counteroffer. Thus, it is always best to start the conversation with your current employer before accepting an offer, even though for practical reasons, you may want to wait until you have an offer in case your current employer reacts poorly to the news. This does not leave much time for your current employer to counter, but at least you are giving them the opportunity to do so before committing to an outside offer. If they do successfully counter in time, you can still decline the other offer without having to unprofessionally rescind an earlier acceptance.

Whether you leave or stay, once you accept an offer or counteroffer, you should stop looking for other opportunities for the near future. If you have effectively sought and negotiated your new situation in accordance with your broader career objectives, you should be comfortable committing fully to your new job until the next critical juncture in your career.

Exit gracefully from your current employer when you do move

Because life is unpredictable, you should maintain good standing in as many relationships as you can. Former colleagues can become powerful advocates in the future or serious obstacles depending on the relationship you maintain with them during and following your exit from the company.

You should make every effort to leave the company in positive standing (including being eligible for rehire) and maintain that positive standing after leaving. This begins with handling counteroffers well. Informing the company before accepting a competing offer is a good starting point. However, if you have no intention of seriously considering a counteroffer, it is best to let your current employer know you feel that way, so no one wastes time or political capital to fight an impossible battle to keep you.

After you leave, you should avoid making negative comments about your prior employer, especially in public forums like social media. There is no need to hide that you are transitioning jobs, but always frame the move in the context of the positive aspects of the new job rather than by discussing any negative aspects of the prior job. That will help you preserve relationships at your old company and will reassure your new colleagues of your professionalism.

Even after you leave, it is generally smart to maintain contact with key people from your soon-to-be previous employer. While this contact will obviously be less frequent and involve discussing different topics, it is important to maintain that communication to perpetuate the potential for those people to become advocates for you in the future.

Let money be important, but don't let it be everything

It is important to remember that job choices should not be "all about the money." Certainly, the money is important, and this chapter talks about ways to convert non-monetary elements of the offer in to monetary equivalence for simpler comparisons between opportunities. However, it is possible to lose sight of an opportunity's impact on your happiness, fulfillment, and/or long-term success when you are focused solely on money.

Most people find that once an offer satisfies the wealth creation opportunities they are looking for (assuming they set reasonable targets at the beginning of their process) additional wealth creation has much lower impact on their happiness and fulfillment than intangible attributes of the job like culture and the quality of people they work with.

Furthermore, it is not sensible to sacrifice long-term career growth potential for near-term wealth creation. Over time, long-term career growth is likely to return more wealth (and more job satisfaction) than even the compounded value of that near-term additional wealth. So, while it is appropriate to ask a future employer to show you the money, make sure that is not the only thing they show you. Make sure your decision to chase an opportunity is founded on more than just the associated dollars.

* * *

Opportunities to Apply Chapter Concepts
- Within the six primary decision criteria (level, function, industry, location, fit, and compensation) identify a minimum and target value for each.
- Develop a spreadsheet that allows you to objectively compare opportunities in quantitative terms.

WANT MORE HELP?

The recruiting process is complicated, and getting expert support for key aspects of it is not lazy – it is strategic. Such support easily pays for itself when it accelerates your process or generates the necessary edge or momentum to secure a job that meets your objectives.

Careers are uniquely human endeavors, and require human intervention to flourish. The point of this book is to empower you to do this on your own. But we have found that often, two heads are indeed better than one. If you think another head would help you achieve your career goals, contact us – anytime.

The idea that every situation is different is true in most contexts, but is especially true when it comes to careers and job searches. The combination of widely differing personal circumstances and widely differing company situations ensures it will be challenging to apply even general rules to specific situations.

If you like the concepts laid out in this book but do not feel 100 percent confident in your ability to apply certain concepts to your unique situation effectively, it may be useful to seek some outside support, either through your network of advocates or through experts in the field.

Furthermore, to thoroughly apply every concept introduced in the book could generate a massive undertaking, vastly exceeding the necessary effort. This book aims to give you a thorough introduction to different tools which can be helpful in managing your career and landing jobs. Even when you are comfortable doing the heavy lifting yourself, you may value the guidance of an expert in rationalizing and prioritizing the activities you engage in.

Since neither career management nor job searching is anybody's full-time job (at least not on an extended basis), everyone approaches these activities as less than expert. Because successful career decisions and movements have the potential to significantly improve your personal situation, it is sensible for you to seek expert guidance for your specific situation.

Expert guidance is far more than convenient, it makes financial sense. Take, for example, the scenario where a successful job search lands you a $10,000 per year salary hike. Spending $1,000 on expert, individualized support that helps you secure that position just generated a 10X return on your investment (much more if you consider how your earning potential grows over time). Even if your salary increase is "only" $5,000, or expert guidance costs $2,000, your return is still a substantial 150 percent.

Even if you are not looking for a significant raise – and some people aren't – there is value in optimizing your time. Outside support prevents you from wasting time pursuing jobs that would ultimately be poor fits for your career and reduces the number of iterations you make on resumes or cover letters. Such support helps you develop your interviewing skills so you don't have to learn from poor interview performance. It helps you showcase yourself well enough to earn a job offer. We are certain that if you follow the suggestions we outline in this book, you will substantially increase your chance of success in your career. We are equally certain that individualized attention tailored to your specific situation can be even more valuable, often significantly exceeding the cost of that support.

Having read this book, you should be in a much better position to tackle the challenge of owning your career, but if you would like to explore ways to continue your learning and further empower yourself to live your dreams, please visit:

https://livingyourbestcareer.com/

We'd love to help you.

ABOUT THE AUTHORS

This book came together as the result of many years of parallel, independent efforts by the authors to understand the hiring process and identify common behaviors that lead talented people pursuing career advancement to create success and failure. Each author observed from his own unique situation many examples of gifted people pursuing jobs that were great mutual fits for candidate and employer and many more where the fit was one-sided at best.

With a mixture of altruism, curiosity, and hope for eventual commercial purpose, the authors independently began experimenting with individuals to better their understanding of their capabilities and their desires. The authors found that they could greatly improve not only the likelihood of a candidate receiving an offer, but more importantly, increase the likelihood of long-term job satisfaction.

Combining the benefits of their extensive collective experiences, the authors developed the blended approach to career ownership that is chronicled in this book. They hope this book can reduce the need to learn from mistakes as they both made and have seen so many others make before truly taking control of their careers. They aim to empower a wide audience with the skill necessary to enhance their career ownership and efficiently pursue their career objectives as they define them.

Mike Cox

Graduating from Rice University with a degree in mechanical engineering, Mike never anticipated writing a book like this until two weeks before he started to pen it. In fact, Mike could have benefitted from reading this book early in his career as he unknowingly stumbled during the launch of his career.

What was supposed to be a career designing propulsion systems for aircraft manufacturers quickly pivoted to a career in management consulting thanks in part to incomplete research into the defense industry. In retrospect, it is easy to see how Mike could have gone straight to management consulting had he developed and followed a North Star, but instead he ambled through his early career by chance and fortune rather than intention.

After about 10 years of success supporting businesses as a management consultant, he made the seemingly harmless decision to share some ideas with his boss about how the company might improve its recruiting program. Two weeks later, he found himself no longer a management consultant, but an HR person. Though originally intended as a temporary assignment, this small event ended up becoming a seminal redirection in his career.

Tasked initially with rebuilding the company's MBA recruiting program – something he successfully did, growing from only one successful hire the prior year to 17 in his first year holding the reigns – Mike's interest in the hiring process was sparked. Going from his first year in human resources to the second, his gaze expanded from simply attracting the right people to understanding how to keep them. At that point, the seeds for this book began to be sown.

Mike was able to see that success in the roles for which he hired was not an effective indicator for the satisfaction of the individual in the role. Successfully retaining people see more a matter of strength of a mutual "win" Than performance. No matter how successful an employee was, if he/she felt the job they occupied was not taking their career in a direction that they wanted, they would not stay.

Based on this, it became very important to not only assess the fit of candidates to the job, but also the fit the job to the candidate's career ambitions. Mike's recruiting program had proven itself very effective at determining the potential for candidates to adequately perform in the roles it was filling, but it needed to make sure the role would adequately support the candidate's career aspirations if he wanted to retain them longer.

Despite his candidates clearly being the most qualified people to speak to their career objectives, Mike realized that most of them struggled to know what they wanted from their careers. They could extol their capabilities and qualifications much easier than they could describe their needs and wants. This was a big problem and became the impetus for designing pieces of the process that ultimately became this book.

Studying hiring from both the candidate and employer perspectives in the pursuit of finding a repeatable way to consistently generate "win-wins" hires, Mike spent years developing these frameworks and approaches. Even as he ascended the HR ranks to ultimately lead global HR organizations, he retained his passion for helping candidates get into and be successful in the right jobs for their careers.

Jonathan Phillips

Like many people, Jonathan's early career was framed by trial and error and directed more by reaction to unattractive situations than intentional pursuit of attractive ones. In college, he started with getting a bachelor's degree in chemistry only to conclude that he did not want to work in a laboratory all day (the natural next step for the path he was on). He then switched to pursuing a master's degree in chemical engineering only to decide he did not want to work in plants (the natural next step on *that* path). He next moved into technical marketing, and after five years at Shell, concluded that too wasn't the right fit, and instead got an MBA. Five years later, Jonathan found corporate life too constricting and decided to change careers and joined the executive search industry.

In that industry, Jonathan found himself drawn to large consulting firms, building groups by finding partners and then building out their teams. He soon realized that focusing on the success of the candidate made the entire search process far more effective and efficient for his clients. Jonathan redesigned his firm and created new unique methodologies to help candidates figure out how to make the best decisions for their careers. On the client side there was huge benefit as candidates who went through these new processes stayed longer. These lessons Jonathan learned became the basis for much of the content within this book

Working for clients over 20 years has allowed Jonathan to refine these processes and to codify them throughout this book. He also reached out to past candidates to validate not just how they decided to move, but how they were able to stay and be successful when they moved. In some cases, candidate feedback was collected over more than 15 years of their careers, during which time many achieved top leadership status.

Jonathan is a passionate advocate for candidates and derives great satisfaction from talking through their career options with candidates. His support of candidates has achieved many win-win hires that benefit candidate and client alike. He hopes this book will help you realize and achieve the full potential of your career.

APPENDIX A - SELF-DIAGNOSIS AND TRIAGE (WHAT TO READ)

This book is designed to be read flexibly based on the needs of readers not only when they purchase the book, but as they evolve in their careers. We encourage you to read the book cover-to-cover, but we also recognize that readers often have a narrower focus. With that in mind, we crafted the chapters to be readable and useful even if you haven't read the other chapters. This enables you to read only the chapters most relevant to your immediate situation (although we really hope you read and find value in the whole thing).

If you are aiming for maximum impact with minimum reading time, the following tables should help you focus on the most relevant text. Simply look for a description of you and/or your current situation and turn to those chapters. Of course, if you're really in a hurry and want customized, personalized support, visit https://www.livingyourbestcareer.com/support/ for details on how to leverage the support of trained career advocates.

By specific topic

Applicant tracking systems – Chapter 14
Coaches – Chapter 4
Counteroffers – Chapter 18
Cover letters – Chapter 15
Engaging your network – Chapter 12
Finding opportunities – Chapter 12
Headhunters – Chapter 4
Integration planning – Chapter 16
Interviewing techniques – Chapter 17
Interview sample questions – Appendix B, Appendix C
Offer comparison – Chapter 18
Offer negotiation – Chapter 18
Personal board of directors – Chapter 12
Personal branding – Chapter 7
Personal criteria for jobs – Chapter 6
Resumes – Chapter 14

By seniority demographic

If this sounds like you	Then you're probably	And you should
30+ years of work experience	In the late stages of your career, trying to ensure you are positioning yourself well for retirement and/or the legacy you want while beginning to work less and/or on more specific topics	Read chapters 3, 6, 12
20 – 30 years of work experience	Interested in maximizing income to address high family expenses while giving yourself as much flexibility late in your career as possible	Read chapters 1-3, 6, 9, 12
10 – 20 years of work experience	Recognizing that you have a valuable professional identify and increasing number of outside influences on your career, and want to make sure you are balancing all effectively	Read chapters 1-4, 6-8, 12
<10 years of work experience	Unsure where to get started, how to be successful achieving your ambitions, and interested in avoiding decisions you will regret later	Read chapters 1-9

By job situation

If this sounds like you	Then you're probably	And you should
Unexpectedly unemployed	Scrambling to find employment quickly and are willing to make sacrifices in value to career in order to speed to employment	Read chapters 11-18, Appendix B
Facing pending unemployment	Interested in setting yourself up for an efficient, focused job search	Read chapters 4, 6-7, 9, 11-18
Unhappy in current job	Ready to develop a plan to move into a healthier situation	Read chapters 1-4, 6, 9-12
Happy in current job but investigating new opportunities	Preparing to be agile in responding to opportunities	Read chapters 1-4, 6-10
Happy in current job but want to ensure I remain happy and achieve my career goals	Looking for signposts that let you know when action needs to be taken to continue your positive progression	Read chapters 1-6, 8
Beginning my career	Hoping to build a roadmap for your career and to master techniques that will enable you to successfully secure meaningful employment	Read the whole book

By job search issue

If this sounds like you	Then you're probably	And you should
I know that I am a great fit and fully qualified for this role, but even though I get interviews, I don't get job offers	Not articulating a clear and compelling brand and/or Failing to prepare well for an interview	Read chapters 4, 7, 13-17, Appendix B-C
I think my resume looks great and I regularly get compliments on it (maybe even paid a professional to do it), but I still don't get called in for many interviews	Not tailoring your resume to specific opportunities and/or Not providing enough or compelling context with your submission and/or Not effectively utilizing your advocates to support you	Read chapters 3-4, 7, 12-14
I want to make a change in profession and think I am being ignored as a candidate because although I am qualified, my profile is unusual	Not providing enough or compelling context with your submission and/or Not effectively utilizing your advocates to support you and/or Pursuing a path which is incoherent with your long-term objectives	Read chapters 1-4, 6-8, 12-17

APPENDIX B - 10 INTERVIEW QUESTIONS YOU MUST BE ABLE TO ANSWER

Sometimes you find yourself with an opportunity to interview on short notice or on the losing side of a bout with procrastination. Either way, you may be short on time to prepare for an interview that you want to do well in. There is no silver bullet or cheat code that will take the place of thorough preparation, but when under a time crunch, be able to answer the following questions effectively.

Every company and interviewer will have his/her own specific objectives related to any interview questions. Therefore, there is no best answer. The guidance below is meant to help you understand what *most* companies hope to understand when asking each question.

Why should we hire you?

This is one of the most versatile questions, making it also one of the most common. Interviewers can ask this question and listen for very different things, and it is impossible for you to know with certainty why the question was asked.

The simplest reason for asking this question is purely practical. If the interview goes well, the interviewer will have to convince somebody else to hire you (or are least continue your recruiting process). Your answer can equip the interviewer with a good argument to make on your behalf if he or she decides to support hiring you. The answer can become their "elevator pitch" for hiring you.

The interviewer might also be looking for insight into your character. Answering with high levels of deference and/or humility can show a lack of confidence and/or leadership potential, while answering with extreme conviction and/or self-focus might seem arrogant or pompous. It is generally a bad idea to claim you are the best candidate? After all, how could you objectively justify that? However, you should use your understanding of the role and your prior accomplishments and skills to confidently assert that you would be a good fit for the role and be successful.

Simply being qualified for the role is only justification for *considering* you, it is not justification for *hiring* you. Deciding to hire you will be based on you having unique - not just minimum - qualifications. Your answer to this question should highlight those unique qualifications. This is not the time to comprehensively show you meet the minimum requirements. Instead choose only the most compelling or unique reasons and share that small subset.

Why do you want to work here?

Usually this question aims to test your conviction and the depth and authenticity of your interest in the job. Accurate assumptions about the benefits and rationale for you taking the job show high levels of interest and preparation, while inaccuracies or lack of detail in your rationale conveys poor preparation and/or limited interest in the job.

This question is typically a powerful indicator of the ease of attracting and retaining you. When the company has a unique value proposition for you personally, it becomes much more likely that you not only will accept an offer but will remain with the company for an extended time. However, if your reasons for wanting an offer are limited or lack distinction from other opportunities, it suggests to the company that it may struggle to retain you.

Just as the company does not want to hire somebody who has only the bare minimum qualifications, they prefer to not hire somebody who is interested in the position only because they need a job. They would much rather hire somebody who is excited by their *specific* job and motivated to do well.

Companies could reasonably argue that it is not their responsibility to make sure that the job they offer is a good fit for you. They would be right. That's your responsibility and one that Chapter 9 helps you accomplish. Still, many companies do take an interest in confirming you have done the analysis to prove hiring you would be a mutually good decision and one which is likely to land them a long-term employee.

Furthermore, the company wants to ensure that they can deliver on your expectations. If your rationale for working for the company is based on flawed assumptions, it is much better for both sides to correct those misunderstandings before reaching the point of an offer. If the company cannot deliver the expectations you have for it, then you are likely to be less motivated and more difficult to retain than if it can confidently support you in achieving your objectives. And you really shouldn't be accepting the offer if you know this to be the situation.

Why did/are you leaving your last/current job?

Employers want to hire people who they are confident will work for them long enough that they create a return on the investment made to hire the person. Understanding what inspired you to leave your last job helps a prospective employer assess what it must do to retain you, if it makes an offer.

Employers hope to hire people who are inherently loyal but are considering joining a new company because they believe that new company can improve their situation in a unique and specific way. Thus, your answer should not present you as flippant or overly demanding. It should describe a situation which would not be present – or at least would be significantly diminished – at the potential employer, and it must be coherent with your overall story and brand.

This question tends to worry people who were dismissed from their prior job(s) rather than leaving on their own terms. While it is true that having been fired from a prior job is likely to raise concerns for the employer, this not an insurmountable hurdle. Furthermore, there is a difference between being fired for cause (like engaging in illegal activity) and being laid off for economic reasons related to company performance.

While you should not lie during an interview, you need not feel obligated to address the question in a way that is unflattering to you. Like a politician, you could respond with an answer to a slightly different question that is more flattering such as "Why are you excited about future opportunities now that you are leaving/gone from your last job?" However, if you are asked the question in a way that obligates you to answer directly, there are still ways to address the issue gracefully. For example, "Company A decided to eliminate the department for which I was working, leading to the elimination of my position. While this was unfortunate, I am focusing on the positive that this series of events led me to find this opportunity, about which I am extremely excited." This example acknowledges that you were laid off from the last position but identifies this as having been outside of your control while also quickly returning the conversation to a forward-looking, positive subject.

However you choose to address this question, it is generally good practice to avoid disparaging your previous employer, even if the reality is that you are leaving because you hated something about the job. Saying that your priorities have shifted, and X, Y, and Z are now very important to you and you are seeking opportunities that better align with those priorities presents you as a thoughtful professional. Saying that Company A was full of awful micromanagers who were rude could instead make you appear vindictive, high-maintenance, or petty.

What sets you apart from other candidates?

Interviewers asking this question generally are looking to find reasons to hire you. They need to convince both themselves and other stakeholders. This question requires you to not only fulfill the requirements of the job, but also stand out from other qualified candidates.

It is in your best interest to answer this question with something unique, rather than superlatives. Claiming to be the smartest, most dedicated, hardest-working, etc. may sound to you like a compelling argument, but it presumes that you can assess the other candidates (you cannot) and that you know the criteria on which the interviewer would base such an assessment (you do not). So, while the concept is attractive, the credibility of such statements is generally very low.

Instead, position your answer around something you can reasonably expect to make you memorable and different in an objective way. Specific uncommon experiences, awards, qualifications, obscure skills, and other attributes that other candidates are unlikely to have are generally more powerful as answers to this question.

It is frequently effective to tell a story when answering this question, especially if you can connect unique qualifications or experience with a unique vision for the future. For example, "I would borrow concepts from my time in a different industry to help address this particular challenge where our industry has often struggled. I think by using my deep expertise on ABC topic, I will be able to accomplish X." This example would obviously replace the generalities with specifics in a real-life context but provides an example of how you could set yourself apart without making claims you cannot necessarily substantiate.

What are your salary expectations?

This simple question is one of the most dreaded. Candidates assume that too a high number will disqualify them from consideration, and that too a low number will leave money on the table if they are hired.

The reality is that both are possibilities; however, if you are being honest with yourself about your expectations, neither is a tragedy. If a company cannot afford what you expect to be paid, then the job is not the right fit for you. You do not want to put yourself into a job that cannot pay you what you expect because you will be unhappy, unmotivated, and will continue to look to move jobs.

However, if you leave money on the table, what is the real harm? You may never know for certain money was left behind anyway. And if you were certain money had been left on the table, you are still earning what you expected and because you know that the company can pay more, you have the potential to receive a raise. Also, for reasons of internal parity, some companies will offer the same salary for the role regardless of a candidate's salary expectation.

Companies ask this question to avoid wasting their time interviewing candidates who might decline an offer because the remuneration was insufficient to meet expectations. When a company has a clear budget in mind for a role, which almost always is the case, they want to avoid spending time recruiting people who they could accurately predict would decline an offer.

Many candidates opt to defer the salary discussion until later by finding ways other than sharing a salary expectation to assure the employer that time is not wasted. This strategy can work if it leads to the company continuing the recruiting process. In other cases, the strategy simply delays the answering of this question until later in the process and candidates will still need to provide an answer.

Answering directly requires a clear understanding of what you need and want from your financial package. Many candidates are not comfortable answering this question because they lack that clarity. However, if you have gone through the north star exercise in Chapter 6, you should have that clarity.

Even with that knowledge, you still must make a strategic decision when answering the question. Any figure between what you need (your minimum) and what you want (your target) could be a sensible answer. Higher numbers risk you falling outside of the range that an employer would accept but provide a more useful anchor if you receive an offer and choose to negotiate.

When faced with the question, some people mitigate the risk of "pricing themselves out of consideration" by explaining that expectations could change depending on the rest of the total rewards – the vacation time, benefits, bonuses, etc. This sort of answer tells employers that you are not anchored to a number but are instead considering options based on total package. Answers like this can encourage an interviewer to keep you in consideration even if your number is higher than the company is prepared to offer. However, this strategy is hard to execute if answering the question as part of an electronic submission.

Fundamentally, deciding how to answer (or dodge) this question is a personal strategy, but one you should think through before any interview.

What are your long-term career goals?

This multipurpose question provides the opportunity to address a variety of topics. Frequently, employers ask it to estimate how long you could stay with them if hired. They want to be convinced that if they hire you, your career can progress in a way that will avoid unwanted attrition for them and involve you meeting your goals.

This question also speaks to the how meticulous and introspective you are. Free-spirited, creative thinkers may not have very specific long-term goals, whereas detail-oriented people may have precise ones. People with general ambitions are sometimes easier to please with career growth opportunities than people with very specific expectations, but people with specific ambitions are often more thoughtful and deliberate in their actions.

Ultimately, having an authentic, interesting story that is coherent with your overall brand and how you have presented yourself is all that is required to effectively answer this question. Do not make this question more difficult by trying to anticipate what you think the employer would like to hear.

What is your proudest achievement?

In addition to creating an opportunity to differentiate yourself from other candidates, this question forces you to provide insight into what motivates you. Companies want to feel confident not only that they can attract and retain you, but that they will be able to motivate you to perform at your best. Understanding what you are proud of helps employers anticipate how naturally they will be able to motivate you within their compensation and cultural structures.

While there are not many "bad" ways to answer this question other than fabricating or embellishing achievements, some answers will be more compelling than others. Your answer need not be professional in nature, but if it is, and especially if it is relevant to the job, you stand a better chance of creating positive impact with your answer.

Also, it is helpful if you can explain *why* the achievement was so meaningful. Most people would not be impressed by somebody who claimed the completion of a 5k race as their proudest achievement. However, once that person explains that three years before the race, she was paralyzed in a car wreck and told she was unlikely to walk again, the context changes significantly. Hearing she was proud of the 5k because it was the represented her beating the odds through countless hours of physical therapy and determination shows an impressive level of determination, commitment, and resiliency that would certainly be attractive to an employer.

What are your weaknesses?

Contrary to what many candidates think, this question is not an attempt to have you undermine your own candidacy. Instead, the company is usually seeking to understand your levels of introspection, self-awareness, proactivity, and ownership. The weaknesses you identify are rarely of material concern to the interviewer. All people have some weaknesses. How people deal with their weaknesses varies widely – and that's what the question aims to identify.

Companies worry about employees who are not aware of their weaknesses because it suggests those employees will require significant oversight to identify weaknesses and support to address them. Similarly, candidates who are aware of weaknesses, but are ineffective at addressing them quickly, cause an additional burden on management.

Being fearful of or embarrassed by weaknesses makes people prone to hiding or avoiding them, limiting the scope of how such people can be used in an organization. On the other hand, people who view weaknesses as opportunities to learn, grow, and advance are more flexible – especially if those same people are effective at identifying and proactively addressing those weaknesses.

In rare cases you could share a weakness that disqualifies you from consideration, such as if you were applying for a customer service position and stated that you have a short fuse and get angry quickly. In such a situation, your weakness would likely prevent you from being effective in the job, but in a case like that, you probably should not have been pursuing the job at all because it is a poor fit for you.

Many people believe that the best way to answer this question is to offer a strength that is rebranded as a weakness. For example, "I care too much" or "I work too hard." Before planning to use such an answer, recognize that the only way to address these weaknesses would be to "care less" or "work less." So, either you must be willing to say that you recognize your weakness but are doing nothing about it, or you share that you are working to care less or work less, which an employer probably will find unattractive. Furthermore, you need to be prepared to give examples of when you cared too much, and how it hurt a previous employer. Unless you are prepared to give an example of your "weakness" actually causing harm and a plan for addressing your "weakness," you probably should pick a different, more authentic weakness.

A frequently effective recipe for addressing this question involves sharing a weakness, how you came to be aware of it, what you are doing (or did) to address it, and how you are making (or made) progress.

How would your last boss/supervisor describe you?

This may simply be a practical question aimed at understanding what it is like to work with you. It may also be an attempt to gain insight into your level of awareness and emotional intelligence. The content of your answer will address the first objective while the rationale you use to justify the answer will address the latter.

Employers want to hire employees who understand how their actions impact others because that awareness typically improves office dynamics. Employers also are interested in understanding what you think is important to them. They expect that you will pick a description you think flatters you – because why wouldn't you – and therefore gain some insight into your values.

At first, this seems like it should be an easy question to answer well. After all, it is very unlikely that the interviewer has asked your last boss this question to compare with your answer and even if they did, you are speculating, so how could you be expected to answer accurately? However, you should give this some thought because you need your answer to align with the rest of your story (interview, resume, cover letter).

If you have consistently been emphasizing your people skills both on your resume and in answers to other interview questions, but then suggest that your boss would describe you as a "computational genius who is amazing with analytics and building models," an interviewer is likely to question the authenticity of either description of yourself. Similarly, if you claim your boss would describe you as a compelling leader, yet your resume fails to describe you succeeding in leadership roles, there will be a confusing disconnect. If you are inconsistent, either you have low emotional intelligence or the information you have provided should not be treated as credible – or both.

However, if you can give a description in line with the other information you have been providing and a thoughtful justification for that answer, you give the interviewer an opportunity to imagine being your boss and imagine you in their workplace.

What gives you satisfaction in the workplace?

This question seeks to determine whether the company's natural operating behavior and culture will inspire top performance out of the candidate. If the company doesn't think it can easily and naturally provide satisfaction to you, it may conclude that you are unlikely to contribute to your full potential, and/or will likely leave the company after only a short tenure.

Understanding your North Star as introduced in chapter six should be very helpful in answering this question. In many ways, this question is very beneficial to the candidate. It essentially takes the place of you asking the employer if they can provide you the most important things to satisfy you if you accept the job.

There are at least two effective ways to approach this question, both of which rely on having a foundational understanding of your North Star. If you feel confident in your understanding of the employer, you can select something that appeals to you about the job to underscore the message that this job is a good fit for you.

Alternatively, if you are less certain about the fit of the company for you, you can select something that is either very critical to your job satisfaction or something which is perhaps less important to you (but still important) which you have little knowledge about how the company handles. This second approach risks making you look like a worse fit for the role, but only if the role also is a worse fit for your career than you initially expected. In this scenario, you potentially exchange some standing as a candidate for improved decision-making – a trade-off you should be happy to make.

APPENDIX C – SAMPLE INTERVIEW QUESTIONS TO HELP YOU PREPARE

The element of surprise is your enemy during an interview. Familiar questions lead to confident answers. Unfamiliar ones cause you to lock up and fumble your answer. Seeing and preparing answers to many questions reduces the likelihood of surprise in interviews.

You can't anticipate every question a prospective employer might ask, but it's a good idea to anticipate some questions and prepare answers for them as part of the interview process.

The goal of answering anticipated questions should not be to memorize answers. Memorization requires effort that is more effectively spent considering a wider range of topics than committing a small set of answers to memory. Not only is it impossible to anticipate which questions you will be given the opportunity to answer, but attempting to give memorized answers is more likely to fluster you if you struggle to remember exactly what you want to say. As bad, memorized answers tend to come across as inauthentic. We think a better way is to review and practice many questions.

When candidates struggle with a question, it's often because they are trying to understand the rationale for the question while they're trying to answer. Even when they have an interesting response, they get tripped up trying to figure out what's behind the question. One way to counteract that is to consciously force yourself to think only about delivering an accurate and compelling answer.

The following questions are generic and therefore potentially applicable to most job interviews. You're not likely to receive any of these questions verbatim in an interview, but you probably will get some version of at least a few of them.

Rather than trying to answer all the sample questions, look for questions that would have surprised you or questions that look particularly relevant to the job you are seeking, and focus on answering those. Don't forget to apply the concepts from Chapter 17 when developing answers for these practice questions:

Behavioral questions

Questions in this category are meant to help an employer anticipate how you will react in situations they can imagine arising for you if they hire you into the job. They generally assume past behavior is a good predictor of future behavior. It is important to not only share *what* you did, but *why* you did what you did to give the interviewer the insight he or she is likely looking for.

- Give an example of an occasion when you used logic to solve a problem.
- Give an example of a goal you reached and tell me how you achieved it.
- Give an example of a goal you didn't meet and how you handled it.
- Describe a stressful situation at work and how you handled it.
- Tell me about how you worked effectively under pressure.
- How do you handle a challenge?
- Have you been in a situation where you didn't have enough work to do?
- Have you ever made a mistake? How did you handle it?
- Describe a decision you made that was unpopular and how you handled implementing it.
- Did you every make a risky decision? Why? How did you handle it?
- Did you ever postpone making a decision? Why?
- Have you ever dealt with company policy you disagreed with? How?
- Have you gone above and beyond the call of duty? If so, how?
- When you worked on multiple projects how did you prioritize?
- How did you handle meeting a tight deadline?
- Give an example of how you set goals and achieve them.
- Did you ever not meet your goals? Why?
- What do you do when your schedule is interrupted? Give an example of how you handle it.
- Have you had to convince a team to work on a project they weren't thrilled about? How did you do it?
- Give an example of how you worked on team.
- Have you handled a difficult situation with a co-worker? How?
- What do you do if you disagree with a co-worker?
- Share an example of how you were able to motivate employees or co-workers.

- Do you listen? Give an example of when you did or when you didn't listen.
- Have you handled a difficult situation with a supervisor? How?
- Have you handled a difficult situation with another department? How?
- Have you handled a difficult situation with a client or vendor? How?
- How would you describe your ideal cultural environment?
- How has your tolerance level changed over time?
- Do you enjoy training and mentoring?
- What do you do if you disagree with your boss

Motivation questions

These questions are a subset of the behavioral questions which help to identify ways in which your behavior is influenced. Again, the *why* can be as or more important than the basic answer to these questions.

- Out of all the jobs you have had, which one was your favorite (or least favorite) and why?
- Tell me about your three greatest objectives and why they are important to you and to your company.
- Tell me how you were able to get traction at each of the last two companies you joined.
- Tell me about your career goals for the next 2 to 5 years.
- What is the biggest indicator for you of success in your professional life? How do you, personally, measure your success?
- What makes you think you need a change now?
- Think of a time when your work seemed boring or monotonous. How did you handle it?
- Share with me a time when you felt your most motivated at work. Why was that?
- Share with me a time when you went above and beyond the call of duty. Tell me about the details and why you did it.

Background/Skill/Competency Questions

These questions are typically designed to confirm that you a have the necessary skills, knowledge and/or capabilities to perform the job effectively.

- Tell me more about [insert item] which I see you have listed on your resume/CV?
- How did you learn to [insert skill]?
- Have you ever done [X]? Can you give me an example?
- Describe your typical approach for solving [insert particular problem/challenge].
- There are multiple schools of thought on [insert topic]. To which school of thought do you consider yourself most aligned?
- What led you to leave [insert previous job]?
- Your resume/CV says you delivered [X] during [Y project]. To what aspect of your efforts would you attribute that success? How might you do things differently with the benefit of hindsight?
- When was the last time that you conducted business in [insert foreign language] which you have listed as fluent on your resume/CV?
- Tell me about the feedback you received in your most recent performance review.
- What do you believe differentiated you most from your counterparts in similar roles?
- What is most recent skill you have developed or significantly improved? What are you working on building/developing right now?

Emotional Intelligence Questions

Emotional intelligence questions aim to demonstrate to what degree you are aware of how your behaviors influence other people and how their behaviors influence you. Again, the *why* and *how* of the situation are often more insightful than the *what, when,* or *who* so don't be too narrow in your response.

Questions that reveal self-awareness

- Tell me about a time when you knew that your conduct was inappropriate in a meeting or interaction with another.
- Share with me an experience where you found you had to adapt your personality to work well with someone else.
- Describe a time when you felt you were unfairly criticized and how you handled it.
- Tell me about a job you had in the past that you felt you outgrew. How did you know?

Questions that reveal self-control

- Tell me about a time when something was better left unsaid. What were the details?
- Think of a situation in which you said something that you later regretted. Give me the specific details.
- We have all had bad days, share with me the last time you found yourself angry at work. What happened and what triggered it?

Questions that reveal social skill
- Think of a co-worker that irritated you the most. How did they push your buttons? What did you do about it?
- Think of a time when you had to work with a headstrong co-worker and tell me how you handled it.
- Tell me about an experience when you had a new team to work with. How did you assimilate yourself to the group?
- Think of a time when you involved others in a task when it would have been easier to do it yourself.

Questions that reveal empathy

- Give me an example of a time when you had to deliver the same bad news to more than one person. Tell me how you went about it.
- Tell me about a time when you used humor to diffuse a tense situation.
- Tell me about the toughest constructive criticism you've had to give someone else.

Questions that reveal stress tolerance

- Give me an example of a time when you had to balance multiple projects for different people with conflicting deadlines. How did you handle it?
- What types of things in the past have created the most frustration for you? And the least?
- Recall the last deadline you had to meet but couldn't. What was the outcome?

Questions that reveal flexibility

- When was the last time you had to act when there was no policy or formal procedure to do so? Tell me what you did.
- Tell me about the biggest professional risk you have taken.
- Give me an example of a time when your creativity helped you achieve a seemingly out of reach goal.
- Think of a time in the past when you didn't have the time to make something perfect, so you had to sacrifice quality for speed. What happened?

Questions that reveal problem solving

- Recall a time when you disagreed with a directive you received from your supervisor.
- Give me an example of a time when you had two different deadlines to meet for two different people and you couldn't do both. What did you do?
- What is the most difficult decision you have had to make? How did you arrive at your decision?
- Think of a situation when you got conflicting information from two independent sources. What did you do?

Questions that reveal influence

- Recall an experience when you felt you were inspirational to someone else at work.
- Tell me about a situation in which you had to negotiate a successful outcome between two conflicting opinions.
- Think about the most influential person you have worked with. Share with me a specific example of their influence in action.

Questions that reveal optimism

- Discuss a time when you were wronged for doing what is right. What impact did it have on you?
- We've all had times when things at work don't go our way. Think of a time when it happened to you and what the circumstances were. Give me a specific example.
- Tell me how your behavior positively influenced another?

Made in the USA
Columbia, SC
10 December 2018